Firestorm
Typhoons over Caen, 1944

FIRESTORM

TYPHOONS OVER CAEN, 1944

by

Graham A. Thomas

SPELLMOUNT

British Library Cataloguing in Publication Data:
A catalogue record for this book is available
from the British Library

Copyright © Graham A. Thomas 2006

ISBN 1-86227-345-6

First published in the UK in 2006 by
Spellmount Limited
The Mill
Brimscombe Port
Stroud
Gloucestershire GL5 2QG

Tel: 01453 883300
Fax: 01453 883233
E-mail: enquiries@spellmount.com
Website: www.spellmount.com

1 3 5 7 9 8 6 4 2

Printed in Great Britain by
Oaklands Book Services
Stonehouse, Gloucestershire GL10 3RQ

Contents

Acknowledgements		ix
Foreword by Craig Cabell		xi
Author's Note		xiii
Introduction: Typhoons and D-Day		xv
I	Operations	1
II	Softening Up – May 1944	3
III	Setting the Stage	16
IV	The 'Bombphoons' 197 Squadron June 1944	27
V	197 Squadron July 1944	41
VI	197 Squadron August 1944	53
VII	The Typhoon Described	63
VIII	609 Squadron June 1944	72
IX	609 Squadron July 1944	88
X	609 Squadron August 1944	101
XI	198 Squadron June 1944	108
XII	198 Squadron July 1944	127
XIII	257 Squadron July 1944	140
XIV	257 Squadron August 1944	154
XV	The Fall of Caen and the Falaise Gap	161
Appendix I: The Prisoner		170
Appendix II: Sir Alec Atkinson		175
Appendix III: Correspondence Between Montgomery and Eisenhower		179
Appendix IV: Analysis of Air Support for 'Operation Goodwood'		183
Endnotes		189
Bibliography		197
Index		201

This book is dedicated to all the pilots who flew the Typhoon during the Second World War and to the ground personnel who kept the mighty beast in the air. Without a doubt they made a significant contribution to the liberation of Europe. They fought and died so that we may be free. God bless them all.

Acknowledgements

We would like to thank Sir Ken Adam, Tom Annear, Derek Lovell, Richard Armstrong, Sir Alex Atkinson, Mark Crame 609 Squadron Association historian, the National Archives, 197 Squadron Association, RAF Museum Hendon, Imperial War Museum, Trenchard Lines Library at Upavon, Spellmount Publishing and Craig Cabell for making this book possible. The artwork on the front of the jacket is by David Barlow, chief designer and illustrator of the MOD inhouse magazine, *Focus*.

Foreword by Craig Cabell of Focus, the House Journal of the Ministry of Defence

I marvel at the amount of books concerning the Second World War. Tens of thousands promise insights and revelations appertaining to a war that lasted slightly over five years. What activity busied this small blue world of ours, what hurt, torture and downright cruelty pervaded the lives of millions, all because of the insane dreams of one man?

We – the general reader – thirst for more knowledge of that difficult time because we want – *need* – to understand why such atrocities happened, we need to know why brave family members had to die senselessly and finally, understand how close the Allies came to being beaten by the Nazis. Perhaps there are a million other 'whys?' as there are a potential million other books begging to be written. Are there any revelations left concerning the Second World War?

Yes there are, as Graham A. Thomas and I found with our own book *Operation Big Ben – the anti-V2 Spitfire Mission, 1944–45*. Surely everything to be said about the Spitfire had been said? Actually no, and with the help of veteran Big Ben Spitfire ace Raymond Baxter, Graham and I wrote a whole new chapter in the annals of Spitfire history. It is a book we both feel extremely proud to have written and we were both overwhelmed by the positive response throughout the media.

As I turned my attention to more ancient history and the study of Middle English, Graham continued his own exploration of the Second World War. As a fellow reporter at *Focus*, the House Journal of the Ministry of Defence, it was easy to detect Graham's passion for aircraft and in particular the Second World War. His father fought with some distinction with Monty's glorious Eighth Army and a sense of passion and duty has prevailed in Graham.

For those who don't know Graham, he is an English-Canadian: born in England, raised in Canada. His perception comes from that foreign perspective of the English whilst succumbing to the peculiarities of his birth place: in short he can analyse English history for the strange beast it is, but still sympathise with the mentality that implemented it. That is why Graham's books are keen and informative. From his analysis of Furies in Korea to his current project concerning the operational duties of Typhoons – the one you hold in your hands – Graham has always concerned himself with the nitty-gritty of authentic material and actively sought first-hand interviews to support the documentation.

Yes, Graham has found obscure documentation and offers insightful facts that have hitherto been forgotten. He has then applied his sound reasoning and natural story-telling talents to reach into a whole new chapter of Second World War history. This is a very difficult thing to achieve (look at all of those Second World War books on the market and those that grace the shelves of collector's shops), surely there is little more to write about?

Ah, but there is. It is here and backed up by those ever diminishing, but vitally important, eye-witness accounts told to Graham in the interview room. It is difficult to criticise Graham's impunity and dogmatic pursuit of the truth behind the story that has previously been hidden in the shadows.

There is something else you need to know before pull out your wallet – or purse – and purchase this new book: you are in for a full, informative, but most painful read. Not only is the detail of a day-to-day job that was difficult and dangerous to the individual documented, but the story forms part of that so important, larger struggle for freedom that the Western world undertook so imaginatively and passionately. We look back on the Second World War with the cosy feeling of knowing 'we won'. But please remember whilst reading this book that the real people whose lives we drop in on don't know that the war will end and that they – somehow – will be the victors. We won't tell them, we will simply smile and enjoy the ride, shaking our heads in admiration and nodding in gratitude.

Are there too many books concerning the Second World War? I don't think so, because the underdog won at enormous cost and we must constantly be reminded of that fact. Also, what the Nazis did sickened the whole of mankind and we must ensure that a so-called 'super-race' never rears its ugly head again in any bastardised form.

Here's to the next ten thousand books concerning the Second World War and the never-ending pursuit of finding the truth that slumbers in historical shadows.

Craig Cabell
London, 2006

Author's Note

This book is about the gruelling war of attrition experienced by RAF fighter-bomber pilots over the battlefields of Normandy. It is a snapshot of history looking at the air war up to the point where the Allies took Caen, closed the Falaise 'Gap' and began to push the Germans out of Normandy.

The sources used in this book were, by and large, the squadron histories written by intelligence officers from reports on individual sorties written by the pilots as well as from debriefings that took place after operations. Though the events were fresh in the minds of the pilots they are still subjective, from the pilots' point of view, and therefore cannot be cast in stone. We have checked and corrected French place names recorded in the squadron histories so far is possible, but as can be imagined precise spelling was not a priority at the time. We apologise for the certain errors.

This book is not an academic work. There was no objective individual in the cockpit with the pilots, no one standing on the wing watching the events. These are facts, events, missions and operations as the pilots remembered them and in the heat of battle each pilot could see the event slightly differently.

However, the histories are the best record we have of day-to-day operations and must be taken to be as close to fact as possible. This book is a living history because it is based on the pilots' experiences, what they saw and what they felt. The veterans interviewed supplied their thoughts and feelings from their experiences as young men and it is their story.

My desire to write this book partly came from the fascination with the Hawker Typhoon, a large, heavy aircraft that is unlike any other. Its huge chin radiator intake makes it so distinctive. The 24 cylinder Napier-Sabre engine pushed it beyond 400mph.

But it wasn't just the aircraft that drew me to this book. It was what the men who flew the machine did with it. What makes this history different from others is that it brings the reader right into the action day by day, day after day. We can see from interviews with pilots like Derek Lovell, Sir Kenneth Adam, Sir Alec Atkinson and others just how hard it was for the RAF pilots pounding German ground positions in the mighty Typhoon. We see their determination, their bravery and their fear. (For many of the sorties described, not only squadron leaders but the names of all pilots have been given; we realise that this may slow the narrative and apologise for this, but felt it to be important.)

The Typhoon was a rock steady gun platform even in the steepest and fastest dive. But it had vices, vices that in the early days of its production cost the lives of many pilots. It had a bad habit of shedding its tail in a steep dive. And if a pilot ever took his oxygen mask off he'd be gassed by carbon monoxide from the exhaust that blew into the cockpit. Most of the problems of the aircraft were ironed out (although the carbon monoxide one never was) and the aircraft found its true calling as a low-level ground attack fighter.

Although the exploits of Typhoon and Tempest squadrons has been documented before, the men who flew this gruelling war of attrition are still unsung heroes. People remember the Battle of Britain and the romance of the agile Spitfire. But for the pilots who slogged it out in the skies over Normandy there is still very little recognition. Yet their contribution, like those of the Battle of Britain, was immensely important in winning the war.

Firestorm goes deeper into the background of the operations and culminates in the final aerial bombardment that helped Montgomery to capture Caen and allowed the Americans to break out. We look at the relationship between Ike and Monty and analyse the effects of heavy bombing on the city itself.

Firestorm is a window on the character of total war. If we do learn by our mistakes and by history, let us fervently hope that this kind of costly, bloody war of attrition never happens again.

Graham Thomas
2006

INTRODUCTION

Typhoons and D-Day

"After the Hurricane, the Typhoon was like someone hitting you up the backside with a sledgehammer. You took off, and by golly you had to hold on to full left rudder and full left rudder trim. It was about 1500 feet before I worked out how to pull the undercarriage up."

Warrant Officer Derek Lovell 197 Squadron

The morning of 6 June 1944 thousands of Allied troops, packed tightly into landing craft, sailed across the Channel from England for the assault on Fortress Europe. Afraid, anxious, the men in those boats waited while their little crafts approached the beaches. Who would die on the sand and in the surf and who would live through the onslaught about to unfold? How bad would the enemy fire be?

Many of the men were sick as the landing craft bounced and rolled with the swell of the sea. For many, thoughts must have turned to loved ones far away from the death and carnage.

When the landing craft reached their various points along the beaches and the ramps went down, the troops stormed ashore facing whatever the German defenders could throw at them. But they were not alone. Above them and in front of the troops, fighters, medium bombers, and fighter-bombers of the allied Expeditionary Air Force pounded German defensive targets with rockets, bombs and cannon fire.

Typhoon fighter-bombers roared in over the beaches to hammer German gun positions. Pilots of No. 257 Burma Squadron, 197 Squadron, 609 Squadron, 56 Squadron and the rest of 146 Wing ranged over the beachhead and headed further south attacking enemy transport. As they flew, they could see the flashes from the warships shelling German gun positions. The Typhoons roared south attacking tanks, trucks and staff cars.

At 1705hrs on 6 June, a section of six Typhoons from 257 Squadron took off on an armed recce and roared across the Channel. Over Caen, they spotted two tanks and strafed them with their 20mm cannon. Turning south-east of Caen the section followed the main road, attacking 4 heavy trucks. One of them was destroyed and the rest dispersed. Suddenly, one of the Typhoons broke off from the section, spotting a lone tank in a field. He roared down onto the hapless vehicle to spray it with cannon fire when the pilot saw, at the last minute, an identification strip being unrolled in the field by the tank crew. He pulled up sharply and rejoined his section.

Typhoons from 197 Squadron loaded with bombs took off at first light from Needs Oar Point in the New Forest and headed for France. Squadron Leader Taylor led one section and Wing Commander Baker the other. Climbing to 8,000 feet they roared over the beaches and headed for their targets. That day 197's Typhoons bombed enemy trucks, tanks, railways and gun positions. Split into A flight and B flight, each with eight aircraft, they would take it in turns to drop their bombs on the enemy. Throughout the day Typhoons with rockets and bombs attacked enemy positions. They stopped when there was no light left and then the night bombers took over.

Up and down the beaches ahead of the landing troops RAF Typhoon, Spitfire and Tempest squadrons attacked anything that moved. Light and medium bombers pounded bridges and railway lines on the approaches to the beachheads to slow down German reinforcements coming up to the front.

Over the next few days the Allies' foothold on the beaches slowly expanded as they fought their way inland, broadening their areas of operations. For the Americans their objective was the town of Cherbourg with its natural harbour that would make landing men and materiel much easier. For the British their objective was Caen.

RAF pilots had been flying almost continuously, weather permitting, in the months preceding D-day and they would continue to harry and attack the enemy almost non-stop afterwards. There was no start or stop of a specific operation: every day they flew, attacking designated targets and targets of opportunity.

"The first sortie I did was on the 14th of June," explained Derek Lovell, former Typhoon pilot with 197 Squadron during an interview in 2005. "We dived-bombed a bridge at Broucourt in Normandy flying in from Needs Oar Point. The thing about that was I suddenly saw these black puffs and I realised it was flak and it was firing at me."

Much has been written over the years about D-day and the effectiveness of Allied air power over the Germans that will not be dealt with in detail here. This is about the days and weeks after D-day and the Battle for Caen. It is about the pilots of Typhoon squadrons like 257, 197 and 609, and the gruelling daily grind of attacking ground targets on sortie after sortie, braving increasingly accurate flak and what was left of the Luftwaffe. But just how effective were the attacks by Typhoons, Tempests, Spitfires and Mustangs on the enemy?

In a top secret document, an intercepted cable from the Japanese ambassador in Berlin to Tokyo said, "In view of the too great superiority of the enemy's air force, a deep advance into Normandy by the Germans would result in their having their rear communications cut by the enemy's air force and supplies would be difficult."

The same report predicted the Germans would see progress with regards to beating back the Allies by August. Fortunately, they were proven wrong.

D-day itself was a massive undertaking. Two American infantry divisions landed with two British and one Canadian division on separate beaches. The British and Canadians established beachheads south-east of Caen, their objective to secure enemy airfields and protect the Americans while they captured Cherbourg. Air power played an important part in the invasion. Since 1939, the RAF had fought the Luftwaffe continuously and the air superiority they enjoyed on D-day had been hard won. Now the shoe was on the other foot as the RAF vastly outnumbered the Luftwaffe. It was thought by RAF planning staff that the Germans would have 850 aircraft to use against the assault including medium bombers, but the actual number was between 600 and 700. Against this the Allies had nearly 12,000 operational aircraft plus a pool of trained pilots all ready to go into action.

The spearhead of the assault was the air bombardment of coastal defences. More than 5,833 tons of bombs were dropped by 1,136 allied bombers on the German gun positions, making it less hazardous for the troops to land. Before the troops landed from the sea, several thousand were dropped from the air in a huge armada of transport aircraft. The Americans dropped two divisions and the British Sixth division also went in by air. More than 1,166 American transport planes were used in the airborne assault with the British using 462 transport aircraft. The Americans dropped 17,262 soldiers of the 82nd and 101st Airborne Divisions while the British dropped 7,162 soldiers in the greatest airborne assault ever undertaken up to that time. The task of organising the airlift was in the hands of the Allied Expeditionary Air Force and their pilots flew 2,346 sorties from the evening of 5 June to the morning of 6 June. Indeed, over a 48-hour period from 2100 hrs on 5 June all the air forces involved in the assault flew a total of 22,929 sorties. All the daylight airborne and re-supply missions had fighter coverage so in the first two days of D-day not one Allied aircraft was lost due to enemy aircraft.

For the invasion 153 day-fighter and 18 fighter-bomber squadrons had been assembled and allocated to different tasks throughout the assault. 54 squadrons were directed to cover the beaches while the landings took place, 36 squadrons were designated for directing air support, while 33 squadrons were assigned to offensive fighter operations and bomber escorts. Another 33 squadrons were part of the striking force while another 15 were to attack shipping in the Channel during the landings. There were 60 squadrons of Thunderbolts, 46 Spitfire squadrons, 24 Mustang Squadrons, 21 squadrons of the American twin-tail P38 Lightning, 18 Typhoon squadrons and 2 Tempest squadrons. Their duties ranged far and wide, providing continuous cover over the beachhead, escorting day-bomber and troop carrier formations and giving close air ground support to the troops as well as ensuring a strike force was available whenever it was needed. With no Luftwaffe to protect them the German soldiers hated the Typhoons.

"We used to come in at not far short of 500mph," Lovell recalled. "Then we'd drop our bombs, heave up full throttle, full left rudder and pull off."

Flak was with them on every mission so they would fire their cannon as they pulled out of their dives. For the troops on the ground the fighting would be fierce. For the RAF Typhoon, Spitfire and Tempest pilots their war of attrition, of pounding the Germans day after day with rockets, bombs and cannon fire would be just as hard. "In the battle of Normandy itself," Derek said. "I think 350 Typhoons were lost and 151 pilots were killed. The rest baled out, were taken prisoner or managed to get back to the squadron."

This was the beginning of the battle for Caen.

CHAPTER ONE

Operations

Before we look at the daily operations of the squadrons listed in this book it is necessary to put the missions they flew into context. Throughout the various books, papers and other documents used to research this work certain references to missions or "shows" kept cropping up defining the types of air operations carried out by the RAF over France.

The fighter sweeps, or operations, carried out by Typhoons before D-Day and in 1942 and 1941 by Spitfires and Hurricanes were several, comprising anywhere from just two aircraft to entire Wings. Largest of these was the *Ranger*, which consisted initially of one Wing and later of two or three Wings. Aircraft flying Rangers would fly along the coast of France near German airfields to lure the enemy into the air.

Ordered at Command or Group level, the Rangers were elaborate, with one squadron flying at low level and with a covering squadron to the side and slightly higher with the third squadron flying top cover so they could dive from height onto the enemy. Rangers were not particularly successful as the Germans knew what they were and avoided them wherever they could.[1]

Rangers were still being carried out by the RAF in 1944 and by this time, the Germans had developed a sophisticated radar network to pick up the incoming daylight and night bomber raids so these types of large-scale fighter sweeps aimed at hitting the Luftwaffe became less and less successful.

Rodeos were sweeps by single squadrons of RAF fighters run at Station level with Group authority, usually within 24 hours notice. Despite being briefed to fly a predetermined course pilots were encouraged to attack targets of opportunity such as shipping, railways, road traffic, enemy aircraft and airfields, troop concentrations and gun emplacements.

The *Rhubarb* was the smallest defined fighter attack carried out by RAF fighters over France. It could have up to four aircraft involved but usually only two aircraft flew these missions. Sanctioned at the Flight or Squadron Commander level, Rhubarbs were often spur of the moment sorties during periods of inactivity where pilots would fly out and attack targets wherever they could. Throughout the war, RAF pilots flew thousands of these Rhubarbs and their tally of destroyed road and rail vehicles, aircraft on the ground, bridges, ships and coastal vessels, port installations and so on far exceeded the score of targets destroyed or damaged during the much larger, more formal raids.

One of the least effective missions was the *Circus*, which saw bombers flying out with a close escort cover by fighters. Sometimes, the bombers did not have bombs but flew out to bring German fighters up for combat against the RAF fighters flying top cover. They did not attract much enemy reaction, so were relatively ineffective.

Finally, there was the *Ramrod* mission, which saw several squadrons of bombers escorted by at least a Wing of fighters (and sometimes up to four Wings) they were set against specific targets and resulted in some very large air battles in the days when the Luftwaffe was still a force to be reckoned with.[2] The attrition rate of air combat on the Eastern Front had severely weakened the Luftwaffe and its effectiveness against the increasing allied air attacks was diminishing all the time. By May of 1944, the month before D-Day, the Allies had virtual air superiority over Normandy and Caen.

Perhaps the most common operation was the *Armed Reconnaissance Patrol*. By D-Day and beyond some Squadrons referred to them as *Tactical Rhubarbs*. Usually these patrols would follow a briefing on a specific sector defined as a patrol line between landmarks such as villages or towns behind enemy lines that were easily identifiable. Aircraft would fly between 3,000 and 5,000 feet and their main objective was to look for any surface movement that would indicate the Germans were moving their forces up to the front line, or later, retreating from the front line. Once a target was spotted the patrol leader would then radio the position to a forward control van who would be up at the front with the Allied forces and depending on the nature of the target and the weapons the Typhoons would be carrying, the forward control would direct the Typhoons to attack.

CHAPTER TWO

Softening Up, May 1944

Before D-Day occurred, Typhoons were attacking a wide variety of targets, 'softening up' the German's ability to mount an effective resistance by destroying or damaging roads, rail lines, bridges, radar installations, radio communications and much more.

May 1944 opened with drizzle and low cloud making operational flying for the Typhoon squadrons impossible. It wasn't until late the following day when, at 1720hrs, a section of rocket-firing Typhoons of 198 Squadron led by Squadron Leader Bryan took off from their base at Thorney Island on a Ramrod mission to attack the bridge over the Douve River at Pont L'Abbe. Over the target, they peeled off and fired their rockets, seeing one direct hit and several near misses.

No flying took place for 197 Squadron 'Bombphoons' until the 3rd, when seven Typhoons took off in the evening led by Flight Lieutenant Button. Over France, they dive-bombed a Noball target[3] with great success braving heavy flak over the target.

On the 3rd Wing Commander Brooker led 12 aircraft from 198 Squadron to attack railway sheds at Formbrie on a 123 Wing Ramrod. They attacked with rockets and cannon fire, their projectiles ripped into the sidings and sheds causing smoke and debris to go in all directions. When they left the sheds were burning furiously.

For 609 Squadron operations for May began on the 7th as the run of bad weather cleared and the first show of the day saw eight Typhoons take off at 1045hrs to attack shipping in a lock East of Le Havre. Led by a Belgian, Flight Lieutenant L.E.J.M. Geerts, they attacked powered barges in the lock, pumping 64 rockets into the area, spraying it with cannon fire. But they saw no results from their attack and returned to base.

Later, Flight Lieutenant Geerts and his wingman Warrant Officer C.K.E

Martin roared into the air at 1335hrs on an armed recce to attack ships in the Tancarville Canal. Together, they fired 16 rockets into the target area, hammering the bridge and lock gates. Staying low, they strafed several ships and barges in the canal west of the lock with cannon fire and returned to base at 1440hrs.

In the evening, ten Typhoons from 609 Squadron went back to the Tancarville Canal to attack the shipping and barges Geerts had seen earlier. At 4,000 feet the Typhoons peeled off, rolling into their dives firing their rockets at ships in the marshalling basin, recording their projectiles strike the vessels. One was claimed as sunk, while four more rockets hammered one large ship leaving it burning. Two more hits were seen on the bow of another vessel. Two more direct hits were seen on two other vessels that were rocked by the explosions of the rockets.

In 198 Squadron's official history there is an interesting entry for 7th May 1944. "In the evening a party was held at the Kings Beach Hotel, Pagam, in honour of Squadron Leader Baldwin DSO, DFC & Bar[4], our newly departed C.O. and a very good time was had by all. The pilots of the Squadron presented Squadron Leader Baldwin with a silver tankard that read: Squadron Leader Baldwin, DSO, DFC & Bar by the pilots of 198 Typhoon Fighter Squadron in appreciation of good hunting."

The following day, operational flying for 198 Squadron took place at 0955hrs when the new CO, Squadron Leader Niblett led a section of Typhoons on a Ramrod to attack a bridge at Elbeuf. The Typhoons attacked along the length of the bridge, diving down and releasing their rockets at low level. Pulling out of their dives, they fired short bursts of cannon fire and saw their rockets and cannon shells striking the whole length of the bridge including the road at either end.

On May 8th, ten Typhoons from 197 Squadron flew up to Tangmere to take part in a Ramrod with the Wing[5] where they attacked the marshalling yards at Bethune which was successfully bombed with several hits and much damage done.

While 197 Squadron was attacking the marshalling yards 609 Squadron Typhoons did not fly. However, the following day 12 rocket-carrying Typhoons from 609 Squadron, together with aircraft from 183 and 198 Squadrons, attacked a railway bridge over the Seine near Rouen led by 609 CO Squadron Leader Wells.

The Typhoons swarmed down on the target firing their rockets from one end of the bridge along its entire length. In all, 256 rockets[6] were fired by the three squadrons. Rocket after rocket ripped into the bridge as the Typhoons attacked. A fire started in the centre and several railway wagons were left smoking in the northwest end.

"This day everyone is ordered to carry revolvers," recorded the diarist for 609 Squadron in their Squadron history. "To make the day exceptional tea arrived for the first time."

The same day, eight Typhoons from 197 Squadron led by Flight Lieutenant Button went out to bomb targets in the Dieppe area. Taking off at 1010 hours, Button climbed the section rapidly to height and turned the formation towards the Channel. Crossing the coast, he dive-bombed the target and levelled out, firing short bursts of cannon fire before climbing quickly out of range from enemy gunners. But they observed nothing significant owing to the ground smoke and dust raised by their bombs.

In the afternoon, Squadron Leader Taylor led eight aircraft on another Ramrod mission with the Wing to bomb railway marshalling yards in Rouen. They released their bombs just as the Germans opened up with heavy flak. Strafing the yards as well, they hit buildings and rolling stock with their cannon shells. The pilots saw their bombs strike targets inside the target area and the mission was considered to be a success.

At 0915hrs on the morning of the 10 May, eight Typhoons of 197 Squadron led by Flight Lieutenant Button took off from Needs Oar Point and headed for a Noball (V1) site near Abbeville. The Typhoons swooped down onto the target, plastering it with bombs with excellent results. They claimed several explosions from direct hits.

Also on the 10th 12 Typhoons from 609 Squadron led by Squadron Leader Wells with aircraft from 198 Squadron led by Squadron Leader Niblett on a wing Ramrod mission attacked railway lines near Le Coudray. Wing Commander Brooker took the formation across the Channel flying at 8,000 feet. They peeled off 3 miles west of Bosc-Le-Hard heading for the target area, dropping to 5,000 feet. During their attack they encountered heavy and accurate flak and the formation spread out to avoid the flak bursting all around them. A sudden burst near Squadron Leader Well's aircraft threw him up 40 feet. "He thought his nice new craft was messed up but all was well," wrote 609 Squadron's diarist. Wing Commander Brooker's aircraft was hit causing damage to the petrol tank but he was able to carry on with the mission. Another Typhoon received a hit that blew a neat hole through the port roundel.

Undaunted the Typhoon pilots peeled off in 30 degree dives on the target, releasing salvo after salvo of rockets and firing short bursts from their cannon as they levelled out. At least two rockets smashed into wagons in a siding leaving them burning fiercely while others were near misses. The pilots claimed several rocket hits on the railway line.

At 1930hrs that evening 609 Commanding Officer Squadron Leader Wells led 12 Typhoons from 609 Squadron on a Ramrod to attack a radar installation at Cap D'Antifer. As they crossed the French coast, the enemy gunners opened up and Flight Lieutenant Wood was hit, forcing his machine into a dive; his aircraft crashed into the ground and exploded. There was no sign of a parachute.

Flying Officer P.L. Soesman, a Canadian, was also hit and started going down. "Over the R/T he said he was baling out," recorded 609's diarist.

"He was most calm and collected and made a good get away but failed to inflate his dinghy and was seen swimming in the water," wrote the diarist. The target was covered by smoke, dust and debris. Yet through the smoke, they saw their rockets hammering home, hitting buildings and sheds adding to the confusion on the ground. Still the flak came up at them.

Wheeling away, heading for home, Squadron Leader Wells and Flying Officer J.A. Stewart D.F.C. orbited over Soesman until lack of fuel forced them to return to base. A Walrus and some Spitfires arrived to take their place and continue the search but there was no sign of Soesman.

On the 11th a section of eight 'Bombphoons' from 197 Squadron were airborne 0920hrs from Needs Oar Point to Tangmere for another Ramrod mission. Led by Flight Lieutenant Button, the Typhoons took off at 1100 hrs from Tangmere with the rest of the Wing, climbed to height and headed out over the Channel. Their target on this show was the marshalling yards at Douai. Bombers and fighters attacked the target. Explosions ripped through the yards from a few direct hits that smashed the lines, hit buildings and destroyed some rolling stock. All the aircraft on that raid returned to Tangmere unharmed. The eight aircraft from 197 Squadron landed at Manston for refuelling and headed back to base at Needs Oar Point.

Aircraft from 198 Squadron took off at 1905hrs to attack the radar station one mile south west of Le Tréport. They headed across the Channel to their target. Rockets shot from their rails and smashed into the target area pounding it several times. Smoke and debris flew in all directions as the rockets exploded on impact and shells from their cannon tore into the buildings. All the aircraft returned to base though some light flak was encountered.

Heavy weather on the 12th kept operational flying to a minimum but a window of fine weather opened up on the 13th and 197 Squadron laid on a rush mission to bomb targets in the Rouen area. Several Typhoons took off crossing the Channel at 400mph, located their targets and pulverised them with bombs despite the haze over the area. After that, no more operational flying took place that day as bad weather closed in.

While bad weather of 12 May kept the dive-bombing Typhoons of 197 Squadron on the ground the rocket-firing Typhoons from 609 Squadron had a very busy day indeed.

The first operational flight of the 12th took off at 1030hrs on a Ramrod mission to attack a strip of railway track south east of Dieppe. Led by Wing Commander Brooker, several other Squadrons also took part in this raid including aircraft from 198 Squadron. Peeling off into their dives, they fired their rockets, plastering the area with explosion after explosion. The pilots reported seeing strikes all along the rail line. Flight Lieutenant Geerts of 609 Squadron claimed a direct hit while Warrant Officer Martin, attacked a gun position, raking it with cannon fire as well as firing a salvo of rockets at it. The sky was filled with flak from enemy gunners but they all returned to base safely.

In the afternoon, Wing Commander Brooker led a formation of aircraft from 609 Squadron, 198 Squadron and others on a Ramrod to attack a radar installation at Courseulles-Sur-Mer near Caen. They formed up over Ventnor then tore across the Channel towards France. Visibility over the area was very bad and the Typhoons orbited for some time searching for the target. Finally, low on fuel, they attacked enemy gun positions at Port en Bessin scoring several hits, starting fires as the rockets exploded, covering the target with smoke.

Bad weather over the next few days kept the dive-bombing Typhoons from 197 Squadron on the ground but 609 and 198 Squadrons continued to fly. Ops began at 1040hrs when aircraft from 609 Squadron and 198 Squadron headed across the Channel on a 123 Wing Ramrod against enemy road convoys. Climbing to 7,000 feet they crossed the French coast at Fecamp, turned and followed the Seine River, peeling off south of Rouen where they ran into intense flak. Nearing the co-ordinates, the Typhoons peeled off only to find the enemy vehicles weren't where they were supposed to be. Moments later, they found several soft-skinned six-wheeled lorries and attacked them, firing salvos of rockets and leaving six of the vehicles completely destroyed, and others smoking.

Flying Officer Stewart from 609 Squadron was hit by flak over Fleury. Over the R/T the other pilots could hear him saying his engine was cutting out. Losing height rapidly, he baled out and his parachute was seen to open, though none of the pilots saw where he landed.

The afternoon target proved to be elusive when Wing Commander Brooker led a 123 Wing Ramrod to attack enemy convoys sighted between Yvetot and Totes. They didn't see the transport so they attacked the rail line south of Dieppe. Releasing their rockets they dove on the target but they saw only a few projectiles hit the line while the majority of rockets burst in the surrounding fields. Visibility over the area was very bad and the weather conditions deteriorated to the point when flying was impossible.

Bad weather stopped ops until the 18th when Typhoons from 609 Squadron and 198 Squadron led by Wing Commander Brooker, fitted with long-range fuel tanks, took off at 1520hrs on an armed recce to attack road convoys in the Mayenne–Fougeres area. They climbed to 9,000 feet, crossing the coast at Courseulles-Sur-Mer and dived through the clouds down to 6,000 feet but saw no enemy transport. Instead, they attacked the railway junction at Folligny, their rockets smashing into the turntable and destroying a goods train. More projectiles burst on some oil tankers leaving them blazing. Several rail wagons were blasted to pieces by the rockets and strikes were seen on the tracks and sidings.

Typhoons from 197 Squadron were back in action again on the 19th when the low cloud and mist had finally cleared. First thing in the morning,

Squadron Leader Taylor took off at 0555hrs on a weather reconnaissance flight over France. Two hours later, Taylor was back up in the air leading a section of eight Typhoons on a Ramrod to bomb a radar station near Caen. Dropping into their dives, the pilots released their bombs and strafed the area with cannon fire as they roared over the target and pulled away.

But one of Squadron Leader Taylor's bombs remained firmly attached to its mooring under the wing and couldn't be shaken loose. He led the flight back to base, reporting his predicament to Control. Retracting his landing gear, he brought the aircraft in as carefully as he could but the bomb, probably jarred from the impact of landing, dropped off as he reached the end of the runway. Fortunately for everyone, the bomb did not go off and Taylor could breathe a sigh of relief.

The 19th for 609 Squadron pilots was very busy. At 0750hrs Squadron Leader Wells took off from Thorney Island leading a section of eight Typhoons and 4 aircraft from 198 Squadron on a Ramrod to attack a radar station near Caen. Crossing the coast east of Caen they encountered a little light flak but as they approached the target the flak became accurate and intense; so much so that Flight Lieutenant Geerts had to take evasive action to avoid being hit. Wells led Red Section while Geerts led Yellow Section. Peeling off, the Typhoons attacked the targets releasing their rockets. The projectiles plastered the area, pounding into buildings, the explosions ripping sheds and vehicles apart, and sending debris in all directions. As they dove the pilots fired bursts of cannon fire at low level as they neared the target levelled out, raking the structure with shells. Squadron Leader Wells scored at least one direct hit that was seen by Gibson who saw a huge red flash and plenty of smoke.

While this raid was going on, Flight Lieutenant Davies of 609 Squadron took off on an armed recce, leading three other Typhoons for targets in the Caen–Alencon area. Unable to spot their targets due to 10/10ths cloud cover, the Typhoons headed south and attacked rail lines south east of Caen. Rolling into their dives, they fired salvos of rockets at the rail line, cutting it, forcing a goods train to stop because it had no track left to continue. They then roared down onto the train strafing it with cannon fire. All four Typhoons landed safely back at base at 1010hrs having encountered no opposition.

The evening operation began with Squadron Leader Wells of 609 Squadron and Squadron Leader Niblett of 198 Squadron flying a Ramrod mission to attack six large railway sheds west of Formerie. Heavy cloud over the target forced the formation to break up as they attacked through holes in the clouds firing their rockets into the target area. The pilots saw direct hits as they levelled off, their rockets slamming into the engine sheds, sidings and tracks exploding on impact. 609 Squadron diarist takes up the story. "The CO remarked on the great deal of damage already done by 609 on their attack of the third of April. He said this time they left the place in a shambles with plenty of muck flying about from the explosions."

Flight Lieutenant Geerts (609 Squadron) released his rockets that shot into the centre of the target and exploded while he fired his cannon as he levelled off. Geerts saw explosions from the rockets tear through the target area and flames shoot high into the air. Pilot Officer J.D. Inches had two rockets hang up as he dove on the target. Struggling with it he finally managed to fire off the two remaining rockets but they disappeared out of sight, well beyond the target.

After such a successful day the 20th was a disappointment for pilots of 197 Squadron. Low cloud over France again made accurate bombing difficult and it wasn't until the 23rd that the Squadron was able to attack targets in France again.

Both 198 Squadron and 609 Squadron were operational that day. At 1720hrs Wing Commander Brooker led a section of 198 Squadron Typhoons to attack the railway junction between Caen and Clemont. Fitted with long range tanks again they dove on the targets obtaining good results and landed back at base safe and sound.

Pilots of 609 Squadron managed to get airborne in the afternoon of the 20th, when Flight Lieutenant Davies led a Ramrod attack on a rail junction at St Just-en-Clausser but several pilots didn't reach the target and had to abort their flights. Warrant Officer Bavington lost one of his long range tanks while taxiing out and Flight Sergeant Bryant managed to get airborne but thought he too had lost a tank when he saw his streamer[7] in the circuit so he turned back. Warrant Officer Seguin had engine trouble and never left the ground. The remaining five aircraft reached the target and pounded it with their rockets seeing several strikes on the lines and all aircraft returned safely, though Canadian Flying Officer J.D. Inches couldn't jettison his tanks.

At 0915 hours on the 23rd, 197 Squadron CO Squadron Leader Taylor led a section of eight Typhoons from 197 Squadron on a Ramrod to attack a radar station at Cap D'Antifer. As they released their bombs the Typhoons strafed the target area seeing their cannon shells striking the structure and surrounding area.

At 1045hrs Flight Lieutenant Button led a section of four Typhoons from 197 Squadron to St Valery where they dive-bombed an RDF station. One bomb was a direct hit on the station that also suffered several strikes of cannon shells as the aircraft roared in.

The same afternoon of the 23rd, Flight Lieutenant Johnson led a section of eight Typhoons back to the radar station at Cap D'Antifer. All the aircraft plastered the target with bombs as they came out of their dives, and then sprayed the installation, buildings and huts with short bursts from their 20mm cannon causing dust, smoke and debris to rise high into the sky.

For pilots of 609 Squadron the 23rd was busy. At 0745hrs Squadron Leader Wells led a section of eight aircraft along with another eight from 198 Squadron back to the RDF station near Bayeux. The Typhoons roared across the Channel and crossing the coast climbed to their attack height, then spotting the target they peeled off, rolling into their dives firing their rockets. Salvo after salvo shot from the rails under the wings of the Typhoons and ripped into the target area. Explosions thudded through the installation as the rockets found their mark.

Enemy gunners peppered the sky with flak as the Typhoons climbed away, then returned, this time roaring in low, raking their area with cannon fire. Flying Officer Gibson's aircraft was hit by flak and his port under cart cover was blown off but he arrived back at base along with the rest of the flight at 0855hrs.

At 1015hrs Wing Commander Brooker led a 123 Wing Ramrod that included aircraft from 609 and 198 Squadrons to attack the radar station at Saint Valery. Brooker's aircraft developed engine trouble just after crossing the coast and he had to turn back to base, finally baling out 25 miles from Beachy. An hour later he was picked up by an RAF Walrus search and rescue flying boat and returned to Thorney Island. The rest of the flight continued on to the target. Strikes were seen on buildings and at least two direct hits hammered the Freya with the trellis from the eastern Freya completely destroyed. Flak burst all around them as they attacked and Warrant Officer Bavington was hit in the tail. All aircraft returned safely to base at 11.35hrs.

In the afternoon an armed recce was mounted by four Typhoons of 198 Squadron to attack enemy transport south of Caen. Taking off at 1530hrs they roared across the Channel and crossed the French coast heading for Caen. On the road near Caen they bounced a column of enemy tanks ,attacking them at will, diving on the targets releasing their rockets and strafing them with cannon fire. One tank suffered a direct hit from one of Warrant Officer Mason's rockets, blowing the turret off leaving the remains burning furiously. Warrant Officer Hallett claimed a Tiger tank heavily damaged as it swerved off the road into the woods, minus its tracks after several rockets exploded around it. Another tank was badly damaged and a large transport was completely destroyed and left a burning wreck as the Typhoons plastered it with cannon fire and their remaining rockets. Flying Officer Rainsforth attacked a stationary railway engine leaving it with smoke pouring from it.

The last flight of the day for 609 Squadron left Thorney Island at 1100hrs with Squadron Leader Wells taking a section of Typhoons to attack an RDF station that was obscured by cloud. The four aircraft moved onto a secondary target five miles east south east of Caen, a rectangular building surrounded by scaffolding. The pilots thought it was a gun position under construction. The four Typhoons dove on the target, fired their rockets and watched men running away from the building as they levelled out, raking the target with cannon shells. At low-level, Squadron Leader Wells was very nearly blown to bits as the rockets from another Typhoon exploded very near him. Dust, concrete and debris were sent in all directions as 609's rockets hit home shaking the area with explosions that also disintegrated the scaffolding.

For pilots of 197 Squadron the 24th began with great optimism but ended with bad news. A slight ground mist prevented flying until 0955hrs when Wing Commander Baker led a flight of eight Typhoons on an attack on an RDF station at Pont L'Abbé. The aircraft dropped into their dives, releasing their bombs over the target achieving two direct hits, the explosions from the bombs ripping through the buildings. Then the German gunners, now suddenly awake, opened up with their anti-aircraft guns. The air was thick with bursting shells and Flying Officer Coles, hit by flak, turned away from the target, smoke pouring from his engine, Losing height, the other pilots watched his aircraft head out to sea in a gentle dive. Suddenly it flicked over and dropped into the water sinking immediately. Nothing was seen of him.

That same day, operational flying for 609 Squadron began at 1005 hrs with Flying Officer Holmes leading four Typhoons to attack an RDF station at La Hague. Firing their rockets and strafing the target with cannon fire, they left several buildings smoking after seeing several hits strike home. Light flak came up to them as they wheeled away from the target and headed back across the Channel towards base.

24th of May 1944 was a bad day specifically for 198 Squadron. The first mission of the day was an attack on the radar station at Jobourge on the tip of the Cherbourg Peninsula. Taking off at 0950hrs Squadron Leader Niblett (198 Squadron) led the others and they formed up with four more Typhoons from 609 Squadron and headed across the Channel. The target, a wire screen some 90 feet wide and 45 feet high was in an exposed position on a hill and was heavily defended so they went in at low level. Their rockets shot from under the rails as the Typhoons attacked, with heavy and intense flak bursting close by. Several direct hits were seen on the target but both Freeman and Vallerly were hit and exploded, crashing in flames. In a brief moment, 198 had lost two of its best pilots. Following up behind 198 Squadron were 'Bombphoons' from 146 Wing that reported the building at the base of the target was burning furiously. "That was the one where we lost so many people," Richard Armstrong, veteran 198 Squadron pilot recalled during an interview in 2004. "It was on the end of Cherbourg Peninsula and the only way we could approach it was over the town of Cherbourg which was the most heavily defended area in Europe.

"We crossed the coast as usual at seven thousand feet and dove down to nought feet and then had to fly over Cherbourg town literally over the chimney tops and then fired our rockets and got out. I know I hit the thing. I was with a chap called Johnny Baldwin who was a wing commander and he hit it and so did I. The chap behind me didn't pull out and flew into the tower and killed himself and made a mess of the tower too. Only three of us came back, which was a bit of a surprise."

The Squadron was to have a kind of revenge however later that evening. At 1800hrs aircraft from 198 Squadron joined up with aircraft from 609 Squadron led by Wing Commander Brooker on a Ramrod to attack oil installations at Amiens that was camouflaged to look like a house.

They crossed the coast at 8,000 feet. The first to attack was Squadron Leader Wells of 609 Squadron who attacked north east to south west. Releasing his rockets he pulled out of his dive at 2,000 feet firing bursts from his four 20mm cannon. One of his rockets was a direct hit on a storage tank that erupted into flames from the explosion, issuing a column of thick black smoke that reached as high as 2,000 feet. The target was left burning fiercely from the onslaught of the attacking Typhoons. Pilots reported that the smoke from the fires could be seen by aircraft when they were well on their way home.

On the 25th Squadron Leader Taylor led a section of Typhoons from 197 Squadron to Manston where they formed up with the Wing for a large Ramrod to attack the marshalling yards at Armentieres. More than 200 wagons were parked in the yards when the Typhoons and other aircraft started their bombing runs. All the bombs from all the aircraft landed in the target area – quite a claim – and several cannon strikes were seen.

That same day Air Vice Marshal Cunningham arrived by aircraft at Manston and gave the wing a talk about the impending invasion of Europe.

On the 27th, the weather cleared enough for pilots from 197 Squadron to fly up to Manston for a Ramrod on a radar station near Bruge. Squadron Leader Taylor led his section of Typhoons but suffered engine trouble and had to turn back. The rest of the aircraft from the Wing bombed and strafed the station, with all but two bombs hammering the target area.

Pilots from 609 Squadron were not idle on the 27th as the Squadron was put on readiness. The first show of the day for 609 Squadron was in the afternoon when Squadron Leader Wells leading a flight of eight Typhoons took off at 1725hrs on a Ramrod to attack an RDF station at Berck-sur-Mer. But owing to the haze over the target area, they had difficulty finding their mark and most of the rockets overshot. However, Warrant Officer Martin claimed hits on the station with his cannon.

On the same show, Flight Lieutenant Davies led his section of three Typhoons [8] to attack the radar station at Cayeux and scored several direct hits with their rockets on the Wurtzburg sending debris and smoke in all directions. On the second pass, the three Typhoons roared in at low level, firing bursts from their cannon, destroying the target. Although there was some light flak from the target area, the pilots, as recorded by 609 Squadron's diarist, felt the trip "was wizard."

In the evening, four Typhoons led by Flight Lieutenant Geerts took off to attack the radar installation (Freya) at Berek-sur-Mer again. They fired 32 rockets at the target but smoke and haze from the earlier attack obscured the results so Flying Officer Rowland dropped down to 600 feet and reported that the explosions were very concentrated in the target area so a second attack wasn't made and they were back at base by 2200hrs.

The 28th was hot and hazy. It was Whitsunday and the diarist for 609 Squadron's official history recorded the following: "In Civvy Street we would be off to the sea for a lazy day of holiday." However, for the pilots operational flying was taking place and the first show for 609 Squadron was led by Squadron Leader Wells on a Ramrod, along with aircraft from 198 Squadron with Wing Commander Brooker leading the mission to attack a château at Liessies 20 miles inland from Berck. They took off at 0945hrs and climbed to 8,000 feet heading across the Channel.

Several direct hits were seen on the building as they attacked; firing short bursts from their cannon as they levelled off. Smoke poured from the windows as the rockets exploded leaving the place in ruins. The press later reported that the attack had almost managed to catch Rommel, who was due to arrive at the château at the time the Typhoons got there. Smoke and debris billowed out of the château rising into the air. Heavy flak burst around them and Flight Lieutenant Geerts of 609 Squadron was hit with a small piece in his port leading edge while Squadron Leader Wells of 609 Squadron was hit in the starboard tail plane.

The next sortie took place at 1245hrs when nine aircraft from 198 Squadron acted as a flak diversion over Boulogne for Typhoons from 609 Squadron who were attacking a radar installation on the outskirts of town. The attack was very successful as the 198 Typhoons drew the enemy gunners' fire allowing 609 aircraft to successfully do their jobs. The three targets 609 Squadron Typhoons attacked in the area were Coastwatcher, Freya and Wurtzburg, which were small and difficult to see. The first section attacked North East to South West on the Freya, scoring hits with cannon only. Heavy and light flak peppered the sky and Flying Officer Royston had a piece of flak through his radiator cowling while Warrant Officer Buchanan's starboard panel was blown off by flak; but the Wurtzburg was destroyed and the Coastwatcher severely damaged.

The last flight of the day for pilots of 609 Squadron was at 1555hrs when Squadron Leader Wells led two sections of four Typhoons on a Ramrod to attack two lines of rail wagons near Wavrin. Climbing to 8.000 feet they crossed the French coast and dropped to 6,000 feet before rolling into their dives. Attacking from south south-west to north north-east they roared down on the wagons, firing their rockets. Levelling off at 1,000 ft they strafed the wagons with cannon fire. There were approximately 40 rail wagons in each line that were smashed and ripped apart by the firestorm from the Typhoons. No locomotives were seen.

On the 29th Flight Lieutenant Curwen of 197 Squadron took off at

0930hrs leading 12 197 Squadron 'Bombphoons' to bomb a Noball site. Bomb after bomb from the attacking Typhoons plastered the buildings of the V1 site, bursting on the structures.

Only one operational flight took place for 609 Squadron pilots on the 29th and it was back to the radar installation near Boulogne. The eight Typhoons from 609 Squadron took off at 0945hrs and flew up to Newchurch where they were to start the mission with aircraft from 198 Squadron.

Attacking the target over France they braved the flak as they rolled into their dives, and hammered the installation with rocket and cannon fire. The aircraft from198 squadron attacked an ammunition dump in the vicinity and the aircraft from 609 attached to this flight claimed rocket strikes on outbuildings. Two rockets smashed into the Coastwatcher structure, while more rockets ripped into the Wurtzburg, but smoke and dust prevented anyone seeing the results.

Last sortie of the month for 198 Squadron took place at 1000hrs on 30th of May. Eight aircraft from 198 Squadron took off and split into two sections of four when they crossed the French coast to attack railway yards at Formiere. Attacking with rockets and cannon several projectiles smashed into the target area, causing so much damage that the yards were virtually destroyed. This was the third attack on the yards.

The other section of aircraft from 198 Squadron was directed to attack a radar installation at Le Tréport. Peeling off they dove on the target letting their rockets fly. The area suffered several hits damaging the installation. All the aircraft returned safely to base.

For 609 Squadron pilots only one flight took place on the last day of May. At 0955hrs Squadron Leader Wells of 609 Squadron took off leading seven Typhoons to attack the Abancourt marshalling yards. Climbing into the hot, hazy morning sky, they formed up and raced across the Channel towards the target. One section of the formation scored rocket strikes on the buildings in the marshalling yards while the remainder saw their rockets hammer track and wagons south of Abancourt.

Intense and accurate flak burst all around them as they attacked. Flying Officer Thoroughgood was hit as they left the target area, his aircraft leaking coolant.

"He gained height and headed in the direction of the coast when he abandoned his aircraft and made a successful parachute landing in a large field some 15 miles North West of Formerie and his machine crashed into a large wood," recorded the 609 Squadron diarist. Flying Officer Blanco was also hit by flak and came back with his fuselage in tatters. "He remarked that if he had known the extent of the damage he would have had an accident," wrote the diarist.

Throughout the month of May the tempo of operations had increased as the Allies prepared for D-Day. For example, 609 Squadron had flown 252 operational sorties and 328 operational hours, attacking a wide variety of targets designed to batter and break down the German's continental defences. But there was a price to pay. Five pilots from 609 Squadron alone were posted as missing.

CHAPTER THREE

Setting the Stage

Before we go into the detail of the following day to day operations of the Typhoon squadrons it is necessary to put their actions into context. At this point, we can take a step back and look at the bigger picture. For the Allies, Caen was of immense strategic importance. If the Germans were to stop the Allied landings, bottle them in on the beachhead and push them into the sea, they had to go through Caen. It was a vital road and rail link connecting all the main routes that led to the British bridgehead area from the east and southeast.

The Germans had placed most of their mobile reserves north of the Seine. For them to drive on the bridgehead from the east they would have to converge on Caen. Between Caen and Falaise was good ground for airfields, which is why the Allies wanted it. From there they could attack the Germans by pounding their positions in Normandy and beyond while bombing and strafing them across the Seine. The airfields could also be used to support the British and American Armies as they broke out of Normandy and pushed into France and the Low Countries.

So, we must look at what was going on behind the scenes, at the bitter in-fighting taking place at the highest levels while soldiers, sailors and, in our case, airmen fought and died to liberate Europe from the Nazis.

In the main, we are looking at three major players, General Dwight Eisenhower, the Supreme Commander of the Allied Force, Lord Arthur Tedder, the Deputy Supreme Commander and Field Marshal the Viscount Montgomery, Commander in Chief of Ground Forces.

Over the years, Montgomery's strategy has been criticised; but his plan was straightforward and was agreed to by Eisenhower.

Monty's master plan for the land battle in Normandy was simple. "Briefly it was to stage and conduct operations so that we drew the main enemy strength onto the front of the Second British Army on our eastern flank, in order that we might the more easily gain territory in the west and make the ultimate break-out on that flank – using the First American Army for that purpose"[9].

The British and Canadians were in the east in the Caen sector where taking ground was not as important as it was in the west, as far as Montgomery was concerned. The main need in the Caen sector was to make the Germans commit their reserves so that the American forces would meet less opposition in their advance to gain territory in the west and break out of Normandy.

Caen was therefore of immense strategic importance.

Montgomery's basic principle was to mount strong and persistent offensive action in the Caen sector to draw the German reserves onto the British eastern flank. It was the basis of all their planning according to Montgomery. "Once on shore, I began to get this strategy working and after the heavy battles in the Caen area, and the overrunning of the Cherbourg peninsula, it began to take shape."

But Montgomery was not without his detractors. In his memoirs he states that he never had reason to alter his master plan and while keeping that plan in mind he never worried about keeping to the planned timelines and did not hesitate to adjust the plans according to the battle situation as it developed.

Marshal of the Royal Air Force Lord Arthur Tedder, Deputy Supreme Commander under Eisenhower of the Allied Expeditionary Forces, wrote about the effects of the air attacks in May 1944 on the Germans in his book, *With Prejudice*. "Early in May 1944, there could be no substantial doubt that our attacks were producing the most serious effects. Colonel Hoeffner, who managed Rundstedt's rail transport in France, reported the situation to be critical," Tedder recorded. "The German armies there needed a hundred trains a day from home. In April, the average had been sixty. By early May it was thirty-two.

"As the bombing campaigns of the 2nd Tactical Air Force continued in the run up to D-Day European newspapers and radio broadcasts reported the growing destruction from the air. German propaganda made the most of casualties to innocent civilians and damage to their property. However, allied spies in France reported that the bombing had been fairly accurate and that morale in the civilian population was high."

German coastal installations and defensive positions felt the brunt of allied air power during the early hours of D-Day when some five thousand tons of bombs were dropped on them.

After D-Day, as the Allies established their bridgehead on Normandy beaches, the expected Luftwaffe onslaught never came. In England, D-Day planners had expected the Germans to mount between six and seven hundred sorties a day. In the event, they could barely manage two hundred a day. "We did not realise how well we had done our job," Tedder wrote.

Overwhelming air power was the Allies' strongest card as far as Tedder was concerned. It was their ace in the hole, but for it to be used effectively airfields in France needed to be quickly established. Days after D-Day Tedder began to feel that Montgomery was not pushing fast enough to capture enemy airfields and lead the Allies to a quick victory. He became one of Montgomery's main critics.

It was Air Marshal Leigh-Mallory, Commander in Chief Air, who believed that the heaviest air fighting would probably take place in the Seine area. "We must, therefore, have enough airfields around Caen and the areas west of Paris to operate over the Seine area in strength," wrote Tedder.[10]

The original Overlord plan had a timetable for the capture of the Caen airfields two weeks after D-Day, but Montgomery drafted a revised plan that did not have the same degree of urgency for the capture of airfields southeast of Caen.

In the first days after D-Day and leading up to it, the 2nd Tactical Air Force attacked enemy airfields and roads, rail lines leading up to the beachhead preventing the Germans from rapidly providing reinforcements. The reaction to the invasion by the Luftwaffe was very slow indeed. On 10th June, however, reports came that two-thirds of the German fighter strength had left the Reich for Normandy.

It became clear that the Germans would try to send reinforcements for their forward troops by crossing the Seine from northwest France and Belgium. They would then have to pin down the British troops holding the Caen-Falaise area. "I was sure that the possession of overwhelming air power, and its use before 'Overlord' to disrupt the railway network which the enemy would have to use, had placed in our hands a weapon of the utmost value," Tedder recorded. "Our right course was to strike as boldly and as swiftly as possible while the enemy was feeling the consequences of the paralysis of his railways and our constant harassing of his movements by road. The longer we delayed in securing the area round Caen and beyond it the less became our chances of victory in 1944."

Field Marshall Erwin Rommel reported on 12 June that Normandy operations were "rendered exceptionally difficult and even partially impossible by the extraordinarily strong and in some respects over-whelming superiority of the Allied Air Force." (*Rommel*, Young p 205-6)

At Supreme Headquarters Allied Expeditionary Force (S.H.A.E.F.) it soon became apparent, a week after D-Day, when Caen had not been captured and that a breakthrough on the left was not to be as quick as was hoped for, that victory in 1944 would not take place.

It is interesting to note that Tedder, and many other senior officers at SHAEF, did not seem to understand Montgomery's strategy and were expecting a quick breakout from Caen which did not happen for two months.

In a meeting that took place on 15th June in France, Eisenhower and Tedder assured Montgomery he would have the air support he needed for ground operations. The Germans had all their available Panzer divisions stationed at Caen and the fighting was so fierce that the 7th Armoured Division had suffered a severe setback, according to Tedder's memoirs. So by the 15th, Montgomery ordered another all-out offensive on Caen with all air support available.

On 19th June a gale of such destructive force that it was close to hurricane strength hit Normandy. For four days the weather pounded the beachheads, stopping the movement of men and materiel completely. One of the artificial harbours was ruined while the sea lanes between England and the beachhead were cut off, with many vessels stranded and damaged. Finally, the weather cleared and the landing of supplies could continue.

"As the days slipped by, I could not help being worried about Montgomery's methods of conducting the battle. The principle which we had proved after painful experience in the Mediterranean – that the Army and Air commanders should live side by side, and decide their policies together – had been allowed to lapse. The reason for this was the lack of suitable communications in Normandy that would allow Conningham[11] to control the air forces from Montgomery's headquarters." (Tedder, p 553.)

Tedder was one of Montgomery's main detractors. He felt that the British Army in the east was not fighting hard enough, indeed not prepared to fight its own battles.[12] On 22nd June Tedder told Eisenhower of his fears about Montgomery's slow progress. He felt that the delay in building up the British forces because of the gales in the Channel was an excuse and not a reason for the inactivity on the left flank. "In essence, Montgomery thought the Air Force was not vigorous enough in support of the immediate battle, while Conningham continued to be sharply critical of the Army's slow progress." (Tedder, p 557.)

By the end of June the Americans were poised to take Cherbourg and the British attack on the east flank began. Tedder visited Montgomery on 29th June to provide moral support and push the commander to use all available air power to support his armies fighting in Caen. Intelligence reports showed that the Germans were assembling armoured forces for a counter-attack. The rail line between Nancy, Vitry, and Paris had not been cut and the Germans were using this line to build up their forces. In his memoirs, Tedder recorded his fears about Montgomery's inability to capture Caen. "Now that the Americans had taken Cherbourg, while we had failed to take Caen, it became clear that a breakthrough must be accomplished on the right flank in order that mobile warfare might be established and the whole Front loosened up."

Churchill contacted Tedder wanting to know what airfields were in use in France and Tedder had to report that the British were well behind schedule. As at 27 June 35 fighter and fighter-bomber squadrons were based in France. Five serviceable airstrips in the British sector were available and eight in the American sector were also in use. These were strips created by the engineers as at this time no enemy airfields had been captured. Two airstrips had been abandoned in the east because of enemy shell-fire while three of the American strips were unserviceable for fighters owing to the number of Dakotas being used to bring in emergency supplies.

The plan had been that by the 24th of June, there should have been 27 airfields with 81 squadrons!

Montgomery issued a directive on 30th June that indicated his intention was to hold on in the Caen sector while the American forces broke through from Cherbourg on the right into open country. Indeed, Montgomery wrote to SHAEF stating that the Germans had built up a formidable armoured force in the Caen sector to face the British Second Army and that a counter-attack seemed imminent. He then suggested that the main task of the Second Army was to hold the enemy's forces in the area between Caen and Villiers Bocage, to suffer no setbacks and to develop operations for the capture of Caen.

Tedder wrote that Montgomery's report was not well received at SHAEF and it was hoped that Eisenhower would insist on an early attack. As we have seen, relations between the air forces and Montgomery were not at their best and to alleviate the situation Eisenhower sent a letter to Montgomery on 7th July telling him in a tactful way to get moving.

In his letter, the Supreme Commander passed on information that the Germans had brought up some infantry on the front facing the British Army, giving them the opportunity for withdrawing some Panzer elements for regrouping. A full-dress attack was needed to avoid fighting a major battle with the slight depth still held by the British in the Caen sector.

The letter reflected Eisenhower's feelings that a co-ordinated attack with the whole strength would put the left flank in motion, allowing for the capture of Caen and a break-out by the British and Canadians.

On 7th July Montgomery mounted his attack supported by Bomber Command. In less than an hour, according to Tedder, the Allied Air Forces dropped six thousand tons of bombs in front of the advancing British and by nightfall, the Germans had been pushed back across the river Orme that flowed between Caen and Faubourg de Vaucelles.

At this point Tedder called for an early advance across the Orme to provide elbow room for the Tactical Air Forces. However, Montgomery disagreed and on 10th July issued a directive stating that as Caen had been captured the tactical situation on the eastern flank was in good shape. "His broad policy would remain unchanged," wrote Tedder. "It appeared to Montgomery that we were now so strong and well situated that we could attack the Germans hard and continuously. So long as we killed or captured them in large numbers, our left flank was doing what was needed."[13]

Lord Tedder wrote that Montgomery felt he was not prepared to suffer heavy casualties to secure a bridgehead over the Orme to take Faubourg de Vaucelles on the south of the river opposite Caen.[14]

However, once again the differences between Montgomery and the Air Forces commanders became apparent. Monty's plan as far as Tedder was concerned was too cautious. A bridgehead over the Orme was needed to establish more airfields, give the Tactical Air Forces manoeuvring room and begin much deeper operations against Germans advancing towards the front.

Montgomery's emphasis was on the securing of Brittany and its ports to be used for a massive build-up for an all-out attack in the east. Tedder's concern was that Montgomery did not appreciate the time factor; only a few weeks of summer remained and as far as Tedder was concerned it was essential that the Allies should get across the Seine. Indeed, a message from 21 Army Group on the eve of the attack on Caen stated that the object of the attack was to drive right through Caen and establish a bridgehead beyond the Orme, which wasn't done.

In a report to the Combined Chiefs of Staff, dated July 13th 1945, General Eisenhower stated that the enemy's main concentration of power lay in the Caen sector and had prevented the Allies from breaking out towards the Seine. Because of this, the Allies altered their plans and the Americans were directed to smash out of their lodgement area in the west while the British and Canadians kept the Germans occupied in the East. "Incessant pressure by the Second Army to contain the enemy was therefore continued by Field Marshal Montgomery during July."[15]

Montgomery states that the impression from this report is that because the British and Canadians failed to break out in the Caen sector (east) it was left for the Americans to do so in the west. This indicates that Eisenhower failed to comprehend the basics of the plan to which he had agreed.[16] The plan had *always* been for the British and Canadians to draw the enemy armour into the eastern sector and bottle them up, giving the Americans the chance to break out in the west. Monty's critics were largely situated at Supreme Headquarters well away from the battle and the misconception that the British were not pulling their weight or fighting hard enough or that the battle was a failure because there was no Eastern breakout came from there.

Many of the senior officers, who disliked him, used the misconception to, as Montgomery put it, "make trouble as the campaign developed." Among these were the men in charge of air operations: Air Chief Marshall Sir Arthur Tedder and Air Chief Marshall Leigh-Mallory, Air Commander-in-Chief in command of the British and American Tactical Air Forces. They wanted the high ground between Caen and Falaise for airfields so they could push Rommel out of Normandy. Montgomery was fighting to defeat Rommel in Normandy and by way of that defeat gain the airfields.

By July 1944 the press were also getting impatient about the apparent lack of progress being made by the British and Canadians in the Caen Sector. Operation Goodwood, which began on 18th July, was an attempt to engage the German panzer divisions in the Caen sector while the Americans prepared for breaking out in the west around the Cherbourg area.

The British and Canadian forces had been fighting hard in the Caen sector keeping the bulk of the German armour bottled up but the Americans, delayed by bad weather, only managed to move into the position to launch their breakout from the general line of St. Lo-Perrier, which they should have reached by 11th June but didn't reach until 18th July. The longer the delay on the American front continued, the more Monty ordered the British troops to intensify the fighting in the Caen sector.

When Montgomery signalled the plan for Operation Goodwood, staff at SHAEF breathed a sigh of relief, thinking that finally they would get the battle they wanted, the massive push in the east, the bridgehead across the Orme and more airfields. Tedder promised Montgomery that full weight of the Air Forces would be brought to bear on the enemy in support of Goodwood.

Caen was captured on 10th July. Montgomery recalled, "It was my intention to secure the high ground between Caen and Falaise as early as possible as being a suitable area for the construction of airfields; but this was not vital, and when I found it could not be done in accordance with the original plan without suffering unjustified casualties, I did not proceed with that venture. This was not popular with the Air Command."

The fundamental aim of the plan was still to establish a strong armoured force to the southeast of Caen around Bourguebus in order to keep the bulk of the German panzer divisions bottled up in the eastern flank in order to help the Americans in the west. They reached this high ground when they launched Operation Goodwood on 18th July with an armoured force. Meeting stiff resistance and braving the rain that turned the whole area into a quagmire, Montgomery stopped the thrust on 20th July, the day that the British finally cleared the Germans out of the suburbs of the eastern part of Caen.

Historians are divided over Goodwood and Montgomery's detractors believed it had been a failure, as the man himself explains in his memoirs. "Many people thought that when Operation Goodwood was staged it was the beginning of the plan to break out from the east towards Paris and that because I did not do so the battle had been a failure."

There was never any intention to break out from the bridgehead on the eastern flank. By July 1944 the Allies had superiority on the ground and in the air against the Germans. In the Caen sector the beachhead was narrow, only a few miles deep and every day men and materiel were being unloaded at the beachhead, pouring into Normandy. The question has to be asked. Why did Montgomery wait so long before mounting a massive offensive in the Caen sector? He states that he didn't want to take the casualties in his memoirs, but his critics believed he could have taken more action without suffering horrendous casualties.

From D-Day right up until the "Falaise Pocket" the Typhoon squadrons were flying every day, weather permitting and attacking any German target they could find. Lord Tedder firmly believed that air power, the continuous attacks by fighters, fighter-bombers and heavy bombers, ensured the allies would not lose their beachhead while Montgomery stalled.

The Germans tried to rope off the British and Canadians in Bocage country some 15 to 20 miles inland from the beachhead. It was a successful policy only because the Germans were committing their entire force, including reserves, to this operation; and the cost in men and materiel was high. Though the enemy were able to prevent any substantial advance by the British and Canadians in the east and south of Caen they were not able to counter the thrusts in the west because they were so fully committed. Operation Goodwood, an armoured offensive against the Germans in the Caen Sector, forced them to commit even more reserves into the fighting to stop what they thought was a British break-out from that area. Severe weather had hampered the American advance and supply lines since D-Day and they finally managed to reach the break-out line by the 18th. The break-out was due to be launched on the 20th, the same day that Montgomery ordered that Operation Goodwood be shut down. But bad weather again held them back until 25th July, when Operation Cobra[17] was launched.

While all of this was going on, the Typhoons were knocking out bridges, trains, rail lines, crossroads, attacking enemy vehicles, armour and supplies wherever they could. By 19th August the Battle for Normandy was won and all remnants of the enemy had been swept from the area.

On the 18th when Goodwood began, heavy bombing enabled a breakthrough to take place but by the afternoon of that day, the British had only managed a three-mile thrust. By the following day, the Germans had counter attacked from several different directions.

It was then that Tedder decided Goodwood had failed. The captured airfields he craved so much had not been captured, which meant they could not attack the Germans across the Seine.

So much did Tedder dislike Montgomery and believe he was dragging his feet that on 21st July when SHAEF received news of the attempt on Hitler's life by some German generals, he went straight to Eisenhower urging him to act at once with Montgomery. Eisenhower sent Montgomery a letter on 21st July stressing that time was short until the onset of winter, that greater room was needed for the armies to manoeuvre and that the Brittany Peninsula must be captured and the entire front go on the offensive.

Eisenhower's letter, according to Tedder, was a disappointment and in his book wrote that he had wished to have seen the letter before it was sent to Montgomery because it did not contain a direct order. Montgomery could evade its implications.

On 23rd July Montgomery sent a letter to Eisenhower replying that "There had never been any intention to stop offensive operations on the eastern flank." After receiving this letter Montgomery issued a new directive to his commanders but Tedder thought this directive lacked the vital emphasis that would get him his airfields. Tedder's reservations were very real indeed. Despite overwhelming superiority in the east, the British were still unable to exploit that advantage six weeks after D-Day. One beach and the only port of any size were still under enemy artillery fire. The original objective of seizing good airfield ground southeast and northwest of Caen had not been reached and some airfields were still under shell-fire.

Despite Eisenhower's emphasis on the time factor in his letter to Montgomery and after scrutinising Montgomery's subsequent directive, Tedder was still convinced that Montgomery did not appreciate the time factor at all. "Nor could I see any indication of the bold offensive action which the time factor justified and our strength justified."

Tedder was shocked by the satisfaction that Montgomery evinced in his reply to Eisenhower's letter. He could not see any grounds for satisfaction in the eastern sector. After all, they still did not have the necessary airfield space needed to drive the Germans back across the Seine. If anything, Tedder saw a return to the cautiousness on Montgomery's part in his directive. Montgomery directed his commanders to create a limited extension of the line around the eastern flank while keeping the British front east of the River Orme as active as possible. Indeed, Montgomery wanted the Germans to believe that the British were contemplating a major advance towards Falaise and Argentan and would build up their main strength to the East of the River Orme. [18]

Tedder had no faith in this plan at all. Interestingly, he had every faith in the Americans that they would break through in the west despite the difficult terrain but he had no faith in Montgomery. "On the other hand, the country in which wide and rapid sweeps could be made was that lying to the southeast of Caen," wrote Tedder. "I felt that some more specific action was needed if we were not finally to lose our advantage."

Tedder then suggested to Eisenhower two things – one that he, (Eisenhower) should set up a Tactical Headquarters in France and take control of the two Army Groups. The second suggestion was that he tell Montgomery that his directives to his commanders should give clear and unmistakable orders for decisive action.

Eisenhower again wrote to Montgomery telling him that a general offensive was needed because of the evidence SHAEF was receiving that the Germans were using SS troops to ensure effectiveness in other units.

After the attempt on Hitler's life there appeared to be confusion and doubt in the German ranks and this opportunity should be exploited.

In *With Prejudice*, Tedder wrote that the Americans were beginning to grumble that Eisenhower was too soft on the British. At the same time, a German document fell into the hands of the Allies that showed the enemy's view of the British Second Army. The report said that tactical reconnaissance carried out by aircraft and tanks preceded every engagement and this was usually supported by heavy artillery fire. The report also said that British attacks usually took place only after an artillery barrage of anything up to three hours.

One of the report's greatest criticisms was that the British never exploited the opportunities after they achieved a success. The weakest moment, according to the report, for the British infantry was when they had to fight in close combat without artillery and that was the moment the Germans should attack. Any close quarter fighting between the British and Germans, the report stated meant that the British either retreated or surrendered. [19]

The report drew attention to the fact that there was continual attack from Allied single and twin-engined fighters. "There was no resistance by our own aircraft and therefore the enemy had undisturbed opportunity for flying low in search of our supply routes." Tedder quoted the report in his book. "Since 13 June artillery reconnaissance has been used and fighter-bombers and fighters against our anti-aircraft and artillery positions."

Although Tedder was deeply dissatisfied with Montgomery's handling of the Caen sector in the east, he felt that the air war against the German military in Normandy was going well.

In the west, despite the difficulties of the terrain, the beachhead had been widened with the fall of Cherbourg and on 25th July, the Americans began their offensive which led to the breakthrough from the Cherbourg peninsula across the St. Lo-Perrier line. The first day the going was slow but on the 26th the Americans broke out and rolled south towards Coutances and Avranches and beyond. A huge amount of air power was thrown into this battle with the air forces bombing just ahead of the Army. Some bombs landed on Allied troops.

While the Americans were pushing out, Eisenhower turned to Churchill, appealing for him to get Montgomery moving. The American press were now openly criticising the British for holding back and allowing the American forces to take all the casualties and do all the fighting.

In a letter to Montgomery, General Alan Brooke stated that as a result of the mounting criticism taking place that Montgomery should attack at the earliest possible moment on a large scale. The Germans, he wrote, should not be allowed to move from the British front to the American front.

Before receiving this letter, Montgomery had already adopted the policy of bold aggression. In a telegraph to Eisenhower he stated he had told his commanders to throw caution to the wind, take any risks and accept any casualties and step on the gas.

By the 31st of July the Americans were able to move infantry units into the forward area to consolidate any gains while their armour continued to attack the enemy. The Canadians were fighting intensely, keeping the Germans from breaking out of the Caen sector and rushing to stop the American advance.

On 2nd August, Eisenhower told Montgomery that German resistance in the Avranches area had collapsed and that all allied armoured divisions should be attacking the enemy's flanks.

However, the Germans tried to counter-attack from Mortain to Avranches to cut the American lines of communication. This move provided the Americans with the opportunity to swing round to the south and attack the German flank. If the Germans did manage to break through to Avranches the allied troops left to fight on would be helped by receiving 2,000 tons of supplies dropped every day by air.

The counter-attack by the Germans was halted by the Allies and the American enveloping movement and the British attack on the left boxed in a large German force in what has since been called the 'Falaise Pocket', or the Falaise Gap.

Eisenhower then decided to make a wider envelopment of enemy forces by pushing towards the Seine and east of Paris, resulting in a large number of German troops being sealed off by mid-August. Allied air forces mercilessly pounded the Germans caught in the pocket. The Germans lost nearly half a million men and a mass of equipment in the Normandy campaign.

But before this happened and while all the machinations were taking place between Montgomery and Tedder, the pilots flying their Typhoons continued to fight day after day, pounding enemy targets wherever and whenever they could.

They knew nothing of what was going on at the higher levels of command, nothing of the letters, signals and telegrams from Eisenhower, to Montgomery to Tedder and to the SHAEF staff. All they knew was that they had to keep fighting.

CHAPTER FOUR
The 'Bombphoons' 197 Squadron, June 1944

"The Typhoon was a marvellous gun platform and could take a lot of punishment and get back." These words were from veteran Typhoon pilot Derek Lovell who flew with 197 Squadron over Caen in June, July and August of 1944. Interviewed in his home in 2004 he provided an interesting and entertained insight into the life of a fighter-bomber pilot during the hard and bitter struggle in Normandy. He talked fondly about flying and fighting with the Typhoon. "We used to say it forced its way through the air rather than flew. It had been designed to take on the 190 but it was not good at height. It hadn't got the power at that height. It operated at its best up to10,000 feet. It just didn't match up to the 190 above that."

Lovell volunteered at the end of the Battle of Britain but wasn't called up until June 1941. "We were training at Swift Current, Canada, for a bit on Tiger Moths then the unit moved to Bowden, north of Calgary where we finished our elementary flying and some of us went to Medicine Hat, Alberta and flew Oxfords there," he said. "We started flying in September and got our wings in April. Half of Medicine Hat was Harvards and the other were Oxfords. Then I got sent to instructor school at Trenton, Ontario on Harvards. After that I was posted to Kingston, Ontario on Harvards, at an RAF station with Fleet Air Arms pupils. I'd come back from Canada where I'd been an instructor for a year on Harvards at Kingston, Ontario."

Once in England he went to Harrogate where he was interviewed and asked what he had done his service flying on. Once they heard he'd flown on Oxfords they decided to send him to Bomber Command. "I said 'hang on a minute I haven't done twin engine flying in months and I had 500 hours on Harvards'. Rather cheekily I said I wanted singles, night fighters. The next day I was posted to Wotton in Norfolk[20] and you had to get there by train from Harrogate and it took all day. When I arrived at the adjutant's office he said the unit moved yesterday to Wrexham North Wales." After Wrexham Lovell went to the Tactical Exercise Unit at Telling outside Dundee flying Hurricanes. "I was posted to 84 Group Support Unit at Aston Down and was then introduced to the mighty Typhoon."

Lovell's first flight in the Typhoon was a memorable one. "After the Hurricane with the Merlin the Typhoon with the Napier Sabre engine was like someone hitting you up the backside with a sledgehammer. It was about 1,500 feet before I worked out how to pull the undercarriage up. It was very nice to fly. One had heard all sorts of stories about Typhoons so one was a bit apprehensive. After a couple of flights at Aston Down I was posted to Needs Oar Point with 197 Squadron."

Lovell joined 197 Squadron as a Warrant Officer on 11th June and a few hours after he arrived he was in the air. "After four or five hours I started on my first op from Need's Oar Point in the New Forest," Derek Lovell explained. "There were about 12 airfields in the New Forest at the time. The first time I went as a No. 2 to the CO Squadron Leader 'Butch' Taylor. We always used bombs, never rockets. On the main runway you were over the sea in seconds."

The first day of June 1944 was unremarkable considering they were only five days away from D-Day. According to the diarist[21] who wrote the squadron history for this period only practice flying was laid on for that day.

The next day, however, was a very different story. The first operation took place in the late afternoon when 16 aircraft from 197 Squadron took off from Need's Oar Point and flew to Thorney Island where they joined up with the rest of the Wing for a big attack on the radar station at Cap D'Antifer.[22] The 16 aircraft of 197 Squadron, led by Wing Commander Baker, took off with the rest of the wing at 1800hrs for a low level bombing attack on the target. Crossing over the coast, the Typhoons headed for the radar station as Baker led his aircraft in at tree top level.

Bombs fell from each of the Typhoons exploding into buildings, gun emplacements, vehicles and huts. Troops on the ground were caught in a firestorm of shells as the fighters, their bombs gone, raked the target area with cannon fire.

The entry in the squadron history for the day's work at Cap D'Antifer read, "Altogether a most successful show and all our aircraft returned safely."

Most of 197's operations were Army support, attacking bridges, roads, junctions, and tank concentrations. "We flew a lot of low level bombing," Lovell said. "When I mean low level I mean rooftop and below with 11 second delayed fuses. You'd watch the CO and his No. 2 go in and start counting 11 and by the time it came your turn you had a few seconds left. Usually we got a flight in before all of them went off."

On 3rd June, Squadron Leader Taylor led 12 aircraft at 1755hrs back to the radar station at Cap D'Antifer. This time they attacked the remaining structures from height, diving-bombing with precision. Bomb after bomb fell on the target, causing explosions and fires that destroyed the RDF station. There is no indication from the history of any flak being fired at the Typhoons and the aircraft all returned safely.

The next day the pilots were put to use painting black and white stripes on all the aircraft. This unusual activity took the whole day and no operational flying took place. "We hope that this proves to be the starting point of big things," the squadron diarist recorded.

The weather on the 5th of June was fine. The squadron was placed at readiness and the squadron diarist recorded that "it seems that the 'Big Show' will not be starting yet and that the camouflage is just to fool 'Jerry'."

At 1100hrs, Flying Lieutenant Jolleys took off, leading Flight Sergeants Byrne, Richardson and Tapson, Pilot Officers Watson and Jones, Flight Sergeant Kyle and Flight Sergeant McFee on a Ramrod to attack a radar station at Abbeville. After dropping all their bombs the fighters returned to base at 1225hrs. Twenty-five minutes after they landed, Flight Lieutenant Johnson DFC and Pilot Officer Reid took off on an Air Sea Rescue patrol in search of Squadron Leader Ross of 193 Squadron who had baled out of his stricken aircraft earlier in the morning. During this patrol, Johnson sighted several ships passing south west of the Isle of Wight.

That evening, with light still remaining, six Typhoons took off from Needs Oar Point on a Ramrod mission against an enemy HQ in a château near the village of Bolbec.[23] Squadron Leader Taylor led Flight Sergeant Richards, Flight Lieutenant Jolleys, Flight Sergeant Gilbert, Pilot Officer Trott and Pilot Officer Reid roared in at low level, attacking the house, hammering it with bombs and cannon fire. The pilots reported several direct hits from their bombs on the château before they climbed away and headed back across the Channel to base and a cup of tea. On the way out and on the way back the Typhoons frequently altered course to avoid large convoys heading towards the Cherbourg area. "We wondered if this is going to be the invasion or are we still trying to fox the Hun," wrote the diarist.

A few hours later they found out. At 2130hrs the pilots were called into the officer's mess where Wing Commander Baker briefed the pilots that the following day was D-Day and their missions for that day were laid out. The final entry for the 5th of June states, "We all went to bed tonight with very high hopes for the morrow."

D-Day itself for 197 squadron pilots was busy enough, but the subsequent days were even busier as the allies tried desperately to hold the beachheads. Flying began at 0710hrs with Wing Commander Baker leading Flight Sergeants Ellis, Kyle and Tapson, Squadron Leader Taylor,

Flying Officers Oury and Matson, Pilot Officer Jones and Warrant Officer Bratt on a low level attack on a German General Headquarters southeast of Bayeux with successful results.

Later that day at 1750hrs Flight Lieutenant Johnson led Flight Lieutenant Curwen, Flying Officer Trott, Flight Sergeant Richards, Flight Lieutenant Jolleys, Pilot Officer Taylor, Flying Officer Potter and Pilot Officer Reid on an armed recce to the Caen area attacking several targets of opportunity with cannon fire and bombs. Squadron Leader Taylor was up later in the evening at 2150hrs leading eight Typhoons back to the Caen-Bayeux area where they attacked heavy transport vehicles on several secondary roads with cannon fire and bombs.

Flying on the 7th began even earlier than D-Day with Flight Lieutenant Johnson leading Flight Lieutenant Curwen, Flying Officer Potter, Pilot Officer Reid, Flight Sergeant Clark, Flying Officer Mahaffy and Flight Sergeants Gilbert and Price on an armed recce in the Lisieux–Bernay area. The Typhoons took off at 0600hrs and roared across the Channel to the target area where they attacked transport vehicles and farm buildings but lost Flying Officer Potter on the mission, presumably from ground fire, though there is no mention of what caused him to go down in the squadron history.

Later that morning at 0855hrs Squadron Leader Taylor led Pilot Officer James, Flight Sergeant Kyle, Flight Sergeant McFee, Flight Lieutenant Jolleys, Flight Lieutenant Backhouse, Flight Sergeant Richardson and Flight Sergeant Ellis on an armed recce of eight aircraft back to the Lisieux –Bernay area where they attacked railway sidings and hammered the rolling stock, causing severe damage.

At 1855hrs Flight Sergeant Clark led Pilot Officer Taylor, Flight Sergeants Gilbert and Richardson, Flight Lieutenant Johnson, Flight Lieutenant Curwen and Flying Officers Trott and Mahaffy across the Channel on an armed recce south southeast of Falaise where they successfully attacked a road-rail bridge and hit several transport vehicles with good results.

The next day was just as busy, with flying getting underway early. Flight Lieutenant Jolleys took off at 0730hrs leading Sergeant Farmiloe, Flying Officer Oury, Flight Sergeant Ellis, Squadron Leader Taylor, Flight Sergeant Tapson, Pilot Officer Watson and Flight Sergeant Byrne on an armed recce to La Cambe. In the area around the village, the Typhoons struck, hammering tanks and enemy troops with bombs and cannon fire. Three tanks were hit by bombs, their turrets and tracks smashed from the blasts totally destroyed. Others were caught in the murderous firestorm of cannon shells as the Typhoons dove on their targets. As the attack ended and the Typhoons climbed away, the pilots reported seeing a large column of black smoke rising from the woods they'd just attacked west of the village.

At 1100hrs it was Flight Lieutenant Johnson's turn to lead another section of Typhoons on an armed recce to the Caumont–Falaise area where they successfully attacked enemy tanks, transport vehicles and troops.

The final sortie of the day was inconclusive. Getting airborne at 1800hrs from Needs Oar Point, Flight Lieutenant Jolleys leading Flight Lieutenant, Flight Lieutenant Backhouse, Flight Sergeants Kyle, Tapson and Richardson, Sergeant Farmiloe and Flight Sergeants McFee and Ellis, the Typhoons roared across the Channel at low level and at high speed. Their goal was a reported concentration of German Tiger Tanks in the Aunay–Villiers area. The Typhoons attacked the tanks at low level, each one firing short bursts at the targets. They could see their shells striking the vehicles but through the dust and the smoke and the waning light, they could not see how effective their attack had been. They turned back for home without knowing if they had destroyed the tanks or not.

There was no flying on the 9th due to bad weather and on the 10th the Squadron was put at the disposal of the 30th Division for whenever they needed air support; by 1300hrs the Squadron had not been scrambled. But at 1355hrs four Typhoons of 'A' Flight took off led by Flight Lieutenant Jolleys on an armed recce to the Caen–Falaise area where they attacked railway rolling stock in a siding near Noyers. Shells from their cannon tore into the rolling stock as they attacked. Leaving the target area they headed for home but not before they had successfully shot up enemy troop and gun positions.

In the evening, at 1830hrs, Squadron Leader Taylor took Flying Officer Trott, Flight Sergeant Clark, Pilot Officer Reid, Flight Lieutenant Curwen, Pilot Officer Jones, Flight Sergeant Gilbert and Flight Sergeant Richards on an armed recce in the Caen area. South of Caen, they spotted an armed convoy and immediately attacked it. Several vehicles, including a gun and trailer, were destroyed. Other vehicles were left smoking from the onslaught and enemy troops were killed as the aircraft tore overhead strafing them with cannon fire.

The weather on the 11th was clear over Britain and operational flying began early. Squadron Leader Taylor taking Mahaffy, Trott, Richards, Curwen, Jones, Gilbert and Reid from Needs Oar Point at 0620hrs on an armed recce over the beachhead. But once they reached France cloud cover from the beach upwards in various layers prevented any of the targets from being picked out and the mission was scrubbed.

This was the day the Warrant Officer Derek Lovell joined 197 Squadron. Warrant Officer Bratt and Warrant Officer Hall, a Canadian, also joined this day.

Lovell described what a normal day flying and fighting in a Typhoon was like as part of B Flight. "A batman would wake you up at half past three in the morning for a briefing," he recalled. "You strap on the .38 Smith and Wesson, go down to breakfast and at that time of the morning your stomach says no way so you have some sweet tea. Then down to the ops tent for briefing. Then from there clamber onto the CO's jeep, nine of you, eight and a spare man. We were given synchronised watch time.

"You brought your Mae West, helmet and parachute. The ground crew put your parachute in because it was quite heavy with the dinghy. Before tying on your Mae West you went for a panic pee near the tail wheel of the aircraft with orders not to hit the tail wheel because it was rotting the tyres. You'd go through the cockpit drill then put your fingers on the buttons, looking at your watch listening for the CO to start. You'd hear him start and then you fire your aircraft and make sure all the pressures built up, taxi out looking for your place in the queue following the CO from his place in his bay, Head to the end of the runway, turn 90 degrees run the engine up, make sure all was in working order, 15 degrees flap, down to the runway. We took off in pairs down the runway, full throttle, wheels up, flaps up and then the squadron would form up and climb to 8,000 feet into a finger four battle formation.

"Crossing the French coast your eyes were on swivels in case there was anything about. Approach the target, which you had seen on the map. As soon as you came across the front line up came the flak. They'd all bang away at you. You get into echelon starboard and the CO would go 120 degrees past the target, peel over back to it and that got you into a 60-degree dive. The next, No 2 would count three, then No 3 would count three and then you would count three and then follow down, Aim at the target, release the bombs, heave back full left rudder, full throttle and then rendezvous at 8,000 feet, reform and come home. When you came near base you'd get into two sections of four, line astern and you'd go down the edge of the runway and the CO would peel off and if you got it right all four of you peeled off before reaching the end of the runway and you came round and landed. By the time the CO had landed the second flight had come round and landed. Left right left right, so you landed and taxied to dispersal, debriefing and then off to breakfast. That was a B flight operation."

Flying began early on the 12th with Wing Commander Baker leading an armed recce with three other aircraft to the Caen–Conde area where they attacked several heavy motor transports with good results.

Flight Lieutenant Johnson led Flying Officer Mahaffy, Flying Officer Trott and Pilot Officer Taylor on the squadron's next armed recce to the Caen–Argentan–Flers area where they attacked several vehicles, leaving a staff car and truck smoking. Despite this, the bombing results were not so good.[24]

Lovell, Bratt and Hall did some local flying, practice formation flying and practice dive-bombing on this day.

At 2100hrs with the light beginning to fade, Squadron Leader Taylor took off from Needs Oar Point, leading Flight Sergeant Ellis, Flight Sergeant Kyle, Flying Officer Oury, Pilot Officer Watson, Flight Sergeant Byrne,

Flight Sergeant Richardson, Flight Lieutenant Backhouse, Flight Sergeant Clark, Pilot Officer Reid, Flight Sergeant Gilbert and Flight Sergeant Richards on an armed recce to the beachhead, where they bombed and strafed several enemy targets. Rolling into their dives, Taylor led the Typhoons down onto several motor transport vehicles and enemy troops strafing them with cannon fire. Several vehicles were hit. Wheeling away, the Typhoons then attacked a road-rail bridge with bombs effectively blocking it. As they attacked, light flak from German gunners came up to them and two Typhoons were hit but managed to return home safely. "The bad thing was to be the CO's number two because if you got a little bit too far behind him they'd miss him and got you," Derek Lovell recalled. "It wasn't a healthy place to be. You've got to be behind him and you got out as quickly as you could."

At 1955hrs on the 13th of June, Squadron Leader Taylor led the same section as the day before on a bombing show to enemy positions in a wood east of Caen in support of the Army. Crossing the Channel at low level to avoid detection by German radar, they climbed to 3,000 feet as they approached the target area. They dropped into their dives, levelled out at 1,200 feet and released their bombs with most of them pounding the target area and the remainder falling just east. At the same, time the Typhoons strafed the area with cannon fire. As they roared away, climbing rapidly, Taylor could see that a farmhouse was left in flames but also that Flight Sergeant Richards was nowhere to be seen. There is no indication in the history as to what happened to him. [25]

The following day the weather was fine and 197 Squadron carried out extensive operations. The first show took place at 0925hrs when Squadron Leader Taylor led Flight Sergeant Byrne, Flying Officer Oury, Sergeant Farmiloe, Flight Lieutenant Jolleys, Flight Lieutenant Backhouse, Flight Sergeant Kyle and Flight Sergeant Tapson on a bombing mission in support of the army. Airborne, Taylor identified the target area, near La Seirandiere, with red smoke set off by the British Army. Dropping into their dives the Typhoons bombed and strafed the targets and all but two of their bombs landed in the target area. The pilots saw a huge explosion of smoke and flames billow up into the sky as if an ammunition dump had been hit. As they climbed away, they could see a farmhouse on fire.

Later in the day, Flight Lieutenant Johnson took Price, Gilbert and Pilot Officer Taylor, Curwen, Bratt and Clark on an armed recce south of Caen.[26] The target was a concentration of enemy troops and Armoured Fighting Vehicles. At 3,000 feet Johnson led the flight into their dives, attacking from north to south strafing the targets with short bursts. At 1,000 feet they released their bombs and they could see several cannon strikes on vehicles and personnel, with most bombs in the target area.

Lovell flew his first mission with 197 Squadron at 1615hrs that day. The target was a pontoon bridge near Cherbourg, which they couldn't find so they attacked two masonry bridges instead with no direct hits.

The last flight of the day took place at 2150hrs and was an armed recce led by Flight Lieutenant Jolleys who led Flying Officer Trott, Pilot Officer Jones, Pilot Officer Taylor, Flight Sergeant Clarke, Flight Sergeant Rook, Flight Sergeant Gilbert and Pilot Officer Reid to attack targets in the Villiers–Caen area. The Typhoons patrolled the area searching for transport targets and found several vehicles using a main road. Heavy flak kept the aircraft from diving down to low level so they bombed the road from 3,000 feet achieving two hits and two near misses. Gun positions in the area were also bombed. The aircraft returned safely to base "with pilots twitching."[27]

"On one occasion when we were at Hurn and the weather clamped down with thick fog and the squadron was stood down, a number of us went to Bournemouth," Derek Lovell explained about the need for answering the call of nature while flying. "We'd been there about an hour and the fog had burnt off to a clear blue sky and meanwhile the squadron was brought from stand-down to 60 minutes, 30 minutes, and 15 minutes to report to Ops. The CO was running around trying to find eight pilots. Some were celebrating the promotion of somebody and having a few beers.

"Anyway they set off across the Channel at 8,000 feet and it was chilly and you had some beer, there comes a time when nature calls. People were whingeing over the radio and CO said nobody is to turn back just because you want a pee, manage as best you can in the cockpit but don't hit anything electrical. We were sitting there with cockpit harness, parachute harness and Mae West and it all had to be undone and you had to find the fly buttons: no zips remember. The squadron opened up wide in battle formation while the pilots relieved themselves and did this two or three times there and back. Half an hour across the Channel, twenty minutes there and half an hour back again.

"When you landed the Typhoon surplus fuel from the carburettor would run out the back of the big radiator after you closed it down. When your glycol ran out the engine would pack up. The only way to check whether it was glycol or petrol was to taste it. So when the aircraft landed and the ground crew checked them over the engine fitters would sometimes say, 'Excuse me sir, you seem to have a glycol leak that doesn't taste like glycol.' It only happened once or twice."

On 15th June operational flying began with a Ramrod mission at 1055hrs when Squadron Leader Taylor led Flight Sergeant Byrne, Pilot Officer Watson, Flight Sergeant McFee, Flight Lieutenant Jolleys, Sergeant Farmiloe, Flying Officer Oury and Flight Lieutenant Backhouse to attack factory buildings east of Caen. The Typhoons roared in on the target in two waves of four, first from east to west diving from 6,000 feet down to 200 feet, their cannon strafing the buildings and factory chimneys before dropping their bombs. The second wave dove in on the target from West to East, dropping their bombs at very low level and raking the buildings with cannon fire. Fourteen bombs burst in the target area and cannon shells ripped into the chimneys but they remained standing as the Typhoons roared away and landed back at base at 1205hrs.

That evening a big show was laid on that would see all the squadrons in 146 Wing taking part. Leading this Ramrod was Wing Commander Baker to attack enemy strongholds in the village Fontenay-le-Pesnel. On the way in, they encountered heavy flak. Climbing to 6,000 feet, the Typhoons dove on the target dropping to 1,500 feet, strafing the area with cannon. As they levelled out, they released their bombs. Columns of thick black smoke billowed up from the area. Transport vehicles caught in the open on the road in the centre of the village received direct hits and exploded into flames. As the aircraft formed up one very large explosion was seen in the target area. All of 197 Squadron's aircraft returned safely to base just as the weather began to close in.

The following day Derek Lovell was airborne on a Ramrod mission led by Squadron Leader Taylor with Byrne, Tapson, Watson, Ellis, Richardson, Jolleys, Price, Johnson, Mahaffy and Jones to a bridge near Caen. Diving from 4,000 to 1,500 feet, they strafed the structure with cannon fire and released their bombs as they levelled out. Four bombs burst by the bridge supports and four more pounded into the road approaches. One enemy transport truck caught on the bridge was destroyed by a direct hit. Cannon shells pounded both into the bridge and the approaches.

In the evening, another Ramrod mission was laid on this time to bomb the bridges at Thury-Harcourt south of Caen. Led by Wing Commander Baker the squadron crossed in north of Bayeux, just west of Caen, and the cloud was at 4,000 feet. As the formation turned south, heavy and light flak began to burst amongst the aircraft. The flak was very accurate and immediately they began weaving to avoid the bursts. At the same time the cloud was getting lower so the Wing Commander decided to abandon the sortie and return to base.

"Vampire turn 180 degrees,"[28] Baker called to the squadron. Weaving to avoid the flak he was suddenly lost from view. The Squadron turned but there was no sign of him. "He was found to be missing from the formation and it is not yet known what has happened to him," the diarist recorded.

The 17th was another sad day for the squadron. The first sortie, a Ramrod to the Thury-Harcourt area was abandoned because of poor weather over the sea.

At 1335hrs Flight Lieutenant Johnson led a Ramrod to the bridges at Thury-Harcourt south of Caen. The twelve aircraft split into two sections and attacked two different bridges. Diving from 9,000 feet to 2,000 feet, they released their bombs just as they pulled out of the dive. One direct hit was seen on the bridge and several near misses from the twelve bombs dropped landed in the water nearby. As they dove, they pumped cannon shells into the structures. The next section attacked another bridge, dropping their bombs within 20 yards of the bridge but no direct hits were observed as the bridge was obscured by dust and smoke. All the aircraft returned to base at 1500hrs.

Three hours later, Flight Lieutenant Jolleys took Warrant Officer Lovell (his No 2) Flight Sergeant Kyle, Pilot Officer Watson, Flight Sergeant Tapson, Flying Officer Oury, Flight Lieutenant Johnson, Flight Sergeants Hall, Price, Clark and Pilot Officer Taylor back to the bridges at Thury-Harcourt. However, only a few minutes into the flight and Lovell had to turn back due to mechanical trouble. He landed back at base at 1835hrs 35 minutes after he'd taken off. Three other Typhoons also turned back due to mechanical trouble. Jolleys continued to lead the rest of the flight towards the target area.

Crossing the coast, the section rapidly climbed to 7,000 feet then over the target they dropped into their dives roaring down on the bridges below, firing short bursts from their cannon as they dove. Pulling out dangerously low at 200 feet the Typhoons released their bombs and rapidly climbed away. No direct hits on the bridge were seen but they could see all their bombs had fallen on the river bank on the west side of the bridge. They could also see that Pilot Officer Watson, his aircraft on fire, was unable to pull up and he crashed into a hill and blew up. According to the squadron history Watson was an experienced pilot and very well liked. His loss was a sad blow to the squadron. The final entry for this day simply states that Squadron Leader Taylor had been kept busy all day in intelligence as the Wing Commander was missing. By close of play that day there was still no word of him.

On the 18th the weather over England was very clear and bright so flying began at dawn that morning. Eight aircraft led by Flight Lieutenant Jolleys were airborne at 0510hrs on a Ramrod to attack the same bridges they had attacked the day before. But over the French coast the weather was so poor they had to turn back and abandon the mission.

Later in the day they tried again to knock out the bridges only to be recalled before reaching the target due to bad weather. But finally, as the evening wore on, Pilot Officer Taylor, Flight Sergeant Gilbert, Pilot Officer Reid, Flight Sergeant Rook, Pilot Officer Jones, Flying Officer Mahaffy and Flight Sergeant Kyle led by Flight Lieutenant Johnson were airborne at 1855hrs and attacked the bridges at Thury-Harcourt, this time diving from 8,000 feet down to 3,000 feet dropping their bombs on the southern bridge. Every bomb fell in the target area but no direct hits were seen.

The following day bad weather kept the Squadron on the ground. Wing Commander Baldwin D.S.O., D.F.C. and bar joined the wing replacing Wing Commander Baker.

The 20th was a busy day for the Squadron with the weather in England being very fine but poor over the beachhead. At 1250hrs Squadron Leader Taylor led Flight Sergeant Ellis, Flying Officer Oury, Flight Sergeant McFee, Flight Lieutenant Jolleys and Flight Lieutenant Backhouse, Flight Sergeants Richardson, Tapson, Clarke and Byrne to bomb a Noball (V1) site east of Boulogne.

Dropping into their dives, bombs from the Typhoons pounded the target area with two bursting on the end of the ramp, a near miss on a Q building, and three bursts 100 yards from the ramp. All the aircraft returned to Manston where they were bombed up, rearmed and refuelled. At 1655 they took off again to attack another Noball site at Aix. Diving from 8,000 feet to 400 feet the Typhoons bombed and strafed the target. Four pairs of bombs were seen to explode in the target area while the rest were not seen. All the aircraft returned to Manston and then flew on to base at Needs Oar Point.

The following day bad weather over France ensured that no big shows took place though the Squadron remained on readiness.

On the 22nd Flight Sergeants Richardson and Ellis roared away from Needs Oar Point at 0515hrs heading towards France on a weather recce and reported that the weather was of no use for operations as it was 10/10ths cloud at low level.

That evening, Squadron Leader Taylor led Flight Lieutenant Backhouse, Flying Officer Oury, Sergeant Farmiloe, Flight Sergeant Kyle, Warrant Officer Lovell, Flight Sergeant McFee, Flight Sergeant Byrne, Flight Lieutenant Johnson, Flying Officer Mahaffy, Flight Sergeant Clarke and Pilot Officer Taylor on a Ranger to patrol the area east of Caen to Paris. Though they saw no movement on the road they spotted some rolling stock on the railway sidings at Rambouillet and strafed the rail wagons with cannon fire.

Shells ripped into the wagons, the track and the ground nearby as the Typhoons attacked sending dust and debris flying. Two of the wagons were left smoking as the section climbed away heading for home. On their way, they could see a pall of smoke over Paris left by the USAF B17 heavy bombers who had been blasting targets in the area.[29]

All the aircraft returned home at 2100hrs except for Flight Sergeant Kyle who had turned back shortly after take off.

Dawn brought clear fine weather and a Ranger was laid on for targets in the area south of Caen. Ten aircraft led by Wing Commander Baldwin took off at 0855hrs from Needs Oar Point climbing into the morning sky. Flight Sergeant Ellis, Flight Lieutenant Johnson, Pilot Officer Reid, Flying Officer Trott, Flight Sergeant Hall, Flight Sergeant Clarke, Flying Officer Mahaffy and Flight Sergeant Price formed up with Baldwin and then the formation roared across the Channel. Eight miles north north-west of Evereux the Typhoons attacked a radar station with cannon fire. Their shells hammered the buildings and vehicles. Wing Commander Baldwin then turned his section towards St. Andre where they strafed several wagons in a railway siding with heavy cannon fire but no results were seen as they wheeled away. However, on the road from Breteuil to Lisieux the section caught ten heavy transport vehicles and armoured fighting vehicles out in the open that they immediately attacked. Firing short bursts from their cannon, each Typhoon attacked the vehicles setting three on fire.

Early morning on the 24th and the weather was perfect for flying. At 1020hrs Flight Lieutenant Jolleys was airborne, leading Byrne, Oury, Farmiloe, Richardson, Ellis, McFee, Tapson, Reid and Mason on a Ramrod to the railway junction at Evreux. Climbing to 4,000 feet Jolleys peeled off with the other aircraft in a line astern formation. At 1500 feet they released their bombs and levelled off. Three bombs were direct hits smashing the lines completely.

Later in the afternoon, Flight Sergeant Hall took Pilot Officer Jones, Pilot Officer Reid, Flight Lieutenant Johnson, Flight Sergeant Mason, Flight Sergeant Gilbert, Flying Officer Mahaffy, Pilot Officer Taylor and Flight Sergeant McFee on a Ramrod to a supply dump at Montautour. Bomb after bomb from the Typhoons pounded the area causing several fires and two large transport vehicles were hit with cannon fire. German gunners were active, pumping flak into the air. Pilot Officer Jones was hit in the fuselage as the Typhoons turned away from the target area heading for home and made a wheels-up landing on the beachhead in France. Watching him go down, Pilot Officer Reid landed on the beachhead, ensuring that Jones was alright and then returned to base.

Flying for the following morning was cancelled due to low cloud and poor visibility but by the afternoon it had cleared enough for a Ramrod mission to be laid on to bomb a viaduct south of Beaumont. Led by Squadron Leader Taylor the Typhoons roared into the air at 1350hrs and headed for France. Derek Lovell was one of them, flying No. 2 to Flight Lieutenant Jolleys.

They tore in at high speed and low level, dropping their bombs on the bridge and the railway line, raking the area with bursts of cannon fire. Three direct hits were seen and the rail line was cut. As they climbed away and headed back to base the weather was already closing in. The aircraft landed at various bases along the coast of England due to the deteriorating visibility and bad weather but all managed to get back to Needs Oar Point in the evening.

That day, Flight Sergeants Clark, Kyle, Gilbert and Richardson were given their promotions to Warrant Officer, which was greatly celebrated in the officer's mess.

On the 27th, a simply entry in the Squadron history stated that the Squadron received the good news that Cherbourg had fallen.

At 1145hrs that morning Squadron Leader Taylor led Flying Officer Trott, Pilot Officer Clarke, Pilot Officer Reid, Flight Lieutenant Johnson, Flight Sergeant Price, Pilot Officer Gilbert, Pilot Officer Taylor, Sergeant Farmiloe and Warrant Officer Richardson towards the French coast but due to bad weather had to abort the mission and they turned back to base. But on take off, one of the Typhoons had crashed and Pilot Officer Taylor was killed. There is no indication in the history as to what caused the crash.

The weather closed in the next day and no flying took place. But on the 29th it cleared and at 0710hrs Flight Lieutenant Johnson took Flight Sergeants Mason, McFee and Price, Flight Sergeant Rook, Pilot Officer Clarke, Flying Officer Mahaffy, Warrant Officer Lovell and Sergeant Farmiloe to bomb a railway junction at Pont Authou. Six were direct hits, cutting the lines and several wagons were lifted off the rails by the blasts. Firing short bursts of cannon fire, the Typhoons caused havoc, their shells ripping into the rail wagons and track sending debris and dust in all directions. Ground fire from enemy gunners tried desperately to hit the Typhoons but they were gone before any damage could be done.

The same morning, at1120hrs Squadron Leader Taylor lifted his Typhoon into the air leading Flight Lieutenant Backhouse, Flight Sergeant McFee, Warrant Officer Lovell, Flight Lieutenant Jolleys, Flight Sergeant Ball, Pilot Officer Kyle, Flight Sergeant Byrne, and Sergeant Farmiloe on an armed recce to targets south of Caen. The fighters raced across the Channel crossed the coast and headed for their patrol area. They bombed and strafed a road-rail bridge scoring several near misses. A German tank transport truck was caught on the road and the Typhoons fell on it, raking it with cannon fire but no results were seen due to dust and debris obscuring the target and they headed back to base. No other flying took place that day.

June 30th 1944 was a normal day for the Squadron. The weather was good enough for operations and a Ramrod was laid on for attacking a bridge at Amaye-Sur-Orne. Squadron Leader Taylor led Flight Sergeant Rook, Flight Sergeant Vance, flight Sergeant Mason, Flight Sergeant Price and Pilot Officer Reid across the Channel to bomb and strafe the bridge. They roared into the air at 1810hrs, formed up and headed for France.

Over the target the weather was getting worse and the Typhoons dove on the bridge, releasing their bombs. They saw direct hits on the approaches to the bridge. A German tank was caught out and destroyed as the Typhoons strafed and bombed it, leaving it in flames. Taylor's engine suddenly started running rough as he led the section away from the target.

Searching for a landing strip he managed to put the Typhoon down on a friendly strip near the beachhead where he spent a rough night. He returned to Needs Oar Point the following day. (Needs Oar Point, built by the RAF construction unit in the winter of 1943 and in use from April 1944, overlooked the Solent and the Isle of Wight near Beaulieu river and Lymington. For a few days around June 6th it was probably the busiest airfield in the UK. It was operational for just 11 weeks and then rapidly returned to farmland.)

CHAPTER FIVE

197 Squadron, July 1944

The first day of July 1944 opened with low cloud and rain that remained all day. No operational flying took place but the Squadron began to ready the kit and equipment for the move to Hurn. In the afternoon Squadron Leader Taylor returned to the Squadron.

Poor weather on the 2nd hampered the Squadron's move and no operational flying took place that day. Six aircraft did take off but only Squadron Leader Taylor's landed at Hurn; the rest returned to Needs Oar Point. Transport was arranged to the take the pilots to Hurn for the night.

The next day, though the weather in the morning was still bad, transport took the pilots back to Needs Oar Point where they collected the aircraft in the afternoon and flew them to Hurn as the weather cleared. In the evening, at 1905hrs Wing Commander Baldwin led Flying Officer G.C. Mahaffy, Flight Sergeant C.B. Hall, Flight Lieutenant W.J. Johnson, Flight Sergeant F.J. Vance, Flying Officer L.S. Clarke and Flight Sergeant P.C. Mason on a low level Ramrod mission to attack a rail junction at Thiberville. The aircraft climbed to 6,000 feet and rolled into their dives. Releasing their bombs at the bottom of their dives, the Typhoons levelled off at 100 feet, pumping cannon fire into the target area. Direct hits were seen and all the lines were cut. One heavy transport vehicle was left smoking from the cannon shells that had ripped into it. All the Typhoons returned to base unharmed.

The 4th was a fine day and the Squadron was adjusting to its new home at Hurn. At 1000hrs Flight Sergeant W. D. Bells, Flying Officer A.J. Oury, Flight Lieutenant D.A. Backhouse, Flight Lieutenant E Jolleys, Warrant Officer D.G. Lovell, Pilot Officer J Kyle and Flight Sergeant D.E. Tapson roared into the morning sky, heading for France led by Squadron Leader Taylor. Derek Lovell, again No. 2 to Flight Lieutenant Jolleys, climbed rapidly away from base with the section. Over the Channel they formed up and ran into rain squalls and thick cloud and were forced to abandon the mission. They returned to base at 1015hrs.

The following day the Squadron was placed at readiness and as the weather was continually changing, weather recces were sent out throughout the day. A show with the Wing was laid on for the evening but due to bad weather the Wing had to return and Flight Sergeant D J Price carried out a wheels down forced landing at Needs Oar Point due to mechanical trouble. Pilot Officer L S Clark didn't return from the same sortie and was posted missing.

That same day, three pilots Flying Officer G C Mahaffy, Pilot Officer R M Jones and Flight Sergeant D E Tapson were posted to 84 G.S.U. while Warrant Officer A E James and Flight Sergeant J M James arrived at the squadron. Flight Lieutenant E Jolleys received his D.F.C. that day as well.

On 6th July the weather cleared and Squadron Leader Taylor led Flight Sergeant Ellis, Flying Officer Kyle, Warrant Officer Lovell, Pilot Officer Richardson, Flight Sergeant L.S. Bell, Flight Sergeant D McFee, Sergeant R B Farmiloe, Flight Sergeant J K Byrne, Flight Lieutenant W. O Johnson, Flight Sergeant R H Allan and Pilot Officer B L Gilbert on a Ramrod on a bridge at Grosgay[30]. Flight Lieutenant Johnson led four of the twelve Typhoons as fighter cover as 197 joined up with 257 Squadron's Typhoons for the attack. They dropped into 30°[31] dives, roaring down on the target pulverising it with bombs and cannon fire. 197's Typhoons dropped eight bombs and claimed two near misses on the track at the end of the bridge while Squadron Leader Taylor claimed two hits on the approaches.

At 2045hrs Flight Sergeant Bell, Pilot Officer Oury, Warrant Officer Lovell, Pilot Officer Richardson, Flight Sergeant James and Pilot Officer Kyle took off on an armed recce led by Squadron Leader Taylor to the marshalling yards at Clos-Sur-Risle.[32] They dove on the target releasing their bombs at low level. Eight smashed onto the railway lines, four bursting in the yards cutting the lines while another two burst on a road cutting that as well. They caught three enemy tanks and Armoured Fighting Vehicles near Conches on the road and roared down on them, firing bursts from their cannon but it was getting too dark to see the results. They landed back at base at 2220hrs. Flying Officer Oury returned early due to mechanical trouble.

There was only one operation on the 7th and it was a Ramrod led by Flight Lieutenant Johnson in the early evening where Flight Sergeant Allan, Pilot Officer R M Reid, Warrant Officer C B Hall, Flight Sergeant P c Mason, Warrant Officer A N James, Flight Sergeant P J Vance and Flight Sergeant D Price acted as escort to 136 Wing and also attacked the target. One direct hit was seen among storage tanks, another direct hit on a building on the side of the target with smoke pouring from it and the storage tank appeared to collapse.

Early in the morning of the 8th Flight Lieutenant Johnson and Pilot Officer Reid flew to France to a makeshift airstrip B15 near Ryes as part of the beginning of the Squadron's move to France. They couldn't land and were forced to return to England to land at Tangmere owing to low cloud and rain. Later Squadron Leader Taylor led nine aircraft over to land at B15 but poor weather forced them to return to base. The squadron history describes the airstrip at B15 that was to become the Squadron's first temporary base on the Continent. "Our temporary airfield in France is very rough. It consists of one strip N.E – S.W. and is merely a clearing through cornfields. It has a large dip in the middle, which makes taking off with bombs tricky. The pilots spent their first day in France taking stock of our newly won territory and acquiring souvenirs. The ground crew were augmented by the arrival of an armourer from 266 Squadron."

The following day the Squadron flew to B15 but again the weather played havoc with operational flying and they were forced to spend the night at the airstrip. "It appears that our work from now on will consist of close support bombing for the Army in the Caen sector," recorded the Squadron diarist.

At 1415hrs on the 10th of July, Wing Commander J Baldwin with Squadron Leader D H Taylor led Flight Sergeant Ellis, Flight Sergeant McFee, Flight Sergeant Byrne, Flight Lieutenant Jolleys, Warrant Officer Lovell and Pilot Officer Richardson to attack road targets for the Army. The section split into two groups of four and the first group of 'Bombphoons' led by Wing Commander Baldwin attacked a crossroads claiming two direct hits, while the second group bombed another road but no results were seen. Throughout this operation they experienced intense light and heavy flak but all the aircraft returned to base safely. "We did strafing runs down on the deck if the target was there," Lovell said during the interview. "You wanted to save some of the full throttle to climb up out of the way."

Most of the entries in the history for this period state that the squadron would fly from Hurn to B15 where they would then rearm and refuel and attack their targets from there. For example, the entry for 11th July stated, "today Wing Commander Baldwin led twelve aircraft over to B15 from whence they will operate."

Bad weather had hampered flying operations since D-Day and the 11th was no exception. The Squadron attempted only one operation - a Ramrod south of Caen and at this point they spotted ME109 fighters that promptly disappeared into the cloud cover, which was at 3,500 feet.

The following day, Squadron Leader Taylor led 'A Flight' to B15 where they waited for the entire day for the weather to clear. Finally, at 1935hrs Taylor took off from B15 leading Flight Sergeant Hall, Pilot Officer Reid, Flying Officer Trott, Flight Sergeant Vance, Pilot Officer B L Gilbert and Flight Sergeant Mason on an armed recce to bomb railway sidings near Caen where there were supposed to be wagons loaded with ammunition and petrol. As they dove on the sidings, releasing their bombs they strafed the rolling stock with short bursts from their cannon. Several bombs exploded in the target area and two direct hits cut the lines but no large fires were started, leading the pilots to conclude the wagons had no ammunition or petrol at all. Wheeling away, they spotted two large enemy vehicles on the road and immediately dropped down to tree-top level, peppering the vehicles with cannon shells. As the Typhoons roared over the target they could see several strikes on the vehicles but no fires were started. They returned to B15 safe and sound but the weather had deteriorated to the point where they could not fly back to England so they stayed the night at B15.

Dogfights with the Luftwaffe were rare for the Typhoon squadrons flying close support for the Army but on the 13th some of 197's pilots found themselves with enemy aircraft on their tails. "We did get caught by some 109s and 190s," Derek exclaimed during the interview. "I chased a 190 down to the deck and I pulled out before I hit the deck."

Wing Commander Baldwin led Mason, Trott and Rook on an armed recce in the Lisieux area. Spotting a staff car near Blangy, Flying Officer Trott and Pilot Officer Rook went down to attack it. Cannon shells ripped into the vehicle causing severe damage and as the Typhoons pulled away they were bounced by 15 ME109s.

Suddenly the sky was full of weaving and diving aircraft as they fought for their lives. Aircraft from 257 Squadron came to the rescue and in the general dogfight, Wing Commander Baldwin fired several bursts at a ME109 destroying it completely. Two more were shot down by 257 pilots and a further two were damaged but Flying Officer Trott (197 Squadron) was nowhere to be seen. The last reported sighting of him had been as he made a desperate attempt to evade the ME109 on his tail. Pilot Officer Rook, though badly shot up, managed to land back at B15. That evening the aircraft returned to Hurn for tea and the luxury of a bath. Trott was posted as missing.

On the 15th the Squadron flew back to B15 to start the day's operations. At 1135hrs Flight Lieutenant Jolleys took Flight Sergeant Bell, Warrant Office Lovell, Sergeant Farmiloe, Pilot Officer Richardson, Flight Lieutenant Backhouse and Flight Sergeant McFee took off from B15 on an armed recce to the Lisieux area but 10/10ths cloud at 1,300 feet forced them to abandon the operation. They returned to B3, east of Ryes near St Croix, which according to the 197 Squadron diarist was an excellent strip. "The campsite is also very good but the dust proves to be very trying and damaging to the aircraft."

At 2015hrs on the 16th Squadron Leader Taylor, Flight Sergeant McFee, Sergeant Farmiloe, Flight Lieutenant Jolleys, Flight Sergeant Hall, Pilot Officer Richardson and Flight Lieutenant Backhouse north of Valognes on a Ramrod mission to attack enemy troop positions in an orchard. Rolling into their dives, they released their bombs, strafing the target area with cannon fire as they levelled off. Eight bombs burst in the orchard while the rest exploded on the edges and they saw no movement at all in the target area.

"We flew two or three sorties a day," explained Derek. "We flew normally in finger fours, the CO and on one side is his No 2 and on the other side he's got 3 and 4. You are looking at each other and keeping an eye on his tail. When you went into attack the CO would order echelon port or echelon starboard. The flight leader would go past the target and peel over and go down into a 60-degree dive. Pull the nose up, pull left rudder to make it skid because gunners tend to fire along the line of the aircraft. You pull up at 8,000 feet back into finger fours and go home. You sometimes had to go out to sea to get height and you didn't need to form up but went straight home."

Two Canadian pilots, Flying Officer H.F. Wakeham and Flying Officer W.B.T Smiley joined 197 Squadron that day.

Weather on the 17th hampered operational flying but by early afternoon Flight Lieutenant Johnson led eight aircraft to B3. From there, at1440hrs Squadron Leader Taylor led the first of two close support Ramrod missions each of eight aircraft to attack an enemy battalion HQ at Dourges. At 8,000 feet Taylor, leading Flight Sergeant James, Flight Sergeant McFee, Flight Sergeant Byrnes, Flight Lieutenant Jolleys Flight Sergeant Bell, Pilot Officer Richardson and Flight Lieutenant Backhouse peeled off into their dives screaming down on the target. Releasing his bombs at 2,000 feet Taylor levelled out and thumbed the firing button sending bursts of cannon shells into the buildings, the rest of the section doing the same. Four bombs smashed into the buildings and the rest exploded in the immediate vicinity. Flak from enemy gunners burst around the Typhoons as they attacked.

Later, at 1710hrs Taylor led Lovell, McFee, Farmiloe, Jolleys, Bell, Richardson and James on the second close support Ramrod. The target was a concentration of enemy troops in a wood west of Lisieux. Four of the eight Typhoons dive-bombed the woods releasing a storm of fire from eight bombs on the hapless enemy troops while the remaining four Typhoons came in low, dropping delayed action bombs[33], spraying the area with cannon shells. Intense, heavy flak burst around the Typhoons as they attacked but the enemy gunners scored no hits. Smoke, dust and debris came up as explosion after explosion ripped through the woods.

Lovell explained the types of sorties the 'Bomphoons' of 197 Squadron normally flew. "We flew nearly all ground support or armed recce on opportunity targets. There was flak all the time. I mean a lot of flak. The 40mm and the 20mm flak chased you down and chased you back up again," he said. "Most of the sorties were hairy. I can't remember one where we were not shot at."

What happened to the Typhoon when the bombs were released? "There was a clonk and the aircraft bumped a bit but remember you'd just got rid of the equivalent of two saloon cars from your wings. Rocket squadrons went cab ranking and we tended to go for specific low level targets like bridges, tank parks, railways, German Army HQ, factory at Dunkirk, some guns near Flushing, railway junction north of Brador. We attacked a wood that had a lot of things hiding in there like tanks. We attacked mortar and gun positions, barges on the Seine and a road that we had to break up. The enemy forward troops didn't like us very much and there were reports of pilots getting shot down and being shot by the Germans. They didn't like Typhoons. I have heard playbacks from German tank people seeing Typhoons coming and getting out of the tank and running away."

The following morning at 0855hrs Squadron Leader Taylor led a section of eight Typhoons on a Ramrod on troop concentrations in the village of Brettville-sur-Laige but they were unable to find the target so they dropped their bombs on enemy positions in a nearby village where they encountered heavy and intense flak.

"Villages that were holding up the advance were hit," Derek recalled during the interview "They were in the front line. Church towers were favourite targets because they were used as artillery observation posts. We bombed quite close to the frontline. In some cases we'd take off from B3 climb out to sea to gain height then come back in to get to the target, dive down from 8,000 feet, and release your bombs from 2-3,000 feet to give you a chance to pull out before they went off. You didn't pull back up again you just flew straight home and landed; you didn't bother to reform. The front line was just down the road.

"The Germans could see us taking off from B3 but I don't remember being shelled. At B3 you'd have eight Typhoons taking off; you had to wait to make sure the first two had cleared the runway. There were great clouds of dust as we took off and it didn't take much if you were ten miles down the road to guess that something was happening. A lot of attacks took place in July around Caen and the flak the whole time was very intense."

Later at 1235hrs Taylor led Warrant Officer Hall, Pilot Officer Kyle, Flight Sergeant Allan, Flight Lieutenant Johnson, Flight Sergeant Byrne, Flight Sergeant Vance, Warrant Officer Lovell and Flight Sergeant Price on a Ramrod to attack a concentration of enemy vehicles in a wood near Rapiere where they encountered heavy flak. One Typhoon, flown by Flying Officer Allan was hit by flak and though badly damaged managed to get his aircraft back to base without dropping his bombs. The rest of the section attacked remorselessly, bombing and strafing the vehicles. Out of 14 bombs dropped 11 exploded in the wood. An enemy armoured fighting vehicle was caught on the road and promptly strafed by the seven Typhoons that pumped burst after burst of cannon shells into it. The vehicle exploded and was left smoking when the Typhoons headed back to base, landing at 1320hrs.

A successful operation was carried out later that afternoon. Flight Lieutenant Jolleys lifted off from base at 1450hrs leading Warrant Officer Lovell, Sergeant Farmiloe, Pilot Officer Richardson, Flight Sergeant Ellis Flight Sergeant McFee and Flight Sergeant James on an armed recce to the Lisieux–Bernay–Pont L'Évêque area. One of the fighters returned early owing to mechanical trouble and the rest pushed on and divebombed railway sidings with 14 bombs. Eight ripped into the rail wagons and cut the lines with the rest falling nearby. Continuing the recce, six camouflaged enemy half-tracks were spotted and attacked. Firing a storm of cannon shells, the Typhoons fell on the enemy, roaring in at low level, the pilots fired short bursts from their four cannon pulverising the vehicles. Two of the half-tracks were left smoking, another burst into flames while an armoured vehicle exploded and burned under the onslaught from the Typhoons. "Soon as you were on the target you press the cannon hopefully to catch any flak going on down there, but also it gave you a bit of extra moral support," Derek explained. "If one of your cannons jammed you'd zigzag because of the recoil."

The losses on the Typhoons were heavy because of the close support work they were doing, according to Lovell. "Losses on the bomber Typhoon squadrons were relatively less than on the rocket Typhoon squadrons because they were coming in slower in a shallower dive and going out slower," he explained. "In the Battle of Normandy itself, I think 350 typhoons were lost and 151 pilots were killed; the rest either baled out, or got back and a lot of the time we flew in khaki not blue because leather flying jacket and flying boots so near the front line looks remarkably like the Luftwaffe. They wouldn't hang about thinking, 'I wonder if that's RAF or Luftwaffe'."

On the 19th weather hampered operational flying and the squadron was able to mount one armed recce in the evening with Wing Commander Baldwin leading Flight Sergeant Ellis, Pilot Officer Richardson, Flight Sergeant James, Flight Lieutenant Jolley, Flight Lieutenant Backhouse, Flight Sergeant McFee, Warrant Officer Lovell and Sergeant Farmiloe to bomb railway sidings in the Lisieux area. On the sidings were 10 to 20 freight wagons that were pounded with bombs and cannon fire. Diving on the target they released their bombs with one direct hit cutting the line and the rest plastering the sidings. They returned to base at 2145hrs as the light was rapidly fading.

The weather closed in so much that no operational flying took place for three days but during the lull, on 23rd July, Winston Churchill visited the Wing and gave an informal talk on the progress of the war. "Everyone was cheered by what he had to say and the day will be long remembered by members of the Squadron," the diarist recorded.

On the 24th of July Squadron Leader Taylor was posted for a rest and Squadron Leader Alan Smith took his place while the Flight Commander of 'A' Flight, F/L Johnson became the new Commanding Officer of 257 Squadron. Canadian Flight Lieutenant J.M.C. Plamondon replaced Johnson as Commander of 'A' Flight.

In the early evening of the 24th, Wing Commander Baldwin led a Ramrod on an ammunition dump. Climbing to 9,000 feet Ellis, McFee, Farmiloe, Smith, Bell, Oury, Backhouse and Lovell dove down on the enemy positions in the quarry releasing their bombs at 4,000 feet. Light flak peppered the sky around them as they levelled out seeing all the bombs fall in the quarry and a huge explosion sent a thick column of black smoke into the sky. Climbing and turning, the pilots could see horizontal flashes going off in all directions that suggested ammunition was detonating.

The next day, the new C.O. Squadron Leader Smith opened the throttles of his Typhoon and was quickly airborne at 1125hrs, accelerating rapidly. Behind him Pilot Officer Rook, Flight Sergeants Vance and Allan, Flight Lieutenant Plamondon, Flying Officer Wakeham, Flying Officer Gilbert, Warrant Officer Hall and Flying Officer Reid took off and they formed up for a Ramrod mission on a supposed ammunition dump at Argentan. Boring in on the target area, the 'Bomphoons' released all their bombs and strafed the area with cannon fire. Bombs pounded both sides of the road but no explosions or fires resulted in this attack, only some dark brown smoke was seen. On the same mission the Typhoons strafed a large enemy transport vehicle, spraying it with cannon shells at low level. They left it smoking and landed back at B3 at 1225hrs.

Later in the afternoon, Squadron Leader Smith was leading another Ramrod of eight aircraft when he was hit by flak and forced to return to base before dropping his bombs. The rest of the formation carried on bombing and strafing enemy gun and mortar positions. On this same operation several transport vehicles were strafed.

The 26th was a busy day for 197 Squadron. In the early morning a quarry in the Falaise–St Pierre–Cambrouer area was attacked by Flight Sergeant Bell, Warrant Officer Lovell, Warrant Officer James, Flying Officer Oury, Flight Lieutenant Backhouse, Flight Sergeant McFee, Sergeant Farmiloe and Flight Sergeant Ellis, led by Flight Lieutenant Jolleys. 14 bombs were seen to drop in the area but only 4 exploded. Two bombs burst in the North East corner of the quarry producing thick black smoke. Two staff cars were strafed as the Typhoons flew fast and low overhead, claiming one of the cars badly damaged. During the operation Flight Lieutenant Jolleys' aircraft developed engine trouble and as he struggled to stay airborne he managed to get back behind the lines, into friendly territory and safely crash landed at B14.

At 1530hrs Pilot Officer Rook, Warrant Officer James, Flight Lieutenant Plamondon, Flying Officer Smiley, Flight Sergeant Vance, Flight Sergeant Allan, Flying Officer and E K Necklen took off from B3 led by Squadron Leader Smith, formed up, and then joined up with aircraft from 257 and

193 Squadrons. They headed for the marshalling yards at Bernay. On the sidings there were 15 to 20 rail wagons and the Typhoons headed for these climbing to 10,000 feet where they dropped into their dives. But strong winds made the bombing somewhat inaccurate. Only four burst among the rail wagons, six exploded on the lines and the rest pounded an area south of the target.

It was decided to try to bomb the marshalling yards again later in the day when the wind had died down a little. This time, Wing Commander Baldwin formed up over the sea with Flight Sergeant Ellis, Flying Officer Oury, Flight Sergeant Bell, Flight Lieutenant Plamondon, Flying Officer Wakeham, Flight Sergeant McFee, Flight Sergeant Byrne and Warrant Officer James at 1955hrs. Joined by aircraft from 257 and 193 Squadrons the formation turned inland heading back to the marshalling yards. This time the bombing was more successful with all of them exploding in the target area and eight or nine bursting among the wagons and on the lines.

Late in the evening, at 2225hrs, the new commander of 'A' Flight, Flight Lieutenant Plamondon took Vance, James, Gilbert, Hall, Reid and Price to attack a concentration of enemy tanks in a wood near Ramecourt. In the half-light, Plamondon found the target and led the section into attack dropping all their bombs in the area. Two bursts were seen in the woods but in the darkness they couldn't tell if any tanks had been hit. On the return, three of the Typhoons got separated from the formation and landed at another air strip while the rest made successful night landings at B3 after being shot at half-heartedly by gunners from the British lines[34]. "Wing Commander Baldwin was pleased if not surprised by our success," wrote the Squadron diarist. "The Army also signified their approval."

The 27th was another very busy day for the Squadron as they were engaged in close support operations for the Army in and around the Racquancourt area. The pilots flew 48 sorties with highly satisfactory results. The weather, while more or less co-operating, was never really clear and scattered layers of cloud made bombing difficult.

Operations began at 0635hrs with Flight Lieutenant Plamondon leading Flying Officer Wakeham, Flight Sergeant McFee, Warrant Officer Lovell, Pilot Officer Oury, Flight Lieutenant Backhouse, Flight Sergeant Ellis and Flight Sergeant Bell to attack an enemy tank concentration. Lovell flew on this operation where the Typhoons dropped 16 bombs with 12 exploding in the target area. Strafing the target area as they levelled off the pilots could see their bombs exploding sending dust and debris everywhere. Two miles down the road they spotted some red smoke and what appeared to be vehicles on the road that they didn't attack, believing the smoke to be of enemy origin.[35] The Typhoons landed back at base at 0705hrs for breakfast and a hot cup of tea.

The next show of the day saw Squadron Leader Smith leading Smiley, Vance, Allan, Gilbert, Necklen, Rook and Price on an enemy strong point near Racquancourt. Climbing to 5,000 feet the eight Typhoons dove through a gap in cloud, firing short bursts from their cannon as they roared down on the target. At 2,000 feet they released their bombs and levelled off. Twelve exploded in the target area while the rest were near misses.

At 1925hrs Squadron Leader Smith took Flight Sergeant Ellis, Flight Lieutenant Backhouse, Flight Sergeant Byrne, Flight Lieutenant Plamondon, Flight Sergeant Bell, Flight Sergeant McFee and Sergeant Farmiloe to attack enemy mortar and gun positions. The Typhoons climbed rapidly to 8,000 feet over the sea the huge Napier Sabre engines of each aircraft purring contentedly. Turning back to the coast they headed for the target and dropped into their dives. At 4,000 feet they released their bombs, levelled off and tearing over the target at high speed, peppered it with cannon fire. Ten bombs were seen by the pilots to explode and as they headed back for base, they could see the target area covered with smoke from the attack.

"Pilot Officer Rook and Flight Lieutenant Plamondon had lucky escapes," the diarist recorded in the Squadron history. "The latter was hit by flak and his port tyre came off on touch down. He went round again and successfully made a wheels-up landing. Pilot Officer Rook, hit in the engine, glided down from 7,000 feet and force landed with no injury."

Also on this day Flight Lieutenant Jolleys was posted back to England having completed his tour.

Bad weather in the morning and afternoon of the 28th stopped any form of operational flying. By early evening the low cloud had cleared enough for 'B' Flight to get airborne for some close support work. At 1925hrs Squadron Leader Smith led the same pilots as the day before to bomb enemy gun positions but arriving at the target early they orbited for several minutes and seeing no red smoke from the Army to denote the target they didn't attack. Vectored to an alternate target by the Forward Controllers Smith did not attack as he had insufficient information regarding the position of British troops in the area. The Typhoons returned to base with all their bombs.

At 2010hrs Smith led Flying Officer Smiley, Flight Sergeant Vance, Warrant Officer James, Pilot Officer Gilbert, Flight Sergeant Price, Pilot Officer Reid, Flight Sergeant Allan and Flying Officer Necklen to bomb targets in the Fontenay-sur-Mer area. The cloud base was at 5,500 feet and the Typhoons dove on the target, from this height strafing troops, gun positions and buildings as they roared down on the enemy. Despite encountering 20mm and 40mm flak they pressed home their attack releasing 13 bombs at 2,500 feet. Explosion after explosion pounded the area between a church and a wood as ten bombs burst on the enemy positions. The other three burst outside of the target area. Flight Sergeant Price had two hang-ups[36] and couldn't release his bombs but managed to get out to sea and drop them there while Flight Sergeant Vance couldn't get rid of his bombs until he landed when they fell off, fortunately not exploding as he landed.

On the 29th of July Wing Commander Baldwin lifted off from the runway at 0645hrs and climbed into the early morning sky. Flight Sergeants Allan, Gilbert and Vance, Flight Lieutenant Plamondon, Flying Officer Necklen, Pilot Officer Reid, Warrant Officer James and Flying Officer Smiley took off, forming up with Baldwin over the sea and then the formation turned inland to attack a German gun battery near Bretteville. Aircraft from 257 Squadron joined the formation as they headed for the target. Climbing above the cloud cover they dove through a gap in the clouds at 6,500 feet, roaring down on the target, spraying it with cannon fire before releasing their bombs at 1500 feet. All the bombs plastered the target area and a vivid green flash was seen after the first section of Typhoons had dropped their bombs. A huge plume of smoke rose up to 1500[37] feet in the air as fire ripped through the target detonating ammunition.

The following day the 11th Armoured Division began their big push and the first operation for 197 Squadron was for a section to carry two 1000lb bombs on each of three aircraft. But visibility was so poor that the operation was scrubbed until the afternoon when aircraft from 'B' Flight tried again. Taking off at 1620hrs Squadron Leader Smith led Flying Officer Bell, Flight Sergeant Ellis, Sergeant Farmiloe, Flying Officer Oury, Flight Sergeant Byrne, Flight Sergeant McFee, Warrant Officer James and Flying Officer Wakeham to attack enemy positions. Forming up with aircraft from 257 Squadron they were unable to find the target through the low cloud cover and returned to base with bombs still on.

At 2040hrs Flight Lieutenant Plamondon led Necklen, Reid, rook, Gilbert, Smiley, Vance, James, Smith and Hall to attack a concentration of 400 enemy tanks near Pont L'Évêque. With other aircraft from 257 and 193 Squadrons the wing formed up, now led by Group Captain Gilliam. Attacking the target 50% of the bombs fell in the target area but no positive results were seen.

Weather on the 31st of July was hot and hazy and good enough for operational flying to take place. Flight Lieutenant Plamondon led a section of eight Typhoons to attack enemy positions south of Caumont in support of the 11th Armoured Division.

Again with aircraft from 257 Squadron they attacked the target near Bernay with bombs pounding the area. After the attack, smoke, dust and debris covered the area and it was agreed that the target had been totally destroyed. [38]

In the afternoon, Flying Officer Oury took Farmiloe, Wakeham and McFee as fighter escort for 266 Squadron over the Falaise area. No enemy aircraft were seen and they managed to destroy some heavy transport vehicles caught on the road.

At 1540hrs aircraft from the Wing led by Group Captain Gilliam returned to the wood near Pont L'Évêque that had been so unsuccessful the night before. Leading Flight Lieutenant Backhouse, Flight Sergeant Ellis, Warrant Officer James, Flying Officer Oury, Flying Officer Wakeham, Flight Sergeant McFee, Pilot Officer Gilbert Flight Sergeants Bell, Vance, Byrne and Price from 197 on the raid, Squadron Leader Smith pressed home a determined attack.

All the aircraft from the Wing bombed and strafed the enemy. Explosions from bursting bombs tore through the enemy positions from the 75 bombs that pounded the target area. In the western part of the wood, four to six explosions were seen while to the north two more bombs burst among some huts.

Several Typhoons roared in at high speed low level attacks, strafing a large building north of the huts. The pilots observed several strikes as the cannon shells hammered into the building. After the attack brown smoke was seen coming from the wood rising to approximately 200 feet. But no huge explosions or fireballs were seen, no flashes from detonating ammunition were observed so the attack was deemed to be a disappointment by the pilots. Bad weather scrubbed any more operational flying for that day.

CHAPTER SIX

197 Squadron, August 1944

August opened with good results for the Squadron. Though the weather on the first day was dull and overcast it cleared in the early evening and Squadron Leader Smith was airborne at 2000hrs leading Flight Sergeant Price, Pilot Officer Rook, Warrant Officer Hall, Flight Lieutenant Plamondon, and Flight Sergeants Mason, Vance and Allan on an armed recce to targets in the Vire-Dampierre area. Dropping into a low dive he strafed several trucks with his cannon, setting one on fire then led the flight to bomb several railway wagons on nearby sidings, scoring two hits before being hit by flak in his radiator bath. 16 bombs were dropped on more than 20 wagons during this operation.

On 2nd August the weather was again very hazy in the morning and Squadron Leader Smith led 'B' Flight Warrant Officer James, Flight Sergeant Ellis, Flying Officer Necklen, Flying Officer Oury and Flight Sergeants Byrne, McFee and Bell on a close support mission, attacking enemy gun and mortar positions in a wood. They took off at 1525hrs and headed for the target area but only six of the aircraft dropped their bombs which burst in the north end of the wood.

'A' Flight took off at 1705hrs on a Ramrod to attack enemy infantry and gun positions. But the bombing was difficult due to 10/10ths cloud cover over the target. Smith led the section down through gaps in the cloud dropping their bombs in the wood. They observed six hits but three bombs were hung up and later jettisoned in the sea as the Flight returned to base.

After landing, refuelling and rearming Squadron Leader Smith took off again at 1900hrs, leading Sergeant Farmiloe, Flight Sergeants Ellis and Byrne, Flying Officer Oury, Flight Sergeant McFee, Warrant Officer James and Flight Sergeant Bell on a Ramrod mission to 'Conde Sur Noireau' (probably incorrectly recorded) where the Typhoons attacked a large concentration of enemy tanks. Attacking with aircraft from 257 and 193

Squadron, the Typhoons dropped 25 bombs in the village and on the roads to the north and south. Heavy and light flak came up at them as they dove on their targets firing short bursts from their cannon on the vehicles and troops after releasing their bombs. A flak shell smashed through Smith's port wing, forcing him to turn the section for home as quickly as possible.[39] Several bombs exploded amongst the trucks and tanks but no definite claims of a tank destroyed could be made except one armoured vehicle was left smoking.

The last mission of the day saw Flight Lieutenant Plamondon take off with Price, Mason, James, Gilbert, Rook, Reid, and Allan on a Ramrod to attack an enemy concentration of motor transport lorries near La Chapelle. In the village they spotted some tanks and immediately rolled into their dives, bombing and strafing the enemy vehicles. Four direct hits in the village were seen by the pilots while other hits were seen in a nearby wood. One Typhoon strafed several trucks on the road north of the wood but didn't see the results of the strafing.

On the 3rd of August, Squadron Leader Smith took off at 1340hrs leading Flight Sergeant Byrne, Flight Sergeant Ellis, Flying Officer Wakeham, Flying Officer Oury, Flight Sergeant Bell, Warrant Officer Lovell and Sergeant Farmiloe of 'B' Flight to attack an ammunition dump at Argences inside a factory with aircraft from 193 and 257 Squadrons. The estimate in the squadron history is that 70 bombs in all were dropped and 16 of those were from 197 Squadron. As the attack took place, they saw several bombs hit the buildings creating columns of black smoke, the largest coming from the biggest hut. The last pilot of the mission turned and flew in low over the target seeing explosions still going off but no fire before he climbed quickly away as German gunners opened up. 'B' Flight returned to base at 1420hrs safe and sound.

The last operation of the day was a Ramrod where Smith led Warrant Officer Hall, Pilot Officer Reid, Flight Sergeant Mason, Flight Lieutenant Plamondon, Flight Sergeant Price, Pilot Officer Rook and Flight Sergeant Allan to bomb enemy tank concentrations near Bernay. Diving on the target they released their bombs and levelled off as the German gunners opened up on them. They had enough time to see most of their bombs hammering the target area but the flak was so intense they couldn't hang around to see any more detail.

Bad weather closed in on the following day and didn't clear until the early evening allowing Squadron Leader Smith and Bell, Lovell, Wakeham, Oury, Byrne, McFee and Farmiloe of 'B' Flight to take off at 1900hrs on a bombing and strafing run on enemy guns and vehicles at the village of St Germain. The Typhoons dove on the village strafing the enemy positions encountering heavy and light flak as they roared down on the targets. They could see strikes from their cannon ripping into several buildings and 70%[40] of their bombs burst in the target area. Thick black smoke was seen as they left the area landing back at base at 1955hrs. Again foul weather throughout the 5th kept operational flying to a minimum as only one show was laid on and it was in the evening at 1935hrs where aircraft from 197 Squadron took part in a Wing attack led by Wing Commander Baldwin on an armed recce in the Seine area. They bombed and strafed six barges in the river achieving some very near misses and one small explosion on a barge.

On the 6th bad weather again hampered operations and flying finally got under way in the afternoon. Squadron Leader Smith took off at 1500hrs on an armed recce leading Flight Lieutenant Backhouse, Warrant Officer Lovell, Pilot Officer Wakeham, Flying Officer Oury and Flight Sergeants Byrne, Ellis and Bell Smith towards the Lisieux-Falaise area but weather played havoc with their visibility. Nevertheless, they managed to dive bomb an ammunition dump with great accuracy that produced a large column of thick black smoke. Strafing enemy vehicles on the way back they scored several hits and one burst into flames.

The following day flying began around noon when the weather cleared. Squadron Leader Smith took off at 1300hrs leading Smiley, Reid, James, Plamondon, Necklen, Vance and Hall to attack an enemy strongpoint. The bombing was very successful with 100% hits in the target area. They were flying with 263 Squadron who fired their rocket projectiles at the target first then the pilots of 197 Squadron dove on the target, which they strafed and bombed. The result was a column of smoke rising up to 1500 feet![41]

Wing Commander Baldwin then took Squadron Leader Smith, Warrant Officer Lovell, Flight Sergeant Ellis, Warrant Officer James, Flying Officer Oury, Flight Lieutenant Backhouse, Flight Sergeant McFee and Flight Sergeant Byrne from 197 Squadron on a Ramrod mission to the Montaine area to attack a concentration of enemy tanks with 193 Squadron. The absence of red smoke from the Army to denote the target area forced Baldwin to abort the attack and he carried out an armed recce in search of other targets without much success.

The last flight of the day saw Flight Lieutenant Plamondon leading Necklen, James, Price, Smiley, Vance and Reid from 197 Squadron while aircraft from 193 and 257 Squadrons joined up. This formation was led by Wing Commander Baldwin to attack enemy tank concentrations near Vassy but again no red smoke was seen. They orbited over the area for 15 minutes then Baldwin ordered an armed recce. Two aircraft peeled away dive-bombing and strafing six tanks but no results were seen. Two more attacked some railway wagons 4 miles south of Vassey but no results were seen. The rest of 197 returned to base with their bombs.

"In the night, 1000 heavies go over and bomb south of Caen. Our offensive is going very well,"[42] the Squadron diarist recorded.

The first flight of the 8th took place at 0945hrs saw Squadron Leader Smith take off at 0945hrs leading Warrant Officer Lovell (No 2), Flight

Sergeants Ellis and Bell, Flight Lieutenant Curwen, Warrant Officer James, Flight Sergeant McFee and Flight Lieutenant Backhouse on a Ramrod mission with aircraft from 193 and 257 Squadrons to attack the Bretteville area where they dive-bombed and strafed an enemy HQ in a château. The first four bombs were direct hits. Bomb after bomb hammered the target as the Typhoons attacked then levelled off and opened fire spraying the target area with cannon shells. As the Wing wheeled away back to base, the pilots reported they could see a column of smoke rising to 6,000 feet![43]

At 1120hrs 'A' Flight took off from their base to attack a heavily defended area near Cinqueux. Flight Lieutenant Plamondon led Flying Officer Smiley, Pilot Officer Gilbert, Warrant Officer Hall, and Flight Sergeant Vance while aircraft from 193 and 257 Squadrons joined up. Rolling into their dives, they encountered light flak from enemy gunners. Plamondon sent bursts of cannon fire into the village and an orchard then released his bombs and climbed away. Ninety per cent of the bombs hit the mark and the pilots observed a column of black smoke coming from the target area.

Squadron Leader Smith took Flight Sergeants Byrne, Ellis and Bell, Flight Lieutenant Curwen, Warrant Officer James, Flying Officer Oury and Sergeant Farmiloe to bomb and strafe enemy positions in a wood at 'Le Thiele' (possibly incorrectly recorded name) taking off at 1615hrs but Flight Sergeant Farmiloe crashed on take off but was unharmed. The rest of the flight continued towards the target. Smith looked down on the wood searching for the red smoke that would identify the target area and after a few minutes he finally picked out the smoke and rolled into his dive. The Typhoons released their bombs strafing the target starting a large fire. "This was done with such good effect that we were later congratulated by the Army on driving the Hun out," the diarist wrote.

At 1800hrs Flight Lieutenant Plamondon with Smiley, Vance, James, Gilbert, Necklen, Reid and Hall went back to Le Thiel, strafing and bombing the enemy troop and gun positions still in the wood. All eight Typhoons dropped their bombs in the target area and strafed the road south from the village, damaging several enemy transport vehicles caught in the open. Three fires from the previous attack were seen in the village and more fires were started from their bombing.

The last show of the day was at 1950hrs when Squadron Leader Smith led Byrne, McFee, Lovell, Curwen, James, Oury, Backhouse and Ellis to bomb and strafe enemy positions in the village of Proussy. Together with Typhoons from 257 Squadron, they dropped into their dives, tearing down on the village, firing short bursts from their cannon. The pilots saw a large explosion in the north east corner of the village and several Typhoons came back in at low level, raking the area with cannon fire. Thick black smoke rose into the air from the explosion and the entire target was covered in smoke and dust. They were all safely back at base at 2015hrs.

The following day was not as busy. Squadron Leader Smith was given a well-earned 48 hour leave and left Flight Lieutenant Plamondon in charge of the Squadron. The weather was fine and the first flight of the day was an attack on tanks at Chapouville. Flying Officer Necklen, Pilot Officer Reid, Warrant Officer Hall, Pilot Officer Gilbert, Flight Sergeant Mason, Flight Sergeant Vance and Flying Officer Smiley took off at 1140hrs, formed up over the sea, roared back across the coast towards the target area, peeled off into their dives and pounded the area with bombs. No movement was seen and they achieved two direct hits that cut the road east of the village.

Flight Lieutenant R.C.C. Curwen led 'B' Flight with aircraft from 263, 193 and 257 Squadrons to attack a concentration of enemy tanks in the village of Rouen south of Caen. Byrne, McFee, Farmiloe, Oury, James Ellis and Backhouse roared into the late afternoon sky, leaving their base at 1600hrs. Over the target area they dove on the enemy vehicles strafing them with cannon fire. The pilots reported seeing a large fire in the village with thick brown smoke followed by a huge explosion.

Low cloud on the 10th prevented operational flying until the afternoon when it cleared. Flight Lieutenant Plamondon took off at 1545hrs leading 'A' Flight along with aircraft from 193 and 257 Squadrons. They attacked enemy mortar and troops positions in the village of Ouilly-Le-Tesson, south of Caen. Red smoke from the Army pinpointed the bombing area and 197 dove on the enemy firing short bursts from their cannon as they released their bombs. Half fell on the pinpoint while the rest burst in the target area. Heavy flak poured up from the ground as the German gunners tried to hit the Typhoons but the British fighter-bombers stormed in at low level sending cannon fire ripping into the flak posts on the road into the village.

Later that day at 1745hrs, Flight Lieutenant Curwen led Flying Officer Wakeham, Flight Sergeant McFee, Warrant Officer James, Pilot Officer Oury, Flight Sergeant Farmiloe, Warrant Office Lovell, Flight Lieutenant Backhouse and Flight Sergeant Byrne on an attack on an ammunition dump at Mourieres. Aircraft from 193 Squadron went in first and several detonations of ammunition were seen at the north edge of the clearing as their bombs burst on the target. Then it was 197's turn and they didn't miss. Dropping into their dives they released all their bombs causing more explosions that sent ammunition boxes flying in all directions. Moderate flak was encountered and they attacked again, strafing the area before heading for home.

Flight Lieutenant Plamondon was back in the air at 1935hrs leading Warrant Officer Hall, Flight Sergeant Mason, Flight Sergeant Allan, Pilot Officer Gilbert, Flying Officer Necklen, Pilot Officer Reid, Warrant Officer James and Flight Sergeant Vance on an armed recce in the Falaise –Argentan–Flers area where they bombed and strafed several enemy transport, half-tracks and armoured fighting vehicles. They claimed four vehicles destroyed. South of Falaise two German tanks were strafed and bombed by three Typhoons. No movement was seen so the pilots claimed them as damaged. Flying on they caught several enemy transport vehicles in the open and raked them with cannon fire. No movement was seen from this attack. On the way back to base, the Typhoons strafed three enemy gun posts. They were back on terra firma by 2050hrs.

In the afternoon of the 11th the Wing mounted an important show on an enemy radar station at Beauvais that had been helping their 'E' boats to attack British and Allied shipping. It had to be put out of action. Four Squadrons took part. Aircraft from 193, 263 and 266 Squadrons joined up with Pilot Officer Reid, Flying Officer Oury, Flight Sergeant Price, Flight Lieutenant Plamondon, Flight Sergeant Farmiloe, Pilot Officer Gilbert, Flight Sergeant Allan, Flight Lieutenant Curwen, Flight Sergeant Ellis, Flight Sergeant Vance and Warrant Officer James who took off at 1535hrs with Wing Commander Baldwin leading the formation. Arriving over the target they attacked firing rocket projectiles, dropping bombs and strafing the buildings with their 20mm cannon. The south of one of the main buildings shuddered under the impact of a direct hit as bombs and rockets rained down. Three outbuildings were destroyed and another set on fire as the British fighters fired 128 rocket projectiles and dropped 44 bombs with all but four bombs landing in the target area.

The same day Squadron Leader Smith returned from England and at 2115hrs he lifted his Typhoon into the evening sky, leading Wakeham, Lovell, Farmiloe, Curwen, Byrne, Oury and Backhouse to attack enemy troop and mortar positions at Le Thiele. Wing Commander Baldwin led sections from 193 and 266 Squadrons and the three squadrons formed up, heading for the target. Aircraft from 266 attacked first starting a large fire, and then 197's Typhoons dove on the enemy positions releasing their bombs and firing their cannon. All but one of their bombs exploded in the target area. The pilots could see fires and explosions from detonating ammunition. The rest of the aircraft attacked causing more explosions and several fires. Black smoke was seen to rise up to 3,000 feet.

On the 12th, Squadron Leader Smith took off at 1035hrs leading Flying Officer Smiley, Pilot Officer Reid, Flight Sergeant Allan, Flying Officer Gilbert, Flight Sergeant Price, Flight Sergeant Vance, Warrant Officer James and Warrant Officer Hall on a Ramrod mission south of Falaise attacking four transport vehicles with bombs and cannon fire. The strafing was very accurate and 14 bombs fell in the target area but heavy flak forced them to get out as quickly as they could. The pilots claimed three transport trucks damaged.

A big show was set up to bomb a bridge west of Falaise and Squadron Leader Smith took Wakeham, Ellis, Farmiloe, Curwen, James, Oury and Backhouse on this mission at1435hrs. Four Typhoons took two 1000lb bombs each and they bored into the target at high speed and low level. Hazy weather and the smoke from the exploding 1000lb bombs made it very difficult to see the results. The other four aircraft of 'A' Flight dropped their 500lb bombs and two exploded at the southern end of the bridge with one very near miss bursting on the riverbank beside the bridge. German gunners pumped intense flak into the sky and Flight Lieutenant D. Backhouse was hit and not seen again. Flak burst all around the Typhoons as they attacked and Flight Sergeants Ellis and Farmiloe were both hit. They managed to get back to base safely.

The last flight of the day was back to the bridge that had been attacked earlier. Wakeham, Ellis, Farmiloe, Curwen, James, Oury and Bell took off at 1810hrs led by Squadron Leader Smith. Forming up they climbed to 6,500 feet and headed for the target. Approaching the bridge they attacked from south to north, diving down, releasing their bombs then levelling off at 200 feet. They saw two bombs explode in the road and two more were very near misses sending smoke, dust and debris into the air obscuring the results from the rest of the bombs. Enemy gunners pumped light flak into the sky that burst from 2,000 feet up to 7,000 feet but no one was hit and the pilots all returned to base safely at 2045hrs.

According to the squadron history only one show was laid on for the 13th and it was late in the evening. At 2015hrs Squadron Leader Smith took off with Flying Officer Smiley, Flight Sergeant Vance, Flight Sergeant Allan, Pilot Officer Gilbert, Flight Sergeant Price, Pilot Officer Rook and Warrant Officer Hall to attack an enemy HQ and troop concentration North East of Falaise. They attacked the wood at the north end of the village dropping 80% of their bombs in the target area. Intense flak was encountered in the St Pierre area. The Germans were "more or less caught in a sock."[44]

The first flight of the 14th was at 1100hrs and saw Squadron Leader Smith leading Flying Officer Wakeham, Warrant Officer Lovell, Flight Sergeant Byrne, Flight Lieutenant Curwen, Flight Sergeant Bell, Flying Officer Oury and Flight Sergeant Farmiloe to attack enemy gun and vehicle positions north east of Falaise with aircraft from 263 Squadron. Lovell was flying in 'B' Flight as they attacked. 15 bombs from 197 Squadron Typhoon's found their mark, bursting in the target area. Two large fires erupted from the firestorm unleashed by the Typhoons and a thick column of smoke reached into the air. On the way back to base they ran into intense flak from gun positions near Sassy that went as high as 9,000 feet.

The following morning, Squadron Leader Smith climbed into the sky, leading Lovell, McFee, Byrne, Curwen, Bell, Oury, James and Wakeham on a Ramrod to barges in the Seine near Rouen. This time Lovell was flying as Smith's No.2. Following the contours of the Seine, Smith spotted the targets in the river ahead of him. Peeling off, he led the attack strafing the barges with cannon fire as he dove on them. The flak opened up as they began their attack and all their bombs were dropped. Four direct hits smashed into the barges destroying them completely, while nine were near misses. They attacked in a loose line at slightly different angles causing grief for the German gunners who were also under a hail of shells from the Typhoons. They roared away back to base leaving what was left of the barges sinking.

The target for the Squadron's next flight was a concentration of tanks in a wood east of Falaise that they attacked in close support with the Army. This time Necklen, Vance, James, Gilbert, Hall, Rook, Mason, Squadron Leader Smith, Wakeham, Allan and Price took off at 1600hrs and joined up with aircraft from 193, 263 and 266 Squadrons all led by Wing Commander Baldwin. According to the Squadron history there were upwards of 150 enemy tanks in the wood when the Typhoons attacked. Every aircraft from 197 dropped their bombs in the target area as they screamed down on the enemy, firing short bursts of cannon fire. "With so many tanks in the area we must have destroyed several," the diarist recorded.

On the 16th poor weather kept flying at bay most of the day but cleared in the early evening and at1830hrs Flying Officer Wakeham, Flight Sergeant McFee, Flight Sergeant Byrne, Flight Lieutenant Curwen, Flight Sergeants Bell and Farmiloe and Warrant Officer James along with Squadron Leader Smith roared off the runway into the air and a few minutes later joined up with aircraft from 193 and 263 Squadrons and they headed for a château HQ near Bernay. Four Typhoons from 197 bored in on the target in a high-speed low-level attack, raked it with cannon fire and released their bombs, then climbed rapidly away. The rest of the aircraft dove on the building dropping their bombs with great accuracy. Explosions pounded the target area and two direct hits smashed into the château leaving it burning fiercely. Although they encountered light flak none were hit and they were back at base by 1915hrs.

Low cloud persisted all the morning of the following day playing havoc with flying. By the early afternoon four Rhubarbs were laid on to attack the Germans retreating out of Falaise. Heavy anti-aircraft fire was encountered and Flight Sergeant Vance was hit and had to return to base. Lovell was also hit by flak on his Rhubarb and was forced to return to base early. Three enemy trucks were destroyed southwest at Bernay while two more were attacked and destroyed five miles north west of Bernay. One enemy tank and two other vehicles were attacked and destroyed as they headed south. The first Rhubarb Flight Sergeant Allan and Flight Sergeant Vance left base at 1450hrs, the next one at 1515hrs with Warrant Officer James and Pilot Officer Gilbert, the next saw Pilot Officer Rook and Flight Sergeant Ellis take off at 1540hrs, the next Warrant Officer James and Flight Sergeant McFee took off at 1555hrs and the last with Warrant Officer Lovell and Pilot Officer Reid at 1610hrs. They consisted of two aircraft each and the attacks were low level strafing and bombing runs.

At 1825hrs, Hall, Mason, Allan, Price, Vance and James led by Flight

Lieutenant Plamondon went on an armed recce back to the same area. Again, their targets were enemy vehicles. Tearing in on the hapless enemy at high speed the Typhoons left three trucks, including a petrol lorry and an ammunition lorry, on fire. Three more vehicles, including a truck towing a gun, burst into flame under a hail of cannon shells from the Typhoons. They attacked 12 tanks and as they finished more than 15 FW190s came down on them, Aircraft wheeled and weaved all over the sky as they fought to gain advantage. Three FW190s were badly damaged by cannon fire and broke off the fight diving rapidly away, smoking. Flight Sergeant Price was hit by the explosion of a truck and was seen to bale out too late for his parachute to open; he was last seen by the pilots on the ground beside his crashed aircraft. The rest of the flight returned to base at 1925hrs.

But flying for the day was not yet over. Flight Lieutenant Curwen took Flying Officer Wakeham, Warrant Officer Lovell, Flight Sergeants Byrne, McFee, Ellis and Bell and Warrant Officer James to attack and block the road at Vimoutiers that the Germans were using for their retreat. Lifting off from base at 2100hrs Curwen led the section with four Typhoons carrying 1000lb bombs and the other four acting as fighter escort. Over the target the Typhoons released their bombs, with six exploding in the target area and one landing directly onto the road cutting it completely. But haze and intense flak stopped them from making an accurate assessment of the bombing. They returned to base at 2150hrs.

At 0705hrs on the 18th Flight Lieutenant Plamondon, with Pilot Officer Smiley, Flight Sergeants Vance and Allan, Pilot Officer Gilbert, Warrant Officer Hall, Pilot Officer Rook and Warrant Officer James took off on an armed recce to the Lisieux–Bernay area where they attacked several enemy vehicles leaving several smoking. Flak was encountered up to 5,000 feet and as the flight headed back to base they saw several enemy tanks and armoured fighting vehicles burnt out having been subjected to a firestorm of rocket attacks by the RP Typhoon squadrons.

"On one operation there was a big gun in a tunnel that would come out and fire then go back into the tunnel again," Lovell explained during the interview. "The army got fed up with this so they called up the 2nd Tactical Air Force and so eight aircraft from 197 went in with four at one end of the tunnel and four the other and chucked all the bombs at either end and that was it. They sealed both ends of the tunnel. We didn't hang about to look to see if all the bombs went in." Each aircraft carried two 1,000lb bombs. One section of four Typhoons was led by Smith and the other by Baldwin. His section attacked the entrance dropping all their bombs exploding just inside the tunnel. Tons of dirt and debris fell on the track effectively blocking the mouth of the tunnel. At the other end, almost simultaneously as Baldwin's section attacked, Smith's did the same, bouncing their bombs into the entrance where they exploded. As with the other end, the explosions caused rubble to fall on the track, blocking the entrance and sealing the tunnel. On the way back to base, the Typhoons attacked gun positions in low-level strafing runs. Flak from Pont L'Évêque was intense and Baldwin's Typhoon was hit but he managed to land safely. "Group made special mention of this show and it was also mentioned in the radio news," the diarist wrote in the Squadron history.

Since D-Day 197 Squadron had flown hundreds of sorties and suffered casualties. The Allies had broken free of Normandy and begun their offensive into the heart of Germany. The end of the war in Europe was now only months away and it was in part due to those Typhoon pilots who kept up a constant attack on the enemy, never letting him breathe, always on the attack, hitting him with cannon, bombs and rockets from a fighter that left devastation in its wake.

CHAPTER SEVEN

The Typhoon Described

Much has been written about the mighty Typhoon from its beginnings to the capable and formidable ground attack fighter it became. But to best describe the Typhoon here it is necessary to go to the coal face and talk to the men who were the most familiar with it – the pilots.

However, before that, let's look at a brief history of how the aircraft came into being and how the problems encountered by engineers and pilots along the way were overcome.

The evolution of the Hawker Typhoon began in 1936 as a requirement for a second generation of new high-performance fighters to replace the Spitfire and Hurricane.[45] At the time, no one knew how well the Spitfire and Hurricane would stand up to foreign competition and therefore specification F18/37[46] for the next generation were issued by the Air Ministry. Three fundamental demands were put forward: a target speed of 400mph at 20,000 feet; a weight of fire from its gun armament at least 50 per cent greater than the Hurricane and Spitfire; and the ability for the aircraft to operate from soft, or grass airfields.[47]

At the time the thinking in the Air Council was to provide the RAF with intense fire-power which meant the new fighters were to be armed with four 20mm cannon – an idea that went against Hawker's preference for 12 .303 machine guns.

Even before the first production model of the Hurricane took to the sky (October 12, 1937) chief designer at Hawker, Sir Sydney Camm, was already thinking of the design for new, more powerful fighters that would eventually become the Typhoon and later, the Tempest.

On January 15, 1938 the specifications were sent out to ten manufacturing companies and on April 22 of the same year Hawker's tender was accepted.

For the new fighters to reach speeds in excess of 400mph new engines were needed and there were three in development at the time that were rated at more than 2,000 horsepower. One was the Napier Sabre 24 cylinder inline engine with four rows of six cylinders arranged in an H layout, driving two crankshafts on top of each other. The Rolls Royce Vulture was another 24 cylinder inline engine arranged in an X layout driving a single crankshaft and the third was the Bristol Centaurus eighteen cylinder radial engine, which was not sufficiently advanced to be properly considered but would power the later versions of the Tempest and the mighty Sea Fury.[48]

The Air Ministry ordered Hawker to build four prototypes, two with the Napier Sabre engine and two with the Rolls Royce Vulture. The Vulture powered aircraft was the Tornado and the Napier Sabre powered aircraft was the Typhoon.

The Tornado's first flight took place on October 6, 1939 and the Typhoon's first flight on February 24, 1940. But it soon became apparent that the Vulture was underpowered, overweight and mechanically unsound and as a result of the poor engine the Tornado project was scrapped in favour of the Typhoon.

Though the Typhoon project had been given the go ahead engineers at Hawkers were not to know that the Napier Sabre engine would cause them so much trouble[49] that the initial delivery dates had to be rewritten. The plan was that the first batch of 1,000 fighters ordered by the Air Ministry was to be delivered in July 1940 with the 500th to be delivered by September 1941.

In May 1940, however, the project suffered a setback when Lord Beaverbrook, Minister of Aircraft Production, decided to slow down production on all projects except for five types vital to the Battle of Britain – the Hurricane and Spitfire fighters and the Wellington, Whitley and Blenheim bombers. Nine months were lost as the Hawker factories at Langley in Buckinghamshire and at Gloster's in Gloucestershire were concentrating on the production of Hurricanes. Once the Battle of Britain had been won the need for Hurricanes diminished and Hawker could get on with the Typhoon.

Only three Tornado prototypes were built before the project was scrapped. Though, by 1941 the Typhoon was close to going into production the project was to be plagued in the early days with severe problems, mostly with the engine.

Francis K Mason's excellent book, *The Hawker Typhoon and Tempest*, goes into great detail about the many problems the project suffered. The main problem with the engine was sleeve wear. The sleeves and pistons would break and oil would pour from the engine sometimes blinding the pilots testing the aircraft. Often the engine wouldn't start and cooling the 24 cylinder beast was also difficult. The oil in the engine circulated at 3,000 gallons an hour and if not functioning properly the temperature would soar.

During the early period of Typhoon development the prototype flown by Philip Lucas, Chief Test Pilot for Hawker, suffered metal fatigue when he was diving the aircraft and yawing it from side to side, the fuselage split behind the cockpit. He managed to get the stricken aircraft back on land so the designers could study it and repair it, which they did. A month later it was flying again.

Interestingly, the problem that caused this structural failure had nothing to do with the series of structural failures that dogged the Typhoon later on. Indeed, in the early development stages it was the engine providing the problems. The main problem was distortion of the cylinder sleeves and when Typhoons were going to the squadrons the target of 25 hours between major overhauls was very rarely reached. The reason for this was that the sleeves designed by Napier were not up to standard and often failed to reach 20 hours in bench testing. [50]

By 1943 with production lagging a solution to the problem had to be found. Engineers at Bristol discovered that the sleeves to the Bristol Taurus radial engine could be adapted by machining to Sabre size. While the Napier sleeves were distorting after 20 hours Bristol sleeves lasted for 120 hours without any sign of real wear. With the problems of the engine for the most part solved production could be stepped up.

But this was only the beginning of the problems. The Typhoon's tail section had a tendency to fall off.

Going back to the early days in 1940 after the cancellation of the Tornado, Camm's design team were taxed to the limit when it came to placing the Napier Sabre engine into the Typhoon airframe as, unlike the Tornado that had the huge radiator scoop under the middle of the fuselage, the entire radiator and oil cooler had to be placed forward to the nose, creating the distinctive chin radiator look. Also, the Sabre was much heavier than the Rolls Royce Vulture engine, placed in the ill-fated Tornado, and that additional weight needed to be accounted for.

The rear engine mounts were attached directly to the main wing spar. This, according to Mason's book *The Hawker Typhoon and Tempest*, may have accentuated the effects of engine vibration that the Sabre was notorious for, which created a secondary harmonic to the centre and rear fuselage.

In the early phase of development vibration had been so bad that pilots testing the aircraft were unable to see the instruments. Over the course of the development the engine mounts were modified to the extent that engine vibration was substantially reduced. The pilot's seat mounting went through several different versions until a mounting was found that substantially reduced the vibration coming through the seat while still being comfortable for the pilot.

The first 30 or so Typhoons produced had 12 machine guns and the Sabre 1 engine and were designated the Typhoon 1A. The version that was delivered to the squadrons was the four-cannon 1B that had the car door style canopy.[51] This was a fixed canopy with two hinged doors on either side of the fuselage and a clear panel overhead that also hinged and was attached to the starboard door. Both doors could be jettisoned in the case of an emergency in the air or on the ground if the aircraft turned over.[52]

The problem with the tail coming off in high-speed dives emerged as the aircraft were being tested at RAF Maintenance Units. Two or three fatal accidents occurred in mid 1942 where sudden and catastrophic structural failure occurred. Superficial examination of the remains (the main fuselage section being burned but the tail section some distance from the main section remained intact) suggested that the rear fuselage structure had failed causing the entire tail unit to fall off.

The process of investigation into these accidents lasted from April 1942 to October 1943 with more accidents taking place. The failure occurred at the rear fuselage transport joint and one remedy was to rivet a single steel strip around the transport joint. But it was makeshift only and didn't completely solve the problem.

The cause of the problem was the failure of the elevator mass balance mounting bracket and a modification was introduced to strengthen the bracket as an interim solution. At the time of the tail failures the Typhoon had a tendency to tighten up in a turn at about 4g. After the modification to the mounting bracket was made and introduced to the aircraft further modifications were made by Hawker to the elevators and inertia weights on the control column. By July 1943 the test aircraft was turning at 5g without tightening up and with no excessive stress on the transport joint.

The final solution to the problem was reached in October 1943 when a 16lb control column inertia weight and 8lb elevator mass balance, along with the reinforced mounting bracket, were added to the aircraft. These improvements meant that the aircraft could pull turns of more than 6g at 5,000 feet without any tendency to tighten up and without any excessive strain on the transport joint or elevator mounts at high speeds.

With its problems ironed out, the Typhoon went on to be one of the most effective weapons of the war, driving the German panzer divisions out of Normandy and helping the Allies break out and begin the drive to Germany and the end of the war.

In the absence of the Luftwaffe the Typhoon roamed the skies with air supremacy more or less guaranteed over the battlefields, attacking enemy armour, pounding German tanks with rockets, bombs and cannon fire. Their most dangerous opponent then was not the German fighter pilot but enemy anti-aircraft fire.

Despite the demise of the Luftwaffe, the bravery and heroism of the British and Allied pilots flying continuous close Army support missions to attack any enemy movement on the ground should not be underestimated. To understand why, the best place to go to get an intimate picture of the Typhoon is the pilots themselves.

Sir Alec Atkinson, interviewed in 2004, flew with 609 Squadron from 1942 to 1943 on Typhoons and made these comments about the aircraft. "We were in the first Typhoon wing and at that stage there were two main things that were wrong with the aircraft. One was that occasionally the tail would come off and at that time nobody whose tail came off survived. And the other was that it had a Sabre engine and the Sabre was not very reliable.

"Because of the big nose when taking off you knew there was nothing in front of you before you took off, you just guessed what position you were in and put the wheels up. It wasn't difficult as long as you were experienced."

But the long nose could also be a problem when landing as he explained. "You couldn't see where you were going so you landed on three wheels including the tail wheel which was a three point landing. You put all the wheels down and you knew the position well enough to be able to go down gently. You could do that with the Typhoon."

When the Typhoon was going through all of its problems Squadron Leader Roland Beaumont, CO of 609 Squadron at that time, went to a meeting at 11 Group where the future of the Typhoon was to be decided. "He was by far the youngest officer there and the most junior officer there and he defended the Typhoon and said it was as good an aircraft as any other and it would be quite wrong to scrap it," Atkinson recalled. "Really it was his advocacy that stopped it from being scrapped. And it was just as well it wasn't because when the invasion came the Typhoons were used to attack German tanks and were extremely successful. It was certainly a very war-winning weapon at that stage. The tanks were enabling the Germans to stay in Normandy and the Typhoons really cleared them out."

Flight Sergeant Tom Annear, another veteran 609 pilot described how the rockets were fired when he was interviewed at his home in New Zealand in 2005. "You had two buttons, one for rockets and one for cannon," he said. "You had a switch for pairs of rockets or to fire a salvo. You fired your cannon from the control column and the rockets you pressed a button on your throttle. You had your hand over it and you pressed it with your thumb."

The Typhoon was one of those aircraft that pilots either hated or loved. "I found them absolutely marvellous, very steady aircraft," Annear said. "They were heavy but particularly beautiful when flying formation. When we were coming home from an operation we used to fly together about ten or twelve feet apart and you just sat there unmoving because the plane was so steady.

"I loved the Typhoon. I absolutely loved her. It was easy to fly and very steady and okay, you had to control her but you soon got used to that. When you first flew her, she flew you for the first ten hours. After that you became the boss and after that it was beautiful. It was so powerful and so quick that you'd be a thousand feet in the air before you got your wheels up."

During the interview, Annear compared the elegant Spitfire with the mighty Typhoon. "The Spitfire was slower than the Typhoon. The acceleration on the Typhoon was very quick. I think the fastest that I ever got that I know of was when I was playing the fool once and took it up as high as it could go and put it into a power dive and I had the clock at 625[53] before I pulled it out. The aircraft was still rock steady. I started at five miles up and by the time I was straight and level it was 1500 feet. It was exhilarating. I'd been flying her for several hours before I did something like that. I was fairly familiar with her."

In their dives on enemy targets Typhoons flew at well over 500mph according to Annear. "550 mph was nothing. They were very robust, very solid and could take a lot of punishment. It was an all-metal aircraft and was a very big aircraft for a single. The engine was a 24 cylinder so it had to be big to carry that."

Thinking back to his days in the Typhoon as a member of 198 Squadron, veteran pilot Richard Armstrong talked about his experiences with the aircraft during his interview in 2005. Taking off on the Typhoon was a difficult task if the pilot was not experienced with the aircraft as Armstrong pointed out. "When we were on standby, we did two hours on and two hours off. You had to sit with the oxygen[54] on while you sat in the cockpit waiting to scramble. The majority of the times you just sat there all morning doing nothing except reading a book maybe, but all the time on oxygen.

"It was impossible to see forward when you were taxiing the aircraft. You had to weave around to see where you were going, finally position the aircraft for take-off and then open the throttle, giving full left rudder as hard as you could, otherwise the aircraft would roll to starboard to an alarming degree. Hopefully the tree on the horizon that you'd spotted when you opened the throttle was still in front of you when you had finally raised the tail and could see where you were going. You can imagine it was a pretty frightening experience the first time. In addition you were in the air much faster than you were used to.[55] The aircraft accelerated much faster than the Hurricane. It was a beast that you had to control."

Getting into the cockpit was much more of a procedure than with other aircraft because the Typhoon sat so high off the ground in order for the propeller to turn freely. "As far as I was personally concerned the Typhoon was dependable and could take a lot of punishment. I know that one or two chaps would dispute this. If it had a fault it was difficulty in access," Armstrong continued. "We used to leave the parachute in the bucket seat so we could jump in and strap it on once we were in the cockpit. It was pretty difficult to get in if you were already wearing a parachute because the cockpit was so high up," he explained. "It had a stirrup step to pull down and as you pulled it down, a handhold opened to help you climb onto the wing. There was a black walkway on the wing root which defined the area in which it was safe to walk. It was about a foot wide and stretched as far as the side of the cockpit. The cockpits fitted with canopies[56] were even more difficult than the greenhouse types.[57] On the greenhouse types both the door and the top opened and you just stepped in but with the canopy type you had to drop yourself in from above."

"In spite of this small difficulty the canopy type were much preferred because it gave you much improved vision. You could see through an arc of about 270 degrees. The greenhouse version had struts up to support the top door and the rear view was very poor. You did have a rear view mirror but it was a lot better to be able to turn around and have a good look which, if you were wise, you did very regularly."

In addition to the four cannon, the Typhoon carried either rockets or bombs. 198 Squadron was a rocket-firing Typhoon squadron and according to Armstrong they were fired by an electrical current. "This was supplied by a flex terminating with a simple two pin plug. This was known as "the tail" and hung down at the trailing edge of the wing. Immediately before take-off the ground crew[58] would insert the plug into a corresponding socket at the back of the rocket. Pushing a firing button on the control column would complete the circuit and the rocket would fire. Starting the engine with the tails inserted might inadvertently fire the rockets because spurious currents in the airframe were liable to discharge the rockets. If you could see "the tail" flying out behind the wing you knew that the rocket had gone. It had unplugged itself. The rockets were loaded onto launching rails by two clips, front and rear of the rocket, with four rockets under each wing. When the rockets were launched the front clips would slide off its support first and any lateral or vertical movement of any kind on the aircraft and the rocket would be flipped off its target and sometimes you'd think 'Where the hell has that gone?' whilst the rocket would be hurtling groundwards underneath you. It was something you just had to get used to. Until the rockets were off the rails you couldn't move the aircraft. It was necessary to stay stable without any lateral movement of any kind."

Stability was a word used by every veteran interviewed for this book. All the pilots agreed that the Typhoon was an excellent gun platform and also very fast. "The bubble canopy version of the Typhoon was faster than the car door one, 30mph faster," Armstrong said. "But then they ruined it by putting the rocket rails underneath it which played havoc with the dynamics of the thing."

Many popular war films showing aircraft blasting away at a target are inaccurate according to Armstrong. "They are rubbish. The ammo was like a large explosive bullet about eight inches long, clipped into a long belt. You carried about 11 seconds of continuous firing before the ammo was exhausted. You didn't have much time. If you count 11 seconds on your watch you will see that it isn't very long.

"I liked the Typhoon. Of all the aircraft I flew I felt the safest in it and it was certainly the most effective but you had to pay it due respect. You didn't pay much respect to a Hurricane because she was a lady but with the Typhoon you had to obey all the rules if you wanted to live."

In the early days the engine had to be changed every 20 hours. "The engine problems were finally overcome by designing the engine with internal cooled sleeve valves," Armstrong explained. "I don't know a lot about it as I wasn't an engine chap. I remember that we used to get ATC lads coming in at the weekend and they would ask a lot of difficult questions, such as what was the anhedral of the wing, so we would fob them off with something then get them to wash the aircraft off with glycol. It may sound silly but you could get another five miles an hour that way. Another chap used to file the rivets heads flat which, I suppose, was a pretty dangerous thing to do."

As indicated earlier, the Typhoons that carried bombs and dive-bombed their targets were affectionately known as "Bombphoons" by their pilots. Derek Lovell flew with one of the "Bombphoon" squadrons, 197 Squadron and during his interview in 2005 he talked about the cockpit design of the big fighter-bomber. "It was a Hawker type cockpit that had the undercarriage lever on the left. Compared to the Spitfire cockpit it was very roomy. The early Typhoons were known as coffin door jobs. To get out you had to pull the toggles, then the theory was the door went out but they didn't always go out." Speaking about the Typhoon's Napier Sabre engine he said, "It had about 2500 horsepower. In fact it was two engines, two twelve-cylinder engines one above the other with 24 cylinder sleeve valves."

Unlike other fighters of the time, the Typhoon had a different and sometimes temperamental system of starting the engine. "It was a cartridge start," Lovell recalled during the interview. "You had in the engine, a cylinder rather like that on a revolver that had six cartridges in it. They looked like 12 bore shells and they were blue instead of red. You first primed the carburettor, cylinder head and the pump, set the throttle, oxygen mask on and oxygen on. Before you started the engine you put oxygen on and after you turned off the engine you turned off the oxygen because of the carbon monoxide in the cockpit was very bad.

"You pressed two boosters and one fired the cartridge that turned the prop over and God willing got the thing going. It would turn over a couple of times, usually there was a belch of flames, cough and splutter and she was off. If it didn't start the first time you fired another cartridge. There was a safety valve that was the size of a sixpence and would sometimes blow and you couldn't start the engine. You used to carry a sixpence that was the same size as the valve and you used that. It got me out of trouble

I can tell you. When you got back you reported it to the ground crew and they gave you back your sixpence and put in a new valve."

Lovell continued talking about the merits of the Typhoon. "It was a marvellous gun platform, very stable and could take a lot of punishment and get back. We used to say it forced its way through the air rather than flew. It had been designed to take on the FW190 but it hadn't got the power at height. It operated at its best up to 10,000 feet. It just didn't match up to the 190 above that."

The bubble canopy on the Typhoon had a wheel for winding the canopy back. "Under the wing, there is a step that you pull down, stroll onto the wing, there was a step in the side and then you stepped into the cockpit. The seat was adjustable as you could raise and lower it. You took off with your seat up so you got maximum view. If there was a lot of flak about, we used to lower the seat because there was this theory that there was less of you to be seen."

Talking about some of the aircraft's flying characteristics, Lovell said, "On the Typhoon you needed a lot of height if you did formation acrobatics. Once you got her into a spin she was very difficult to get out of it."

The Typhoon had its limitations but it was a great aircraft to fly. "It was very manoeuvrable," Lovell recalled. "Great thing about it was it was a very stable gun platform and could take a lot of damage. I was hit with flak in my rudder trim with a piece of flak about the size of a shilling. I was very lucky."

Often pilots would attack their targets at very low level, sometimes just above the trees, braving intense and accurate anti-aircraft fire. By 1944 the problems had all been ironed out and the Typhoon was a very effective fighting machine giving its pilots confidence to do the difficult jobs they had to do. They knew it could take punishment; fighting at low level many pilots returned from missions with the aircraft full of holes from anti-aircraft fire, as we shall see in the following chapters.

CHAPTER EIGHT

609 Squadron, June 1944

There was no recoil with the rockets. They just left the aircraft, you saw the trail. It was very fast and you must remember the speeds you built up and then you wanted to get out and not linger around.

Warrant Officer Tom Annear, 609 Squadron[59]

Based at Thorney Island near Portsmouth 609 Squadron was a rocket-firing squadron of Typhoons. Veteran Typhoon pilot Sir Ken Adam described his experiences during an interview in 2004 about flying the rocket Typhoons over Caen.

"I was born in Berlin in 1921. My family was sort of upper middle class Jewish German family. Father was a much decorated cavalry officer in the First World War. When Hitler came to power things changed and in 1934 we immigrated to England. My father was quite a well known man and very interested in sports and had a very famous sports store that he inherited from his father and was very much involved in sponsoring sporting events, exhibitions such as Roald Amundsen's various polar expeditions as well as providing the equipment for several films by UFA. Of course it came as an enormous shock to him when in 1933 Hitler came to power so in 1934 my family left Germany. My older brother who in 1932 had studied in France had seen what was happening and he wanted his younger brothers to leave Germany as he could see no future for them there."

Adam and his younger brother went first to a small public school in Scotland, near Edinburgh. "After six months I joined the rest of my family, my mother, my father and my sister who by this time had left Berlin and settled in London," he continued. "We of course lost most of our money. My mother opened a boarding house in Hampstead and with her income from that managed to give us all a very good education. My younger brother and myself went to St Paul's School after learning English in a prep school. My older brother was already twenty and was studying with the London School of Economics and later was working with a firm of chartered accountants and eventually the stock exchange.

"By meeting somebody in our boarding house in Hampstead who was a Hungarian artist and who was a great friend of the Kordas – probably the most successful film producers of that time – I managed to meet Vincent Korda their production designer. He advised me that if I wanted to get into films I should have an architectural background. As a result when I left school I went to University College, The Bartlett School of Architecture and was articled with a firm of architects CW Glover and Partners. War clouds started gathering and the firm was switched to redesigning and updating the munitions factories, air raid shelters. Captain Glover was also a brilliant man on acoustics and had several books published, which I illustrated.

"We were classified as friendly aliens and after Dunkirk suddenly the whole atmosphere in this country changed and there was a panic reaction to anybody that came from Germany or Austria. My older brother was already naturalised because he was 21 but I was 17 so it wasn't possible. They were going to intern my brother and me. I called Captain Glover and said I can't come to work but he said I was too useful for the war effort so I wasn't interned but my younger brother was sent to the Isle of Man. I then decided that I wanted to do something more active and join the Forces.

In university Adam tried to join the University Air Squadron but was always turned down. "The only Paramilitary organisation I could join was the Auxiliary Military Pioneer Corps, which was formed for refugees from all over Europe. Having been a member of the OTC at St Paul's I got two stripes and was sent to Ilfracombe and became part of the training staff there, which was a very interesting period because there were very many famous people, elderly people in their fifties and sixties wearing British uniforms. But we were not allowed to carry arms. The Government was very clever; there was an excellent staff of officers who had been in the diplomatic services because they were dealing with writers, lawyers, and people from all parts of life.

I still wanted to do something more active and kept volunteering for the RAF. Much to my surprise it must have been May of 1941 when my transfer came through and I was posted to No 11 ITW at Scarborough. It was much to everybody's surprise that I started training in the RAF as I was the first German national to be accepted by the Air Force.

I trained initially in Scarborough and was then sent to No 11 EFTS out in Perth to learn flying on Tiger Moths. I spent some time there and I think I was what is known as a natural pilot. I had it in my bones. After that initial training I was sent to Canada because there wasn't sufficient space in England. They were part of the Empire Training Scheme and I did the crossing on an armed merchant ship called the *Leticia*, which had one gun only. There must have been eight to nine hundred of us and we had a destroyer escort all the way across and nothing happened. On the way back, unfortunately, the ship was sunk by a U-boat. I was lucky to be in Canada.

Once in Canada, Adam heard about an American training scheme called the Arnold Training Scheme and applied for it.

"I learned to fly at a place called Lakeland in Florida. I flew Steerman P.T. 17 biplanes and from there I went to Cochran field in Georgia and flew Vultee B.T.13As and then graduated to advanced flying at Napier Field in Alabama where we flew Harvards."

Adam graduated with flying honours in February 1943. He received his silver wings and his RAF wings and spent two weeks leave in New York where he had an uncle.

"When I came back to my unit I was informed by my commanding officer that British Air Staff in Washington had sent him a telex that pending further investigation aviation cadet K H Adam will revert to the rank of sergeant pilot and has to be posted back to the UK as soon as possible. The reasons for that I never found out. Only in the last few months did I have a letter from somebody who had done some research. There was another pilot who was in Bomber Command who had been looking through the archives and found that as a German you couldn't give the oath to the King at the time nor should you be allowed to fly on operations. He flew two tours in Bomber Command and I joined 609 West Riding Squadron in October 1943, which was at the time the highest scoring fighter squadron. In fact, when I arrived they were celebrating their 200th victory in the air. The squadron had recently re-equipped with Typhoons after flying Spitfires. So I arrived at 609 flying really what was the most powerful fighter of those days."

Adam talked about his first impressions of the mighty Typhoon.

"It had this enormous engine, the Napier Sabre engine and 4 Hispano 20mm cannons and would fly straight and level at 8,000 feet at over 400mph. So it was an incredible aircraft. It had its problems but I really loved it."

What follows now is the day to day operations of 609 Squadron throughout the month of June 1944. Some of the operations Adam flew on, some he didn't, but to get a feel of how it was for pilots and Squadron personnel during those dangerous summer months it is necessary to document all the Squadron's operations.

Before May, the Squadron was sent away to learn to fly and fight with rockets. "The Air Ministry decided, because we were such a powerful aircraft to equip us with rockets for air to ground attack," Adam explained. "We were sent to Llanbedr in Wales equipped with eight rocket projectiles and learned to fire rockets. We only had an electronic gun sight, which was not terribly useful for firing rockets. You had to take into account your angle of dive, your airspeed and allow for wind as well. But going through my logbook I found out that my average error was forty yards. Well if you think that each rocket has an explosive power of six-inch naval guns. If you fire a pair or a salvo you could do a lot of damage."

They were no longer with 11 Group but became part of 123 Wing of the 2nd Tactical Air force with several other rocket-firing Typhoons. "We were attached to the army and had to live under canvas, which was a completely new experience for us. Our intelligence and ops setup was also mobile in caravans."

They flew "Ramrod" and "Ranger" operations. "Ranger was just a couple or sometimes four aircraft flying at sea level across the Channel hopping over the French coast to avoid their radar and shoot up trains, troop concentrations etc.," continued Adam. "It was very successful. We used to do it in mainly bad weather conditions and cloud cover because the Germans used to scramble two or three squadrons of 109s or 190s to go after us. And we just went up into cloud and made our way back."

June began with rain. The first day, operational flying was cancelled due to rain. But on 2nd June the rain cleared and operational flying took place in the afternoon. At 1525hrs Flight Lieutenant Davies led Warrant Officer R.E. Bavington, Warrant Officer M.J. Seguin, Warrant Officer J.D. Buchanan, Flying Officer J.D. Inches, Warrant Officer G.K.E. Martin and Flight Sergeant R.K. Adam on a Ramrod to attack a radar station at Dieppe. Reaching the target the Typhoons rolled into their dives, releasing their rockets as they tore down on the installation. The pilots could see hits on the Eastern Freya, the semaphore buildings, the southern Wurtzburg and a hoarding. Cannon shells ripped into the structures as each Typhoon levelled out, firing burst after burst. Throughout the attack the flak was intense and Flight Lieutenant Davies was seen in a box of flak taking evasive action to stay alive. He was hit under the cockpit by a piece of rocket. They all returned to base safely.

In the afternoon, Squadron Leader Wells took off with Flight Sergeant B.G. Pagnam, Flight Lieutenant E.R.A. Roberts, Flying Officer R.K. Gibson, Flight Lieutenant L.E.J.M. Geerts, Flying Officer P.H.M.K. Cooreman, Flight Sergeant L.E. Bliss and Flying Officer A.R. Blanco on a Ramrod to the radar station at Cap Gris Nez. Their rockets slammed into the semaphore buildings, the Wurtzburg and the hoarding causing severe damage. They returned to base at 1900hrs in time for a party that lasted until the small hours.

"It is to be recorded with sorrow that Squadron Leader Niblett, C.O. of 198 Squadron crashed in flames this day on the French Coast. He acted as flying adjutant for this squadron for some time last year," recorded the diarist.

The following day the Squadron attacked the radar stations again at Dieppe and Cap Gris Nez. At 1520hrs eight Typhoons (Bavington, Inches, Buchanan, Martin, Flying Officer R.S. Royston, Adam and Seguin) led by Flight Lieutenant Davies roared across the Channel towards the target. Attacking with rockets and cannon fire they left the Southern Wurtzburg burning. The Northern Wurtzburg, Freya and hoarding were attacked and left damaged. The next flight of the day saw Squadron Leader J.C. Wells, DFC leading Warrant Officer N.L. Merrett, Geerts, Gibson, Cooreman, Bliss and Pilot Officer Watelett back to the radar station at Cap Gris Nez where buildings and the hoarding were attacked. The Southern Wurtzburg was still left standing. The following day the Squadron lost Flight Lieutenant Davies who was made Squadron Leader and posted to 198 Squadron. There was no operational flying on this day.

"One's reactions had to be pretty good because flying at about 400mph at tree trop level it is amazing how quickly things come up at you," Adam explained. "It was exhilarating but we were worried particularly about high-tension wires. Often some of us came back with bits of tree branches stuck in the radiator scoop underneath."

"We were really the forerunners of today's Apache helicopters," Adam said during the interview. "The Typhoon with that inline engine and the big scoop in front was vulnerable; you only had to have a rifle bullet in your cooling system and the engine seized in no time at all. You could always tell when somebody was hit in the cooling system. They left a white stream of glycol like a vapour trail. Unless you kept your eye on your temperature gauge you weren't immediately aware that your engine had seized. It became pretty dangerous."

On the morning of the 5th Flight Lieutenant Roberts became Flight Commander taking Davies' place. The first flight of the day took off at 0755hrs with Squadron Leader Wells leading Warrant Officer Seguin, Flying Officer R.H Holmes, Flight Lieutenant Geerts, Flight Sergeant Bliss, Flying Officer Cooreman, Flight Sergeant Adam, Flight Lieutenant Roberts, Flying Officer Gibson, Flying Officer Inches, Warrant Officer Martin and Flying Officer Royston to attack the radar station at Vaudricourt. However, low cloud made identifying the target impossible so the Typhoons pushed on to the secondary target which was another radar station at Berck-sur-Mer where the Coastwatcher was attacked but no results were seen.

Later in the morning at 1115hrs they attacked the radar station at Vaudricourt. Again Squadron Leader Wells led the same pilots on the operation as they skimmed across the Channel at high speed, rapidly climbing to attack height and then peeled off into their dives. Rocket after rocket shot from the wings of the Typhoons striking the Freya. Nearby huts were strafed with cannon fire as one section of the Typhoons attacked at low level. Another section attacked the Wurzburg and chimney but smoke and dust from the attacks made judging results impossible.

"We used to reach tremendous speeds diving to attack up to 600 mph and pull out low enough to make sure of hitting the target and at the same time to avoid being damaged by the debris from your own explosion," Adam said.

At 1900hrs Squadron Leader Wells took Bavington, Blanco, Bryant, Roberts, Gibson and Inches on a Ramrod to attack an enemy HQ on the Cherbourg Peninsula at Livetau. Hammering the target with cannon and rocket fire, hit after hit was observed and the building was left smoking as the rockets exploded. Taking off with the same section led by Squadron Leader Wells Flight Lieutenant Geerts peeled off as they crossed the French coast, leading Merrett, Watelet, Flying Officer C.A. Roland and Flying Officer R.H. Holmes to attack a rail and road bridge but they saw no results.

Early morning on D-Day saw the squadron at readiness by first light with calls put in for as early as 0345hrs but the first show of the day didn't begin until 1205hrs. Leading Flight Sergeant Bryant, Flying Officer Holmes and Warrant Officer Buchanan, Flight Lieutenant Roberts took off from base and climbed rapidly into the morning sky with the other three aircraft behind him. Turning for the Channel they roared across at high speed heading for the Radar Installation at Le Havre. Over the target, the four aircraft rolled into their shallow dives, releasing their rockets and strafing the buildings as they levelled off. Climbing away, they could see some of their rockets had plastered the Coastwatcher tower. They headed back to base.

On that day, while the awful and epic struggle on the beaches of Normandy was taking place, 609 Squadron remained on the ground until 1710hrs when Squadron Leader Wells took off, taking Flying Officer Royston, Warrant Officer Seguin, Flight Sergeant Adam, Flight Lieutenant Geerts, Warrant Officer Merrett, Flying Officer Cooreman and Flight Sergeant Bliss on a Ramrod to attack enemy transport on the road east of Lisieux. The Typhoons attacked the vehicles in pairs, diving on the enemy, firing their rockets. Two German tanks were hit by the projectiles and completely destroyed, their turrets being blown off while two others sustained heavy damage. At the bottom of their dives, each Typhoon shot over the German vehicles, strafing them with cannon fire before climbing rapidly away. One after the other the Typhoons came down on the enemy firing their rockets. Three transport vehicles were blown to pieces by the rockets, others damaged and one armoured vehicle was claimed destroyed by the pilots. They left the area with smoke pouring from the destroyed vehicles. The Typhoons landed back at base at 1840hrs.

"The air ministry or whoever decided that every four weeks we could have 48 hours leave and fly our aircraft to Gatwick or Northolt in England.[60] The strange thing is that nobody on the day before wanted to fly on operations because they were superstitious about it and also a number of pilots lost their lives on that day before flying off on leave. I had more or less made up my mind that I wasn't going to be alive at the end of the war so that 48-hour leave was very important to us."

The last sortie of the day saw a loss. This time Flight Lieutenant Roberts took off with Bavington, Martin, Inches, Blanco, Gibson, Watelet and Rowland to attack enemy transport south west of Caen. This time they encountered flak. As it burst around them, they carried out their attacks firing their rockets destroying two armoured vehicles, damaging two transport vehicles and destroying two armoured personnel carriers. As their rockets ploughed into the target area, Warrant Officer Martin was hit by flak. Losing power, he was seen to bale out and land in a nearby field. Flying Officer Gibson was also hit by flak and managed to get back to base.

"We were very effective but we also had enormous losses," Ken Adam said. "I had an operation and was out of the squadron for two months and we lost almost twice the squadron establishment."

The following day, the Squadron was again at readiness at first light. The first show was laid on for early in the morning. Flight Lieutenant Geerts took off at 0725hrs together with Wing Commander Brooker, leading Warrant Officer Merrett, Flight Lieutenant P.D.L Roper, Flight Sergeant Bliss, Flying Officer Cooreman, Flying Officer Gibson, Flying Officer Rowland, Flight Sergeant Bryant, Flight Sergeant Adam, Flying Officer Holmes and Warrant Officer Buchanan. Railway sidings near Lisieux were hit by rockets as the Typhoons attacked. A troop train standing in a siding was strafed and attacked with rockets.

In the afternoon, Squadron Leader Wells took Seguin, Roberts, Bavington, Inches, Pagnam, Royston, Adam and Blanco on an armed recce to Le Breuil where they attacked a troop train and several enemy transport vehicles. They left the base at 1555hrs tearing across the Channel towards the struggle on the beaches. Each aircraft had long range tanks fitted. By 1745hrs all the aircraft had returned. The last sortie of the day saw Flight Lieutenant Geerts take a section of eight Typhoons back to the battle area where they shot up enemy transport, destroying two vehicles and damaging several more.

On the morning of the 8th the Squadron was up again with the first operation at 1130hrs. Wing Commander Brooker led a formation of Typhoons on a Ramrod to the Lisieux–Caen area to attack transport vehicles. Brooker took Flying Officer Rowland, Flying Officer Blanco, Flight Sergeant C.H.T. Cables, Flight Lieutenant Geerts, Warrant Officer Merrett, Flying Officer Cooreman, Flight Sergeant Bliss and Pilot Officer Watelet towards the target coordinates where he peeled off and dove on the enemy convoy. The Typhoons plastered the column with rocket projectiles and cannon fire, destroying an armoured car, staff car and four trucks completely as well as severely damaging two other vehicles. "Ranger operations, with

1 Supermarine Spitfire passing a Hawker Typhoon of 609 Squadron on a
Normandy airstrip. Erk on wing steering.

2 Flying Officers Spain and Spencer of No. 257 Squadron RAF wait on standby in
their Hawker Typhoon Mark IBs, attended by their ground crews, at Warmwell,
Dorset. The further aircraft is JP494 FM-D. (IWM)

3 Flight Sergeant J S Fraser-Petherbridge of 198 Squadron takes off from Thorney Island, Hampshire, in Typhoon Mark IB MN293 TP-D on a sortie over the Normandy beachhead to search for enemy transport. His was one of eight Typhoons led by Wing Commander R E P Brooker attacking AFVs on the Caen-Falaise road. (IWM)

4 Squadron accommodation area; the four gallon petrol cans were used for holding hot water.

5 Rearming a Hawker Typhoon PR-R.

6 Hawker Typhoon PR-B taking off on an armed reconnaissance flight, Kluis. Jan Mathys is the 609 Squadron pilot. PO Mathys would become (in 1976) a Brigade-General in the Belgian Air Force.

7 Crash-landed Typhoon PR-Z.

8 Wing Commander J R Baldwin, leader of No. 146 Wing, with his Hawker Typhoon Mark IB at B3/Sainte Croix-sur-Mer. Baldwin joined the RAFVR and served as ground crew in France during 1940. After bomb-disposal duties in the UK, he transferred to aircrew and joined 609 Squadron in 1942. After steadily building up his victory score he became CO of 198 Squadron in November 1943, leaving them in April 1944 for a staff appointment at No. 11 Group, Fighter Command. He was promoted as wing leader of 146 Wing in June 1944 and on 13 July destroyed a Messerschmitt Bf 109 to bring his score to 16.5 victories. He spent the rest of the war on ground attack duties and in 1945 was promoted Group Captain commanding of 123 Wing. (IWM)

Opposite above: **9** Still from film footage shot from a Hawker Typhoon Mark IB flown by the CO of No. 609 Squadron, showing smoke rising from a burning German vehicle attacked by Typhoons near Vimoutiers. (IWM)

Opposite below: **10** Ground crew watch Hawker Typhoon Mark IBs of No. 175 Squadron as they taxi out for a sortie at B5/Le Fresne Camilly, Normandy. (IWM)

11 Soldiers of the Pioneer Corps laying prefabricated bitumised strips (PBS) for a new runway at B10/Plumetot, as a Typhoon of 198 Squadron takes off. (IWM)

12 Mark IBs of 198 Squadron taxi through clouds of dust on the perimeter track at B10/Plumetot. (IWM)

13 Hawker Typhoon Mark IB JP963 TP-T of 198 Squadron parked by the perimeter track at B10/Plumetot. A bomb-disposal squad explodes German mines in the background. (IWM)

14 Daylight attack on enemy HQ by Typhoons of 609 Squadron, 123 Wing; height 5,000–1,000ft.

15 Rockets shoot away from a 609 Squadron Typhoon during a daylight attack on enemy positions as the aircraft dives from 7,000–1,000 ft.

16 Bird's eye view of a daylight attack on enemy buildings by a Typhoon from 609 Squadron from 7,000–1,000 ft.

17 Rocket attack on a train by 609 Squadron Typhoon aircraft; height 9,000–1,000 ft.

Opposite: **18** Sergeant Ken Adam steps into the cockpit for another op over Caen.

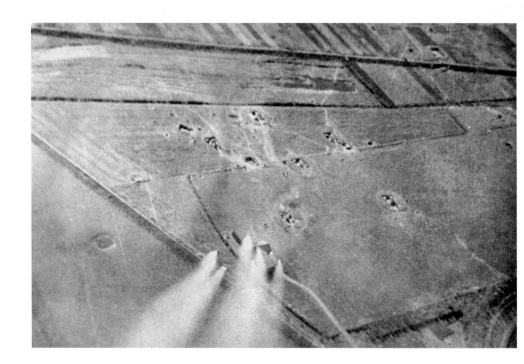

Above: **19** Rocket attack captured by the Typhoon's wing camera. Feedback was of course vital for forward planning of operations.

Left: **20** Warrant Officer Tom Annear seated in his Typhoon takes time out for a photo call while an unnamed member of the ground crew looks on. Does anyone out there recognise him?

just a couple or sometimes four aircraft flying at sea level, cutting across the Channel, hopping over the French or Belgian coast and shooting up trains, troop concentrations etc. were undertaken in mainly bad weather conditions and cloud cover because the Germans used to scramble squadrons of 109s or 190s to go after us. And we just went up into the cloud and made our way back."

The next sortie of the day was in the evening at 1800hrs when Squadron Leader Wells led Royston, Inches, Bryant, Roberts, Harkness, Holmes and Gibson back to the Caen–Lisieux–Falaise area where they attacked several enemy vehicles including tanks. Splitting up, one group of Typhoons rolled into their dives, releasing their rockets into an enemy tank concentration. Three were quickly destroyed as the rockets ripped into the vehicles, causing them to burst into flame. As the rockets plastered the area, more tanks were hit and badly damaged. The Typhoons levelled off firing bursts from their 20mm cannon, raking the enemy tanks with shells. The other section of Typhoons attacked more enemy tanks and huts, claiming two vehicles destroyed.

A long line of enemy tanks were seen on the road North of Amaye so Flying Officer Inches dove down to 200 feet flying along the road, firing his cannon. He was about to break away when he hit a tree that knocked him down onto some telephone wires, which wrapped around his mainplane and rockets causing him to lose his wingtip. Climbing the stricken aircraft to height he managed to form up with the rest of the squadron and landed back at base with French telephone wires and pieces of French road in his aircraft.

Rain the following day kept the squadron grounded. However on the 10th the weather had eased and they were back in the air. Squadron Leader Wells led a formation of 12 Typhoons with Flight Sergeant Pagnam and Flying Officers Blanco and Rowland in his section with Flight Lieutenant Geerts leading Flight Sergeant Bliss and Flying Officers Coorman and Merret and Flight Lieutenant Roberts leading Warrant Officer Buchannan, and Flying Officers Holmes and Harkness. Due to low cloud the first eight aircraft were unable to find the target. Eventually Roberts identified a radar station at Le Havre and attacked it with his team. Several cannon strikes were witnessed along with near misses by the rockets were also seen.

The second flight of the day took place in the early evening. At 1800hrs Squadron Leader Wells was up again, leading Price, Seguin, Inches, Roberts, Bavington, Adam, Bryant, Royston, Holmes, Harkness and Gibson to attack a troop concentration in a wood south of the battle area. Four transports were destroyed from their rockets and cannon fire with several others damaged.

At 2215hrs that same day another formation of Typhoons took off heading to the battle area to attack a concentration of enemy tanks in an orchard. As the light of day rapidly disappeared Flight Lieutenant Geerts led Flight Sergeant Billam, Warrant Officer Merrett, Flight Sergeant Bliss, Flying Officer Blanco, Flying Officer G.L.C.F. Jaspis, Pilot Officer Watelet, Flying Officer Cooreman, Flight Sergeant Cables, Flying Officer Rowland and Flight Sergeant Pagnam rapidly across the Channel to the target. Four aircraft peeled away just before the main attack took place to search for the secondary target that they couldn't find and had to return to base with their rockets.

Meanwhile, the remaining Typhoons attacked the enemy formation, plastering the orchard with rockets and cannon fire but as twilight was giving way to darkness they could not see the results of their attack. The Squadron returned in darkness, the last aircraft landing at 2320hrs. Each Typhoon made a good landing with no excitement. It must be remembered that these aircraft did not have night flying instruments, which makes this mission so remarkable. Rain and low cloud scrubbed flying the next day.

On the 12th four Typhoons climbed rapidly into the early morning sky, lifting off at 0525hrs to attack the radar station at Le Havre. "There was that famous attack of four typhoon squadrons to attack a radar station near Le Havre," Adam described an attack on the radar station at Brunevall near Le Havre that took place on 11 May 1944. "The American medium bombers attacked first and then the Typhoons came in to finish off the radar station. We were still flying in fighter formation and the idea was to cross over the French coast go into echelon starboard and then attack in line astern out to sea. First of all the rockets went through the steel works and didn't do a great deal of damage. The American bombing also hadn't been very effective against the strong concrete fortification.

"As I was crossing the coast I already heard the chatter over the R/T and I knew it wasn't going to be a piece of cake and as we were diving to attack I could see the flak coming up in a line because the German gunners were going for the first aircraft and if they didn't get it they'd get the second or third one. So I slid out a little bit to the side and attacked from an angle, which probably saved my life because we lost two aircraft and one damaged in that one attack. It was the first time we had these losses and it affected all of us quite badly. We all thought nothing could happen to us."

Flight Lieutenant Geerts led Bliss, Cooreman and Cables into their attacks on the station hammering it with rockets and cannon fire. One rocket was seen as a direct hit by the pilots. Cannon shells tore into the target as the Typhoons strafed it at the bottom of their dives. They left the target damaged but not destroyed.

While this attack was going on, Flying Officer Blanco led another section (Billam, Merrett, Pagnam, Jaspis, Watelet and Rowland) to attack the radar station at Cap d'Antifer. Taking off at 0615hrs they roared across the Channel and released their rockets scoring one direct hit, while the rest hammered the target area causing damage. They were back at base by 0710hrs.

At 1340hrs Geerts was up again leading Cables, Merrett, Bliss, Blanco, Cooreman and Pagnum to attack an enemy concentration near the battle area. Seeing the red smoke from British troops on the ground they peeled off, diving down on the enemy, unleashing their rockets. Explosion after explosion could be seen as the rockets hit the target area, Three fires shot up into the sky creating columns of smoke. "Our own troops report that the attack was successful," wrote the diarist. They were all back at base by 1500hrs when the weather closed in and stopped any more flying for the rest of the day.

On the 13th Squadron Leader Wells led the Squadron to attack an enemy concentration north east of Caen in support of the army. It was the only show of the day and the Typhoons took off at 1855hrs. They formed up with another 12 aircraft from 198 Squadron and headed for France. Identifying the target from smoke signals by allied troops the Typhoons rolled into their dive plastering the area with rockets. "The fellows did not think much of the idea as our own troops were very near the target," recorded the diarist. The last aircraft from this sortie touched down at base at 2020hrs.

The first operation of the following day was at 0930hrs when Squadron Leader Wells took on a Ramrod to attack an army support target. Leading Flying Officers Royston and Inches and Warrant Officer Seguin (in his section) along with Flight Lieutenant Roberts, Flight Sergeants Price and Adam and Warrant Officer Buchannan Wells took the formation across the Channel to the target. Orbiting overhead they searched for the pre-arranged signal of red smoke over the target pinpoint but none was seen. Instead, they saw red smoke at a village four miles west of the target and Wells wheeled the formation around to attack the village. 60 rocket projec-tiles hit the area, virtually obliterating the village.

"There was no recoil from firing our rockets," explained Adam. "They left at the same speed the aircraft was flying, accelerating after this to enor-mous velocity leaving white trails behind. We usually attacked in a section of four flying in a loose finger formation. We had learned our lesson after the attack on the radar station. One always knew when a pilot released the rockets too early because they usually whizzed past your aircraft."

The rest of the day turned out to be a memorable one. At 1410hrs the Squadron took off and landed in Normandy at a temporary landing strip B2 near Beuzeville. "The most annoyed man was Flight Sergeant Adam who at 1200hrs was seen lugging his parachute and dinghy out of his machine as Wing Commander Brooker had pinched it and Adam had to stay behind," wrote the squadron diarist.

Brooker and Wells then took part in the next two operations of the day from their French landing strip. While they waited for the next show, the Squadron could hear the guns and watched the Commandos servicing their equipment. Finally, at 1835hrs Wing Commander Brooker took off, with Squadron Leader Wells, Flying Officer Royston, Flying Officer Gibson, Warrant Officer Bavington, Flying Officer Holmes, Flight Sergeant Price, Warrant Officer Buchanan and Warrant Officer Seguin amid the dust and sand to attack a crossroads and two villages held by the enemy. Brooker dropped back as they reached the target and attacked. He went in last, releasing his rockets and strafing the areas with cannon fire. The squadron had removed an enemy stronghold allowing the Army to gain a little ground.[61]

The last flight of the day took place in the late evening. Again with Brooker and Wells airborne at 2155hrs they led the same pilots to attack a rail bridge and rail sheds near Campagne. As they released their rockets, enemy gunners opened up, pumping intense and heavy flak into the sky, forcing the formation to break up. The rockets exploded in the target area, with eight pounding the bridge itself[62] and more direct hits on the rail sheds. Cannon shells from the low flying Typhoons ripped into vehicles, sheds and the road as they strafed the area, the flak getting more intense. "Some of the fellows admitted they were shaken by it," wrote the diarist. With the formation broken up by the flak, the squadron headed back across the Channel to their base at Thorney Island, arriving in twos and threes, the last two aircraft, Price and Holmes, touching down at 2315hrs.

The following day, Squadron Leader Wells led Flight Sergeant Stellin, Flying Officer Cooreman, Flight Sergeant Cables, Flight Lieutenant Geerts, Warrant Officer Merrett, Flying Officer Rowland, Flight Sergeant Billam, Flying Officer Blanco, Flying Officer Jaspis, Pilot Officer Watelet and Flight Sergeant Pagnam to attack the ferry crossing of the Seine at Mailleraye and Duclaire. Airborne at 1705hrs, Wells watched the rest of the section climb rapidly into the sky and form up with him, then he turned the formation and they raced across to France. Coming up on the target they dropped into their dives, firing their rockets and cannon. The jetty at Duclaire suffered direct hits, while the jetty and a boat on the opposite bank were also hammered with rockets. Flak from enemy gunners exploded near the aircraft but none were hit and they returned safely to base. On the next sortie at 1925hrs Flight Lieutenant Roberts led Harkens, Inches, Bryant, Seguin, Adam and Royston on a Ramrod to the radar installation at Cap D'Antifer. There they claimed several hits on the lattice structure as well as encountering flak.

The 16th saw the weather close in and no operational flying. On the 17th the Squadron was up early but there was to be no flying this day as they were ordered to move from Thorney Island to a new base at Funtington by 1500hrs. "Nobody really knew what was what," recorded the diarist, "but finally the airfield got away in lorries and the pilots and Airlift party were left behind to come on the next day." They left early the next morning and landed to find the tents for dispersal already up. The pilots and the rest of the ground crew were busy organising sleeping quarters and at 1255hrs the first show was set up with Wing Commander Brooker leading seven Typhoons on a Ramrod that was cancelled due to bad weather over the French coast.

In the evening the weather had cleared enough for Flight Lieutenant Geerts to take Flight Sergeant Cables, Flying Officer Cooreman, Flight Sergeant Bliss, Flying Officer Blanco, Flight Sergeant Billam, Flying Officer Rowland and Warrant Officer Merrett to attack enemy targets in the Vire–Falaise–Lisieux area. They caught a column of 15 trucks and armoured fighting vehicles on the road between Falaise and Argentan that they immediately attacked. Rockets shot from under the wings of the Typhoons as they roared down on the enemy. The projectiles set eight trucks on fire.[63] Others were damaged by the firestorm of cannon shells from each of the four cannon from the attacking Typhoons. Smoke and debris from the shells and rockets tearing into the vehicles filled the area as the Typhoons climbed rapidly away. They encountered no flak and were back at base by 2145hrs.

"The Belgians on the trip were all talking at one another 19 to the dozen," wrote the diarist. "Manu was so determined to destroy one truck that he almost hit the deck. He claims two lorries. Merrett came back with a hole in his mainplane caused by debris. Price says it is the best trip he has been on so far."

Bad weather made flying the following day impossible and the Squadron was stood down. Flying began on the 20th at 1910hrs when Flight Lieutenant Geerts took off on a Ramrod leading Pilot Officer Watelet, Flying Officer Cooreman, Flying Officer Jaspis, Flying Officer Blanco, Flight Sergeant Billam, Warrant Officer Merrett and Flight Sergeant Pagnam to attack railway targets in the Bernay-Evreux area. They headed for the target area and identified more than 50 stationary wagons near St Hilaise along with four locomotives.

Peeling off, the Typhoons dove on the targets and levelled off at low level strafing the wagons and locomotives with their cannon causing severe damage. At Laigle, Geerts spotted three stationary goods trains and led the section to attack those with cannon fire. Several enemy transport trucks were damaged in this attack as well.

The only other flight of the day was a Ramrod to the Lisieux area. At 2135hrs Wing Commander Brooker was airborne leading Buchanan, Gibson, Seguin, Roberts, Bryant, Holmes and Bavington to attack rail lines and points in this area. Tracks, a signal box and other railside buildings were victims of the rockets fired by the Typhoons as they dove on the targets, firing bursts from their cannon.

The following day, the Squadron moved to Hurn so there was no operational flying but on the 22nd while the squadron facilities were being prepared and everyone working out where everything should go, the squadron was on readiness. One flight took place that day, which saw Squadron Leader Wells taking Flight Lieutenant Roberts, Flying Officers Inches and Royston, Warrant Officer Bavington and Seguin, Flight Lieutenant Geerts, Flying Officer Blanco, Flight Sergeants Bliss and Adam, Flying Officers Gibson and Holmes across the Channel in support of the US troops attacking Cherbourg. They took off at 1200hrs in pairs and formed up over the Channel with aircraft from 198 Squadron.

Over the target, 609 Squadron pilots went in first, meeting little flak. Firing their rockets they saw their projectiles smash into enemy flak positions, railways and road positions as well as a wireless station, causing damage and fires, sending debris flying. Then, as 198 Squadron went in the flak became more intense and Squadron Leader Davies was hit.[64] He managed to make his way over enemy lines before his engine died and he baled out. Unfortunately he didn't have enough height for his parachute to open. "It is with deep regret that we write of the almost certain death of our Dave," wrote the 609 Squadron diarist for that day.

The 23rd was an interesting day for the Squadron. At 0955hrs Flight Lieutenant Roberts lifted into the morning sky climbing rapidly away followed by Flight Sergeant Bryant, Flying Officer Gibson, Flight Sergeant Adam, Flying Officer Holmes, Warrant Officer Buchanan, Flying Officer Royston and Warrant Officer Harkenss. Their mission was to fly an armed recce in the Lisieux–Evreux area but no movement was seen. Four of the eight Typhoons attacked five tank carriers hitting three of them with rockets and cannon fire, destroying the vehicles, setting them on fire.

As these four Typhoons levelled off from their dives and began climbing away from the destruction on the ground they saw the remaining Typhoons caught up in dogfights with enemy ME109F fighters. The diarist takes up the story.

"Flying Officer Holmes in climbing to join formation with the rest of his section, as he thought, discovered they were enemy aircraft. He gets all excited and yells into his mike but nobody understands what he says. He jettisons his rockets and tanks and by this time the fun is on. He gets into position and sees his guns doing their work, striking the engine of one of the ME109Fs but his ammo runs out, otherwise he would have had a victim for sure."

While Holmes was running out of ammunition the rest of the Typhoons were twisting and turning trying to shoot down as many of the enemy aircraft as they could. Canadian Warrant Officer Buchanan had three 109s on his tail and had some cannon fire through his hood with one bullet exploding so close that he was wounded in the arm. Flying Officer Gibson latched onto the tail of a ME109, firing his cannon at it. He saw bits of the enemy aircraft fly off as his cannon shells struck home. But he was unable to see if the 109 went down as he suddenly had a hang up with one of his rockets, and debris hitting his radiator. Peeling away he headed for home, unable to continue the fight.

Flight Lieutenant Roberts attacked another 109 with several short bursts and saw hits all over the enemy aircraft. He watched it go down in a dive then skid along the ground and smash into a hedge exploding. The general feeling after the dogfights was that the Typhoon had outmanoeuvred the ME109F even with rocket rails on, but the pilots were disappointed that all six aircraft engaged were not destroyed. Their claim stood at one destroyed, one probable and four damaged.

The first flight on 24th June was at 0930hrs when Flight Lieutenant Geerts led Flight Sergeant Billam, Flying Officers Jaspis, Hue and Cooreman, Flying Sergeant Stellin, Flying Officer Rowland, Flying Officer Watelet and Warrant Officer Merrett on an armed recce where they attacked railway tracks at Lacelle and railway sidings at Evron with rockets and cannon fire. Rockets strikes were seen on the tracks and on some stationary rail wagons but no enemy flak was encountered and they saw no enemy fighters. However, Flying Officer Watelet was low on fuel and searching for a place to land. With Flying Officer Rowland in company the two Typhoons landed at an American airstrip near Cardonville, refuelled and were in the air again after 45 minutes. This day, Squadron Leader Wells was also posted to 84 G.S.U. at Middle Wallop for special work and Flight Lieutenant Geerts was made up to Squadron Leader to command 609 Squadron.

The last flight of the day took place at 1940hrs when Wing Commander Brooker took Warrant Officer Merrett, Flying Officer Rowland, Flight Sergeant Pagnam, Flying Officer Blanco, Flight Sergeant Billam, Flying Officer Cooreman and Flying Officer Hue on an armed recce to the Domfront–Alencon area where they sighted 20 rail wagons in sidings at Neau. Rolling into their dives, the Typhoons roared down on the sidings, firing rockets and short bursts of cannon fire. Several strikes on the tracks and wagons were witnessed by the pilots as they turned, climbing away. At Sille another 50 rail wagons in sidings were also attacked with some left smoking and damaged while at St Gervais, they attacked another 25 wagons in a factory siding and saw their cannon shells and rockets strike home. Poor weather made operational flying impossible for the next two days.

On the 27th the weather cleared enough for operational flying to resume. The only flight of the day took place at 0820hrs with Squadron Leader Geerts taking off leading Warrant Officer Seguin, Flying Officer Royston, Warrant Officer Buchanan, Flight Lieutenant Roberts, Flight Sergeant Ashworth and Flying Officer Holmes. Forming up, they headed for the Laval–Le Mans area on an armed recce to attack rail and road targets. Buchanan's rockets ripped into several rail wagons, one of which was blown off the track. Geerts went after some rail coaches, attacking them with cannon and rockets. His rockets were near misses but he saw shell after shell tear into the coaches. At Sille they attacked another train that had been bombed before and this time finished the job with rockets and cannon fire.

Flight Lieutenant Roberts, flying top cover, while Squadron Leader Geerts was at low level, encountered three enemy FW190s. Roberts' section was caught in a wide turn as they engaged the enemy fighters. Flight Sergeant Ashworth and Flying Officer Holmes were strung out on the turn as the enemy aircraft came in. Roberts tried desperately to turn as fast as he could. Jettisoning his rockets and tanks he managed to fire one burst from his cannon at an FW190 before turning away.

Coming out of the clouds Ashworth dropped onto the tail of another FW190 firing his cannon as he did, but he suddenly realised he had the other two enemy fighters on his tail. Peeling away he dove down to deck level, making for the coast away from the fight. Unfortunately, Holmes did not return to base.

"The Typhoon had a nasty habit of flipping over on its back in a high speed stall if you pulled up too quickly. It went straight into the ground which meant curtains for some of our boys," Adam recalled.

The next operational flight for June was on the 29th with eight aircraft from 609 Squadron (Flying Officers Rowland, Jaspis, Blanco, Watelet and Cooreman, Flight Sergeant Pagnam and Warrant Officer Merrett) on an 84 Group attack to a railway junction at St. Maske and several hits were seen. At Collanders 12 rail wagons and some tanks were plastered with rockets and cannon fire as the Typhoons attacked, roaring in low after firing their rockets, strafing the sidings, buildings and rail lines.

Confusion reigned as they started returning back to base with some pilots landing at different forward landing strips in France due to low fuel. Once the Squadron had returned to Hurn they discovered that Flying Officer Rowland was missing. "As this is being written on July 4th at B10 at Plumetot in Normandy comes news that a crash has been found and he lies buried on French soil.[65]"

The following day, the 30th the Squadron started packing for a move to France. There was no operational flying that day. After a month of attacking German radar stations and then after D-Day their transport system and other targets in support of the Army, 609 Squadron had lost three pilots – Martin, Holmes and Rowland.

"Eventually, we operated in France where the engineers had built airstrips for us after D-Day and I was sent out first to find out if it was safe for my Squadron to land there," Adam said. "Coming into land I was shot at and thought, what are the Canadians doing shooting at me, a friendly aircraft? So I landed and saw nobody there but I did see some steel helmets in some slit trenches and thought thank God they were our steel helmets. What one didn't realise was that the bomb line was about three or four miles away from the airstrip so the flak had come from the Germans, not from us. I must have spent between 36 and 48 hours in slit trenches and in the medical tent which was dug in before I managed to get back to England. It wasn't the right time to send the whole Squadron over."

CHAPTER NINE

609 Squadron, July 1944

All our operations were in Army support or most of them attacking things such as trains, strong points, troop positions, tanks, HQ buildings – anything that belonged to the Germans that was in the way of the Army they would call us up and they would give us the target and we would just go and attack them. We were the flying artillery because we were rocket firing.

Warrant Officer Tom Annear 2004

On the 1st of July the Dakotas arrived at Hurn to move the airfield over to France. "At 1530 we are off but we leave the pilots behind," wrote the diarist. The trip across the Channel was uneventful and 13 unescorted Dakotas lumbered across without a single enemy aircraft in sight. "We land at Plumetot, unload and then the fun begins. Shells land on the airfield and unloading has to be hurriedly dropped as we take cover."

As they put up the tents and dug in for their first night near the battlefront, they could hear the guns and had their first taste of war close at hand. "We had no such thing as an airfield," Tom Annear recalled. "It was just a wire netting strip on the ground and we had tents over slit trenches which we slept in. We roughed it. We were pretty young and to us it was just a way of life."[66]

On 7th July, the Squadron diarist wrote that the RAF began bombing Caen. "In the evening word goes round that the RAF is going to bomb Caen and at 2130hrs we make tracks for vantage points around the runway. Soon we hear the sound of heavy bombers and then the sky is black with them. The bombs go down around Caen and the flak comes up, a terrible sight. A Lancaster does a belly landing on the strip. Both outer engines are gone and one of the inners is unserviceable and he makes a beautiful landing."

On the 8th the pilots of 609 Squadron finally took off after days of being grounded due to bad weather and flew over to France, but didn't manage to land at Plumetot. Instead they landed at Camilly (Airfield 121) and were immediately scrambled to attack enemy gun positions but were unable to find them. The pilots finally managed to land at Plumetot in the evening.

"A common accident was caused by the airstrips built by our engineers," Ken Adam explained. "They were first covered with a sort of wire mesh which later was replaced by perforated metal sheets called "Sommerfield Tracking". What happened frequently because of their constant use was that they were damaged, causing a tyre to burst on take off or landing and resulting in the Typhoon flipping over on its back. It nearly always proved fatal because of a broken neck. Remember we were sitting with our head above the fuselage under a Perspex canopy. I was lucky landing once with a burst tyre and just ground looped."

The following day the pilots flew to Camilly where they were detailed to attack six tanks southwest of Caen. Squadron Leader Geerts led Flight Sergeant Bliss, Pilot Officer Merrett, Flight Sergeant Pagnam, Flight Lieutenant Blanco, Flight Sergeant Billam, Flying Officer Hue and Warrant Officer Stellin on the raid but found no movement and empty tank pits. Though they saw nothing, they attacked the tank pits anyway and managed to shoot up enemy transport on the road between Tilly and Campagne. Landing back at Camilly they then flew on to Plumentot (Airfield 129).

On the 10th of July operational flying continued and Flight Sergeant Annear arrived from England to join the squadron. He was born and bred in New Zealand and joined the Air Force when he was 20 only after he had been conscripted into the army and his father signed the papers for him to go flying. He joined 609 Squadron as a Flight Sergeant and finished up as a Warrant Officer.

"The condition of joining the RNZAF was to do a tour overseas," Annear explained. "Most people wanted to go to England. All the bomber boys went to England and a high proportion of the single seats went to England. It was just the accepted thing. You had to volunteer. You weren't appointed. Flying and adventure had to be a young fellow's dream. When I jointed the air force I was working in Hamilton, which is about 80 miles south of Auckland.

"I got my wings before I went there. I started flying in July '42 and I left for England at the end of March '43 and I had my wings and was a qualified pilot. All we flew in NZ were Tiger Moths and Harvards. You qualified on Harvards. When we got to England we were shifted to Miles Masters, then on to Hurricanes, then onto Spitfires and then onto Typhoons. I volunteered just for the desire. When I was on the Squadron I was 23. When I joined the Air Force I was still 20."

During an interview in 2004 he described what happened when the rockets fired. "You had very little reaction when the rocket fired because you didn't drop them, they were still going the same trajectory as you so they just flew away in front of you," he explained. "You carried eight and you fired them in pairs, one each side for balance or the whole lot at once. The gunsight for the cannons had two settings and we just flicked the switch. The second setting was virtually 29 feet lower than the one for the cannon. The cannon would fire straight ahead and the focus point for the rockets was adjusted slightly lower so that at 1,000 yards it would be 29 feet lower than for the cannon. It was a reflector gunsight so all you got was a red ring and a dot."

This day they were still flying out of 121 Airfield while Plumentot remained their main base. At 0915hrs Wing Commander Brooker led Pagnam, Stellin, Hue, Flying Officer Watelet, Flight Sergeant Cables and Flying Officer Jaspis on an armed recce to attack an enemy strong point at Amaye-sur-Orne but 10/10 cloud obscured most of the target area. Diving through gaps in the cloud, the Typhoons unleashed their rockets. However, due to poor visibility they couldn't see the results of their attack. They were back at 121 Airfield at 0950hrs. No other flights took place that day.

The following day, Squadron Leader Geerts took off at 1535hrs leading Flight Sergeant Bliss, Flying Office Hue, Warrant Officer Stellin, Flight Lieutenant Blanco, Flight Sergeant Billam, Pilot Officer Merrett and Flying Officer Jaspis to attack an enemy tank concentration south east of Hottot. Spotting red smoke set off by British soldiers to identify the area to attack, Geerts peeled off and roared down on the enemy vehicles. Almost immediately, intense flak came arching up at them. Firing their rockets they roared away as the flak burst all around them. Flight Sergeant Bliss was hit and his aircraft was seen to be pouring black smoke. It rolled over and went straight into the ground. Bliss was not seen to have baled out.

On 12th July the Squadron discovered they were to move again, which caused considerable consternation amongst the pilots and ground personnel. Though they were in France, the Squadron was not busy and pilots were spending time sitting around by the tents waiting to get airborne.

That day there was a show on in the evening. At 2015hrs Wing Commander Brooker led Pagnam, Cables, Watelett, Hue, Jaspis, Stellin and Billam on an armed recce to attack targets in the Cabourg–St Pierre–Falaise area. They attacked a wood near Lisieux, destroying one enemy transport vehicle. Rocket after rocket shot from their wings as the Typhoons attacked in pairs firing short bursts from their cannon. Smoke was seen to rise from the wooded area but they could not see the results. "Strafing was part of the game," Tom Annear recalled.

The following evening, Geerts took 'B' Flight, Flight Sergeant Ashworth,

Flying Officer Gibson, Flight Sergeant Adam, Flight Lieutenant Roberts, Warrant Officer Harkness, Flying Officer Royston and Flying Officer Inches to attack the ferry at Caudebec. Peeling off, Geerts went in first, dropping into a shallow dive with the rest of the formation behind him. Rockets dropped from his wings as he hit the release button and shot away pounding the jetty on the south side of the river. More rockets from the rest of the Typhoons pounded the jetty and the ferry, though the ferry was not badly damaged. The whole area was raked with cannon fire as each Typhoon came out of its dive at low level. Light but accurate flak from enemy gunners burst all around them and Flying Officer Inches was hit but he managed to get back to base safely. His aircraft was flown back to England for repair.

On the 14th there was no flying for the squadron but six enemy fighters attacked transport northeast of the aerodrome. The squadron diarist recorded: "Gunners were quickly on the mark and at least three of the six were shot down in flames; but we lost an oil and petrol lorry and another transport shot up by cannon fire."

The next operational flying for the Squadron was on the 16th when Squadron Leader Geerts took Flight Sergeant Cables, Pilot Officer Merrett, Warrant Officer Stellin, Flight Lieutenant Blanco, Flight Sergeant Billam, Flight Sergeant Annear and Flight Sergeant Pagnam on an armed recce covering Evrecy, Villier Bocage, Amaye, Thury-Harcourt, Avenay St Honorie. Both Cables and Stellin were forced to return home with mechanical trouble while the rest of the formation continued on. In the area south of Forêt de Cinglais they ran into flak. Blanco took his section, Billam, Annear and Pagnam up to provide top cover while Geerts and his No 2 Pilot Officer Merrett dropped down to deck level, braving the flak bursting all around them. Both pilots managed to get hits on enemy transport vehicles. One truck burst into flames as rockets and cannon shells hammered into it while two others were badly damaged. A flak shell went right through Geerts wing and another hit his radiator. As Geerts and Merrett roared in at tree-top level flak burst all around them rocking and bumping their aircraft. They climbed rapidly away joining up with the formation moments later.

On the 17th, pilots of 609 Squadron remained on the ground with no operational flying taking place that day. But the following day was different. The first flight was at 0735hrs with Squadron Leader Geerts at the head of a formation of Warrant Officer Seguin, Pilot Officer Buchanan, flying Officer Inches, Flight Lieutenant Roberts, Flight Sergeant Price, Flying Officer Royston and Flight Sergeant Scott to attack enemy gun positions in the St Ouen-du-Mesmil-Ogar area. Rockets shot away from under the wings of the Typhoons as they battered the target area but the enemy guns continued to fire. They were heavily camouflaged in a wooded area and Pilot Officer Buchanan received a hit from flak in his undercarriage. They were back at base at 0815hrs feeling that the show had been unsuccessful.[67]

The final sortie of the day was led by Flight Lieutenant Blanco on an armed recce to attack targets in the Bretteville-sur-Laise–Falaise–Mézidon area. Leading Annear, Stellin, Cooreman, Adam, Hue, Jaspis and Watelet Blanco attacked enemy transport caught out on the roads. Ripped apart by rockets and cannon shells, one German staff car exploded into flames, while several other vehicles were badly damaged and left smoking. Wheeling away, Blanco was suddenly bounced by eight Spitfires but he quickly managed to turn away and outrun them. "The only aircraft who ever shot at us were our own people. That's not a well-known fact," Tom Annear pointed out. "They didn't recognise us and we had all the recognition but in the air they thought we were German aircraft. If you read the history of the attacks then you can see we lost a few that way."

"There was one incident of friendly fire when we were supposed to escort some Marauders who were bombing Abbeville across the Channel," recalled Adam. "I was very keen to get on one of these shows as we called them. But being a new pilot it wasn't always easy. This time I was on board and when I ran to my aircraft I noticed it was the only one without long range tanks but I wasn't too concerned because we only had to escort the American bombers to Abbeville, which was well within range of the Typhoons actual fuel tanks. Then there was a cock-up and I didn't rendezvous with the Americans over Beachy Head until a quarter of an hour later. As I was crossing the French coast my engine started cutting on mains so I switched over to reserve tanks which was always a dicey thing if your mains were empty and I called my squadron commander and asked him what he wanted me to do.

"He said, 'You bloody fool.' We were flying at 20,000 feet and he said 'Get a homing to Manston, glide as much as you can, reduce your revs and hopefully you'll make it.' The sad part of the story is that he and two other pilots were shot down by a high level escort of American Mustangs or Thunderbolts who thought we were FW190s.

"We weren't aware of any enemy aircraft at that time," Adam continued. "That was before the stripes on the wings. We had an American pilot, Artie Ross, and he was shot down but managed to make a forced landing on a beach somewhere. Then he was sent to all the American fighter stations to show off the Typhoon. They can't have been very happy about it having claimed they'd shot down 190s. But the Typhoon was often mixed up with the 190 but then we got the stripes and things improved."

By the morning of the 19th, instead of flying that day in support of the ground troops pushing out from Caen, 609 Squadron pilots and ground crew were moving their airfield to B7 at Martragny. "We arrive and there is much worse confusion than usual over where we have to bed down," recorded the diarist about the move. "Lorries are packed and unpacked several times and then the trouble starts. There is not enough tentage so at least two pilots sleep out under the stars."

Bad weather and poor visibility made operational flying impossible for the next four days until late in the evening of the 24th when the Squadron got some business. At 2030hrs Squadron Leader Geerts took Flight Sergeant Annear, Flying Officer Watelett, Warrant Officer Stellin, Flight Lieutenant Blanco, Flight Sergeant Cables, Flying Officer Cooreman and Flying Officer Jaspis to attack a German Army HQ at Morieres. Once again, red smoke from British troops identified the target area and the Typhoons rolled into their dives, attacking the building. Rockets shot away from the fighters and pounded into the structure. Levelling off, they strafed the area with cannon fire. Explosions ripped through the enemy HQ causing several fires. The building was completely destroyed. "We sometimes went out and came back late," Annear explained, remembering coming back in darkness. "Only occasionally we had to use a flare path. You were trained to do it and we didn't think about. It was part of your job; second nature to land like that."

The following day, the 25th, operational flying began early. Flight Lieutenant Blanco led a section to attack gun positions near Fresnay. They took off at 0605hrs but the target was obscured by mist and no markers were seen so they aborted the attack.

Later that day, Blanco was up again leading Annear, Watelet, Stellin, Merrett, Adam, Hue and Pagnam. "Sometimes you were scared," Adam recalled during the interview. "I always discussed it openly with my friends because you got to know each other very well. I could never understand that there were pilots who didn't know fear and volunteered for the most incredible things. I was scared at times.

"Obviously when you are attacking a target the fear disappears because you are concentrating on what you are doing because of that incredible speed. It was exhilarating and it had that dangerous fascination."

They took off at 1210hrs to attack enemy mortar positions near Amaye-sur-Orne. Heading for the target they encountered heavy intense flak that burst all around them. "One of the most notable sorties is one we did over the Caen: eight of us went out and eight of us got hit," Tom Annear recalled. "We knew it was a dicey one before we went because of the flak and only one, an Australian, reached the target, for which he got the DFC. The rest of us more or less belted off. In my own case I had my windscreen blown out. The concussion disorientates you and the speed you are going you might be a couple of miles away. After that you've got to recover yourself and I didn't have my goggles down so I had a face full of bloody crap and I could hardly see so I just had to abort it.

"The tears in my eyes helped to clear them. I flew back and landed at the first airfield I came to which wasn't mine and they gave me a bucket of water to wash my face and my eyes out and they kept me there for about an hour. After an hour they released me and I flew back to my own base which was only a few miles away and that was where the doc took me away, syringed my eyes out and cleaned me up."

As the pilots took evasive action they were hit by fragments of exploding shells and one by one were forced to return home without attacking. Australian Pilot Officer Merrett, braving the flak roared in at low level firing his rockets, strafing the target with cannon fire. Flak burst nearby, rocking and bumping his aircraft sending debris into his radiator as he climbed away. He was the last to touch down at base at 1255hrs, his aircraft, like all the others, the worse for wear.

The next show was at 1625hrs with Squadron Leader Geerts leading Flight Sergeant Ashworth, Pilot Officer Buchanan, Warrant Officer Harkness, Flying Officer Inches, Warrant Officer Seguin, Flying Officer Royston and Flight Sergeant Scott to attack an enemy strong point at Rocquancourt. They arrived over the target area but couldn't see any markers. For 30 minutes the section orbited the target area, and then Geerts saw another Typhoon squadron attacking a wood, and peeled off, leading his formation down onto the target as well. Their rockets pulverised the area and one suspected a tank was hit along with several transport vehicles.

The last operation of the day took place at 1920hrs with Geerts leading the overall formation of eight Typhoons. Airborne, they split into two sections of four, with Flight Lieutenant Inches leading Harkness, Adam and Bavington, while Geerts led Price Buchanan and Scott. Locating the gun positions at Rocquancourt, Geerts took his section down on the enemy gun position completely destroying them with rockets and cannon fire.

Inches took his section in on gun positions at Fontenay-le-Marmion obliterating those with rockets and cannon fire. Throughout the sortie they had to brave intense enemy flak. This time none were hit and they all arrived back at base at 1955hrs.

Tom Annear talked about the Germans and what he had heard about their reactions to the mighty Typhoon.

"They would probably be aware that we were in the air and see the smoke from where they were," he said, talking about the early days in France when the Germans were only a few miles away. "But I don't think they had anything that could stop us. Even for the German fighter aircraft we were going too fast for them to upset us really. The only defence they had against us was anti-aircraft fire. Sometimes we'd sneak around the POW cages and we weren't liked. Germans didn't have an answer to us at that time so we were a pretty nasty enemy. When we came on them they knew they were in for a bit of trouble."

26th July was another busy day for the Squadron. The first operation began with Squadron Leader Geerts taking off at 1225hrs leading Ashworth, Buchanan, Harkness, Inches, Adam and Price to attack railway junction and station at Yvetot to Charleval. Diving down to low level Geerts took his section into attack, firing their rockets and strafing the rail yards with cannon. The station received a direct hit. Cannon shells and rockets slammed into stationary rail wagons at Yvetot knocking several off the track, leaving others burning and smoking. Flight Sergeant Price dove through cloud to attack the targets and as he climbed he formed up with Typhoons that were in the process of attacking and he went down again, realising he was with the wrong squadron, but he attacked again until short of fuel and had to land at B9. They were all back at base by 1330hrs undamaged without encountering any flak.

In the evening, Flight Lieutenant Blanco led Flight Sergeant Annear, Flying Officer Hue, Flight Sergeant Stellin, Flying Officer Cooreman, Flight Sergeant Cables, Flying Officer Jaspis and Flight Sergeant Billam to attack a tank harbour in a wood near Racquancourt. Five Typhoons peeled off diving on the wood, firing their rockets. In all, 40 projectiles hammered the area, explosions sending white and black smoke into the air. The other three Typhoons attacked a nearby village, pounding it with rockets and cannon fire before wheeling away and joining up with the rest of the formation.

Pilots of 609 Squadron found themselves involved in a new system of very close support to the army on the 27th. In the thick of the battle a Visual Control Post directed the pilots onto the targets. This meant that sections of aircraft from two up to four were lined up on the runway waiting to be scrambled.[68]

"I'll take you through a controlled sortie," Tom Annear explained during the interview. "When you went out you were under the control of the forward control people. Might only be four of you and you had your number one, two three four. The FC would call you up and say 'in one minute we will put down red smoke on your target. That's what you will hit.' We would position ourselves before seeing the red smoke on the target. The leader would go down first and then a few seconds afterwards the No.2 would go down and then a few seconds after that the No.3 would go down and then a few seconds later the No.4 would go.

"We spaced ourselves far enough apart that you didn't run the risk of firing on your mate ahead of you. Also because you were coming down so quickly you were making alternative targets for the ack-ack because you were spreading the field. You might be a hundred yards to the side of the person ahead of you and so you go down and make your attack. It depended on whether you fired a salvo or if you fired two rockets, then you went back and had another go.

According to Tom Annear, the degrees of the dive didn't make much difference. "You might have one degree or two degrees different angle of attack, which would be immaterial to the target. If I was coming straight in from 120 degrees the other side might be coming in at 178 and the other

182, but it would make very little difference to his line of aim. It wouldn't be noticeable that he was on any different line of attack to you. He would see your aircraft and you were firing more or less to his side. You weren't following him firing straight behind him, you were coming in a different direction to his side."

"We used a system called 'cab rank' in close support of the army," Ken Adam explained. "There were four of us sitting on the edge of the airstrip. I had a grid map and we knew more or less the bombline. So what you did when the ACP fired off a green light, you climbed over the airfield to about 8 or 9,000 feet to avoid the flak and then the controller took over who was in the frontline in an armoured car or tank and he would say fly over to grid reference so and so and in twenty seconds there would be some green or red smoke, so go down and attack, and that's what we did. The whole operation took twenty minutes.

"The moment you took off four more aircraft took your place so the Army had continuous air support most of the time. We were particularly effective against the German tanks, which were superior to our armour and also against 88mm gun positions and so on. But we started having losses and they kept building up because the German anti-aircraft was incredibly efficient. We never had any losses from enemy aircraft because they didn't fly very much in those days."

The first scramble of the 27th came at 1210hrs when Flying Officer Cooreman led Cable, Jaspis and Adam to attack tanks south of Bourguebus. They spied two objects on the road that looked like burnt out tanks and attacked them with rockets for good measure. Then directed by the controller they fired eight rockets at a small tank concentration in the corner of a nearby wood but saw no results.

Thirty minutes later the call came through for Yellow Section to scramble. Roaring down the runway the four Typhoons were quickly airborne heading for dug-in enemy tanks near Frenouville. Pilot Officer Merrett, leading Annear, Billam and Stellin peeled off and dove on the targets. The four aircraft fired 32 rockets that smashed into the road and the surrounding areas, leaving one tank smoking and others badly damaged.

Red Section led by Pilot Officer Buchanan took off at 1730hrs leading Price, Adam and Bavington to attack an enemy concentration near Tilly. They were directed 600 yards southwest of Tilly where they ran into intense flak. Suddenly, Price broke right and down, disappearing through a rain cloud at 2,000 feet, and was never seen again.

Flak fragments hit Adam's tail and forced him to turn back to base leaving Bavington and Buchanan to attack. Firing their rockets, Bavington watched Buchanan go in but he was too low. Suddenly, he pulled up sharply, or was blown up by flak, rolled onto his back and crashed in flames. Bavington, wheeled around, strafing several enemy transport vehicles on the road before returning to base. It had been a terrible raid for the Squadron.

"Our losses weren't funny," Tom Annear recalled. "90 per cent of our losses were through flak. We were told we could expect things to get hot generally but in the air you have no idea. The only time you know there is flak about is when you see smoke and sometimes the gun flashes or the bursts when you are flying a bit higher. At low level you see nothing, you hear nothing you know nothing. It's only when you get hit, the concussion and the noise that tells you you've been hit. Otherwise you wouldn't have any idea that they are even firing at you. That's the only time. You see the gun flashes sometimes but there is no sensation that you are flying into antiaircraft."

The following day was met with low cloud and rain but the Squadron remained in readiness. The first scramble came at 2024hrs with Flight Lieutenant Blanco taking Annear, Hue and Flight Sergeant Ken Adam to attack tanks south east of Rocquancourt. Seeing the red smoke, they peeled off, diving on the enemy vehicles. Rockets shot from under their wings hitting enemy tanks on the road, destroying three of them. Columns of white and black smoke drifted into the air from the burning tanks as enemy gunners opened fire but the Typhoons were gone before they could find their mark. "Tanks would take up the biggest amount of targets in relation to overall targets. Maybe 40 per cent or something like that," Tom Annear explained. "Sometimes you didn't know what you were attacking because you only got a smoke flare on your target and it could be a concentration of artillery that was blocking the army and you couldn't see until you were right down on top of it what it was."

Yellow Section was scrambled at 2046hrs to attack tanks northeast of Rocquancourt. Finding the target Flying Officer Cooreman peeled off followed by Cables, Jaspis and Stellin of his section. Raking the area with rockets and cannon fire, Cooreman saw one of his projectiles smash into a tank, ripping the turret apart and sending up thick black smoke. Three other tanks were destroyed and the four Typhoons landed back at base without incident at 1315hrs. The army sent the Squadron a signal of congratulations on a job well done. "This type of work is very concentrated and with the heavy amount of flak encountered is taking a toll of the pilots," recorded the diarist. "This and the fact that every night is broken by our own AA fire at Jerry kites, is causing signs of exhaustion to become apparent among the pilots."

Flying began on the 29th early when Flight Lieutenant Blanco took Annear, Merrett, Adam, Cooreman, Cables, Jaspis and Stellin on an armed recce in the Pont L'Évêque–Lisieux–Bernay–Laigle–Argentan–Falaise area. Poor weather made the flight abortive but they managed to salvage something by attacking a road junction bridge near Falaise where they ran into heavy, accurate flak. Fortunately, no one was hit and no results were seen of their attack. Six miles south of Lisieux they attacked a railway station with rockets and cannon fire. Shells ripped into the building and surrounding track but they saw no fires or explosions.

In the evening, Squadron Leader Geerts led Flight Sergeant Scott, Warrant Officer Seguin, Flight Sergeant Ashworth, Flying Officer Inches, Warrant Officer Harkness, Flying Officer Royston and Pilot Officer Bavington on an armed recce to the same area. The formation broke into sections with Red Section attacking a small enemy transport truck on the road south of Laguiole, destroying it. Yellow Section attacked 30 rail wagons in the marshalling yards near Laguiole with rockets and cannon fire. The projectiles ripped some of the wagons to pieces causing many to catch fire. Geerts took his section in low, attacking enemy vehicles on the road south east of Evroult, the Typhoons tearing two staff cars and one truck to pieces with rockets and cannon fire. Flames shot out from one staff car as it was blown off the road by their rockets. Over Laigle they ran into intense flak and Flight Sergeant Ashworth was lost.

On 30th July the first show took place in the afternoon. Flight Lieutenant Blanco, leading Flight Sergeant Annear, Flying Officer Jaspis, Warrant Officer Stellin, Flying Officer Cooreman, Flight Sergeant Pagnam, Flying Officer Hue and Flight Sergeant Adam headed for an enemy gun position in the American Sector but it was not identified so they attacked a hut in a clearing completely destroying it. South of the target they encountered six tanks painted yellow and several trucks that they plastered with the remaining rockets and cannon fire though no results were seen.

"We were operating attacking rolling stock, transport and shipping right to the end of hostilities," Adam recalled. "We would circle then attack the target because you were flying too fast. If there were German dispatch riders they would try to get behind a wall or something. It wasn't always easy to find a target. We also had to attack some shipping and so on but really the main function of the Typhoon was close support for the Army."

On one occasion Adam was hit by flak. "I knew I was hit but as long as I kept flying and was able to land I did not realise the extent of the damage. When I landed one elevator was missing and part of the rudder had been damaged. At another time the oil seal on the prop came off on takeoff and I had to jettison the canopy. The only thing you could do was jettison the hood and then you would have to look out the side."

In the evening, Squadron Leader Geerts took Flying Officer Jaspis, Flying Officer Hue, Flight Sergeant Pagnam, Flight Lieutenant Blanco, Flight Sergeant Annear, Flying Officer Cooreman and Flight Sergeant Adam to attack an enemy HQ near Caumont. Forming up with aircraft from 164 Squadron the whole formation was led by Wing Commander Dring. In all, 64 rockets hammered the target area and several direct hits were seen on the building. Cannon shells ripped into the structure.

Explosions from the rockets started several fires and the building was left smoking.

The first show of the 31st took place in the afternoon when Flight Lieutenant Roberts led Seguin, Inches, Adam, Royston, Harkness, Bavington and Scott on an armed recce to the Vire–Flers–Thury–Harcourt area. Splitting into two sections of four Roberts took his aircraft down low to investigate a wood while the other section (Yellow led by Royston) remained on top cover. Bavington turned back with engine trouble but the remaining three continued to fly above the tree tops around the wood when they encountered heavy flak. Royston and Inches were hit but managed to get back to base.

They were up again at 1710hrs with Flight Lieutenant Roberts leading Seguin, Inches, Cables, Royston, Harkness and Bavington to attack enemy troop concentrations south of Caumont. Joining up with aircraft from 164 Squadron. 64 rockets dropped from the wings of the Typhoons and plastered the target but the pilots could not see the results of their attack.

July had been a difficult month for the Squadron. They'd moved from England to a strip in France and switched tactics from attacking radar stations to working in very close support to the army. The Squadron flew 225 operational sorties for 154.5 flying hours and had lost Flight Sergeant Bliss, Pilot Officer Buchanan and Flight Sergeants Price, Ashworth and Jock Adam.

Looking back on his time, Tom Annear believed they were doing the right thing. Unlike soldiers on the ground who sometimes came face to face with the enemy, the pilots never did, it was much more detached. "Well it was war and you were attacking a target, not a person. That was the attitude."

Pilots such as Sir Ken Adam were the lucky ones who managed to come back from the war without serious injury. Tom Annear was not so lucky. He ran into trouble one day, when the Squadron was operating from Holland. "I ran out of motor on an operation and had to crash land but wasn't successful," he explained. "I got her down alright and turned her over and that was the end of my war. I spent four months in plaster."

According to the veteran's agencies he is registered as 60 per cent disabled. "I consider myself very lucky. Outwardly you wouldn't know – it's all internal. I've got limited spine rotation, limited forward movement, limited back rotation. I've just sort of seized up. It was all a result of that crash. It never became normal." His engine cut out around a thousand feet when he was six miles from the airfield. "All of a sudden I looked down and there was no engine – it was very unexpected."

Once the war was over and he was reasonably fit he was discharged. "They wouldn't keep me any longer. I was still in plaster when I left England. I left just before Christmas and they put me in the NZ army hospital in Cairo, Egypt, and was there for three months until March. I had a fair amount of liberty and I was allowed to go and spend an afternoon in Cairo or a day trip."

Tom Annear became a civil servant in his native New Zealand, where he built up a good career for himself with the post office and finished up as the deputy district controller in Hamilton. Sadly, he passed away before this book was published.

CHAPTER TEN

609 Squadron, August 1944

On the 1ˢᵗ of August 1944 an Army signal came through that heartened the pilots, the perfect justification for all the work and sacrifice. "Captured P.O.Ws report that elements of the 21ˢᵗ Panzer Division were very severely handled by Typhoons as they were massing for an attack and as a result of this the attack was never put in. Congratulations 609."[69]

"I kept sort of making changes to my name but it was ridiculous," Ken Adam said during his interview. "I added an 's' to my last name so it was Adams instead of Adam. My German name was Klaus so I changed it to Keith. I was fortunate in as much as my older brother was in intelligence. Remember we had other nationalities, Belgian pilots, French pilots, and Norwegian pilots, Polish pilots; we had a lot of international pilots in the Squadron.

"Intelligence in the UK knew a few days after a pilot was shot down if he was taken prisoner and if any information had been given to the Germans. I wasn't allowed to visit my brother at his H.Q. because of the risk involved in case I was shot down. The Typhoon did an incredible job in close support. Remember we were operating from the bridgehead within two to three months before the British and Canadians broke out at Falaise."

The next two days the Squadron saw much activity with Flight Lieutenant Roberts leading Warrant Officer F.L. Taylor, Flying Officer Inches, Pilot Officer Bavington, Warrant Officer Seguin, Warrant Officer Harkness, Flying Officer Royston and Flight Sergeant Scott on an armed recce to the Mortain–Flers–Conde–Thury–Harcourt area. Taking off at 1435hrs two pilots returned to base early and the remainder pressed on attacking two staff cars parked outside a house with cannon fire.

The second sortie of the day saw Flight Lieutenant Roberts leading the same pilots as the first to attack enemy transport which was located in a village south east of Caen. One AFV was seen and attacked with rockets and cannon fire. After several strikes it burst into flames and was left smoking. Continuing the attack, the Typhoons fired the rest of their rockets into the village which was left a smoking ruin.

Roberts was up again at 2055hrs leading the same pilots to attack enemy transport. Spotting three scout cars at Forest de Heloise they attacked them with cannon and rockets leaving two burning furiously and the third badly damaged. Turning, they spotted enemy tanks and transport vehicles and dove down to low level, firing their cannon and remaining rockets leaving one tank in flames, billowing smoke, and several trucks damaged, before heading back to base.

On the 3rd the Squadron flew six shows despite the grey, cloudy morning. The first flight scrambled at 1246hrs with Flight Lieutenant Roberts took Warrant Officer Taylor, Warrant Officer Seguin and Warrant Officer Harkness to attack a wood with no results seen. The next section, scrambled at 1310hrs with Flying Officer Inches leading Flight Sergeant Scott, Pilot Officer Bavington and Flight Sergeant Adam fared just as badly not seeing any results from their attack due to ground mist.

Adam recalled talking about attitudes to ops and how temperamnt played a part. "I discussed this with a great friend of mine, a famous film cameraman who flew Lancaster bombers during the war. I told him I didn't think I would have made a Bomber Captain. To fly for eight hours or longer, part of the time through heavy flak or fighter attacks. I wouldn't have had the courage or temperament. He said to remember that he had a big crew, able to talk to each other during those long trips. But he preferred to be on his own so that he only had himself to blame if anything went wrong."

Flight Lieutenant Blanco's section, Flight Lieutenant J.N.C. Vandaele, Flying Officer Cooreman and Flight Sergeant Billam scrambled at 1310hrs and attacked some flak positions with rockets and canon fire, silencing the enemy's guns.

The only other show of the day was when Flying Officer Cooreman's section of Flight Lieutenant Vandaele, Flying Officer Hue and Flight Sergeant Pagnam were scrambled at 1952hrs. They soon encountered heavy intense flak and Cooreman was hit. As his aircraft went down, he managed to push back the canopy and bale out. He was back with the squadron the next day.

The only successful flight the following day took place at 2050hrs when Squadron Leader Geerts took off at 2050hrs leading Pilot Officer R.D. Grant, Warrant Officer Seguin, Warrant Officer Taylor, Flying Officer Inches, Flight Sergeant Scott, Warrant Officer Harkness and Flight Sergeant Cables on an armed recce to the Falaise – Lisieux – Argentan area. Catching three enemy transport vehicles on the road, the eight Typhoons peeled off, dropping into their dives, spraying the area with rockets as they levelled off, firing short bursts from their cannon. As each rocket exploded it threw up dust and debris making it very hard to see any results in the waning light. The last aircraft touched down at 2110hrs.

The only flight on the 5th saw Tom Annear's guns jam. Another Belgian pilot, Flight Lieutenant J.N.C. Vandaele led Flying Officer Hue, Flight Sergeant Annear, Pilot Officer Merrett, Flight Sergeant Billam Flight Sergeant Pagnam and Warrant Officer Stellin to attack several transport trucks and tanks but they saw no results. Going in low, Annear, kept his gunsight on the targets, his engine roaring as he raced in on the target, thumbed the firing button on his cannon and nothing happened. Disgusted, he returned to base with the others.

For the last few days the morning had been misty and flying could only take place in the afternoon when the mist cleared. At 1505hrs on the 6th Flying Officer Royston took out Warrant Officers Taylor, Seguin and Stellin, Flying Officer Inches, Flight Sergeant Scott, Pilot Officer Grant and Flight Sergeant Cables on an armed recce to the Falaise – Bretteville – St Pierre area where they attacked several enemy transport vehicles moving on the road south east of Falaise but no results were seen. They encountered heavy flak from nearby woods. Some gun positions were attacked in the evening again without any results being seen.

The following day the morning came out fine but no business came the way of the squadron until that afternoon at 1430hrs when Squadron Leader Geerts led Flight Lieutenant Vandaele, Flying Officer Hue and Warrant Officer Stellin on an armed recce to the Vire–Flers–Domfront–Mortain area. Flight Lieutenant Blanco, leading the other section took off immediately behind the first four but his tyre burst and he shot off the runway, looped in and completely destroyed his Typhoon. Fortunately he was unhurt but the crash blocked the others of his section from taking off. Geerts continued on and at St Barthelemy spotted some tanks and transport vehicles and immediately took his section in low, pulverising the area with their rockets. One tank suffered a direct hit and exploded in flames. A tank transporter was left smoking after receiving the attentions of the Typhoons hammered by rockets and cannon shells. They could not return to base because of Blanco's wreckage and had to land at another strip.

By the 9th they were back at Martragny and everything was back to normal. The first flight saw Geerts leading Flight Sergeant Cables, Warrant Officer Seguin, Warrant Officer Taylor, Flight Sergeant Scott, Pilot Officer Merrett and Flight Lieutenant Vandaele on an armed recce to the Falaise area. They took off at 1010hrs and they spotted enemy tanks moving northwest 6 miles south east of Falaise and were immediately attacked. The Typhoons roared down on the enemy vehicles, releasing their rockets that straddled the vehicles, with some scoring direct hits. Two tanks were left burning fiercely and others severely damaged by the time the Typhoons climbed away.

The same section, led by Geerts, was back up again 1345hrs on an armed recce to the Falaise–Argentan area. More enemy vehicles were caught in the open and pounded by the rockets that exploded all around the enemy vehicles and one smashed into the turret of a tank setting it on fire. Some of the trucks were damaged by debris and cannon shells as the Typhoons came in low and fast firing their guns.

The last sortie of the day saw Flight Sergeant Annear, Flight Sergeant Pagnam, Flight Sergeant Billam, Flying Officer Jaspis, Flight Lieutenant Vandaele, Flight Sergeant Adam and Warrant Officer Stellin taking off at 1640hrs in a formation led by Pilot Officer Merrett on an armed recce in the Falaise area. They attacked enemy transport they found in the open and then turned away; tearing towards a wood thought to contain concentrated enemy transport. Peeling off, they dove on the target area, releasing their rockets. As the projectiles shot away from their aircraft the pilots could see smoke rising from the woods as the rockets exploded causing a huge fire that sent flames and thick smoke into the air.

Typhoons around this time played a large part in preventing the Germans from making any counterattacks.[70]

The 10th began as a glorious summer day but within an hour of sunrise the cloud base began to grow. The first action of the day took place at 0925hrs when Squadron Leader Geerts took Flight Lieutenant Vandaele, Flying Officer Jaspis, Flight Sergeant Adam, Pilot Officer Merrett, Flight Sergeant Annear, Flight Sergeant Pagnam and Flight Sergeant Billam on an armed recce to the St Pierre–Trun–Falaise area. A concentration of enemy transport and tanks was seen at Mont Pinçon and was promptly attacked but no results were seen from their rockets and cannon fire.

At 1240hrs Geerts led the same pilots[71] back to the same target area that included motorised transport and horse drawn transport along with tanks. Diving, they fired their rockets and one truck received a direct hit exploding into flames while others were left smoking. Three horse drawn vehicles were hit and left damaged

The last sortie of the day was at 1830hrs when Wing Commander Dring led seven other Typhoons (Lough, Wallace, Harkness, Royston, Cables, Seguin and Bavington to attack tanks south of Vassay. Seeing no movement they orbited the area for a few minutes then headed back for base when they encountered heavy and light flak near the target area. Lough was hit in the windscreen but managed to land safely.

The following day, Geerts, with Wing Commander W Dring D.F.C. along as well, led Flight Sergeant Pagnam, Flight Sergeant Billam, Flight Lieutenant Blanco, Flight Lieutenant Vandaele, Flying Officer Jaspis and Warrant Officer Stellin on army support duty to attack a château near St Quentin. The château however was already burned out so they attacked some buildings south and left them blazing. Flying Officer Jaspis who had been Flight Lieutenant Vandaele's No.2 on this flight came in to land too fast and overshot. Quickly he pulled up his undercarriage and the aircraft came to a sudden and abrupt stop yards from the edge of the road.

The 12th was a busy day for the squadron. Flying began at 1420hrs when A Flight was scrambled. Led by Flight Lieutenant T. Y Wallace, Flight Sergeant Lough, Warrant Officer Harkness and Warrant Officer Taylor they could not identify the primary target so they attacked a secondary target, a wood northeast of Falaise. Throughout their attack they encountered heavy accurate flak.

Before Wallace's section returned the next flight was scrambled, this time with Pilot Officer Bavington leading Flight Sergeant Scott, Warrant Officer Seguin and Pilot Officer Grant and they attacked the same wood pulverising it with their rockets. As their projectiles smashed into the targets, they could see smoke and flames from the previous attack and more smoke from their own. On the way back to base they reported to Control that they had seen ten enemy tanks dug in south east of Epaney.

At 1645hrs Wallace took out the same formation to attack the tanks previously reported. They dove on the targets, firing 63 rockets and raking them with cannon fire causing a large explosion. They landed back at base at 1735hrs. Wallace came in normally, rolled to a stop and was suddenly run into by one of the new pilots, Flight Sergeant P.W. Lough who came in too fast and took off Wallace's tail. "When we see the accident figures for the end of the month we shall find a big black against 609," wrote the diarist.

The 13th of August marked the beginning of the end for the Germans as they began to retreat. Squadron Leader Geerts took Scott, Seguin, Cables, Wallace, Harkness, Bavington and Taylor to attack the German column of transport vehicles, troop carriers and tanks on the Falaise–Argentan area. "The Hun felt himself safe to move under the cover of cloud and mist but a hole in the cloud gave him away," recorded the diarist. And through that hole the Typhoons attacked, releasing their rockets and firing short bursts from their cannon. Caught on the road the large concentration of enemy vehicles was mercilessly pounded. Four tanks had their turrets blown off as rockets smashed into them. Many other tanks and transport vehicles were attacked and damaged, some burning from the fires started in other vehicles.

Coming in low over a village, Bavington saw that some of the transports were big troop carriers. Firing his cannon and his remaining rockets the resulting explosions caused havoc and carnage sending smoke and flames into the morning air. Smoke from the burning vehicles was rising up to 4,000 feet.

Their rockets expended, 609's Typhoons went in again, raking the burnt and smashed vehicles with cannon fire, catching enemy soldiers on the ground running for cover. "As far as the Luftwaffe is concerned the Jerry tanks and transport have had it. They have left them to their fate," wrote the Squadron diarist. "We are all sorry for the Frenchman who was seen dressed in his Sunday best, going off to Mass who got caught right in the middle of it."

Ken Adam visited the battlefield and had this to say about the carnage. "I was involved in that attack on the S.S. Divisions in the Falaise Gap, which turned out to be a massacre. The day after the attack my flight had permission to visit the battlefield to see the damage we had done.

"It was a traumatic experience for all of us. We were stuck in a slowly advancing armoured column and though we covered our noses with handkerchiefs, the smell of the dead and the animals, horses and cows all with rigormortis with their legs in the air is something I will never forget. The sweet smell of death and the havoc we had caused.

"It was the first and only time I had been in contact with the results of our attack. Sitting in a cockpit diving at tremendous speeds one is removed from the horrors on the ground even though I was aware of destroying tanks and gun positions."

The Squadron diarist summed up the day by saying that "it was a great day for all the squadrons and everybody was like a two year old coming back from a jolly party." Though Ken Adam's comments point to another, hidden reaction.

Ken Adam stayed with 609 Squadron flying Typhoons up to the end of the War. "Every time my wing commander applied for a commission for me it was turned down," Adam explained. "Finally, it was in August '44, I talked to my wing commander Scott, a New Zealander. I used to fly as his No.2 on many occasions. I used to say to him, "Scotty, if I take the same risks or even more risks than anybody else and my commission keeps being turned down I don't think this is right. So unless I get my commission I would like you to post me to Coastal Command where I could fly Sunderlands and have bacon and eggs for breakfast.

"He had a tennis pal from earlier days who was Sir Anthony Eden so I finally got my commission through the good offices of Anthony Eden."
Adam left the squadron in November 1944 to undergo a hernia operation and rejoined it in February 1945 during the advance through Belgium and Holland. Before the Rhine crossing they were stationed at Nijmegen near Arnhem but were unable to support the airborne landing due to adverse weather conditions.

"In November 1944 my younger brother 'Denie' had joined 183 Squadron in my wing," Adam recalled. "As his older brother I could apply for him to join me. He was with me during the Rhine crossing when we had been briefed to attack the German anti-aircraft batteries. We flew off to assist the bombers towing the glider troops. The Germans hardly fired a shot at us because they did not want to reveal their positions, but once we had attacked and broken away the flak started coming from all directions. I will never forget some of the gliders being hit with the troops tumbling out to their death. It was a horrific sight."

609 Squadron returned to the UK in September 1945 and Adam stayed for another year with an extended commission in the RAF at Wunsdorf, the Squadron's last base in Germany. "My job was to organise roughly ten thousand ex-Luftwaffe POWs into labour units to rebuild the airfield," he said. The airfield later became the main supply base during the Berlin airlift.

"Nowadays when I look at the only Typhoon still in existence at Hendon I am amazed at how much larger it is compared to the Spitfire or Hurricane. One feels the power of its enormous engine and weaponry. Even though it was not an easy aircraft for aerobatics in, it was really quite a fantastic aircraft for those days. Until it was replaced by the Tempest and then later on the Meteors or Vampires it was really the fastest piston-engine aircraft. Its disadvantage compared to the Thunderbolts was they could take much more damage than we could because of their radial engine; very often they came back with cylinders missing but we were very vulnerable.

"If you look at the Typhoon you'll find the wing was very thick compared with the Tempest, which was very thin. The Tempest was also faster and more manoeuvrable than the Typhoon. But I think the Typhoon did an excellent job."

CHAPTER ELEVEN

198 Squadron, June 1944

During an interview in early 2005, Richard Armstrong, formerly a Flying Officer talked about flying the Typhoon on operations and life in general during those very dangerous days of the summer of 1944.

In early 1942 he flew Hurricanes with 130 Squadron, a Canadian Squadron based at Baggotville, an RCAF Station in Northern Quebec, Eastern Canada, where they were deployed in East Coast Defence defending a large aluminium plant in nearby Arvida.

"I returned to the UK in June 1943 and after a brief spell in Bournemouth was posted to 198 Squadron who were flying Typhoon 1B's from Manston in Kent. I had said repeatedly, whilst in Bournemouth, that I didn't mind what I did as long as it provided enemy action. I naturally preferred an 11 Group posting, in the southeast corner of England. When I was eventually posted to Manston I couldn't find it on the map. It was with some mixed feelings, when I eventually found it, to discover that you couldn't possibly get nearer to France."

"There is a huge airstrip at Manston, a couple of miles long, which they were just building whilst we were there," Armstrong recalled. "In the meantime aircraft flew from the old grass strip which had an interesting dip in the middle of it. Manston was a front line base and Spitfire squadrons, with bombs attached, used it as a refuelling point prior to taking off for the continent. Many and many a time Spitfires landed, came to the dip which they hadn't anticipated, and lost a bomb. It would go bouncing down the runway after them, perhaps breaking into a couple of pieces to which your immediate reaction would be to rapidly put your hands to your ears. I never saw one explode. The Typhoon didn't have any problem with the dip. It was too heavy. In comparison a Spitfire was very tiny, having much less wingspan and being much lighter."

Originally flying Hurricanes he discovered the Typhoon was a very different type of aircraft. "The Hurricane was a beautiful aircraft to fly although she was terribly slow. Her maximum speed I think was 220mph and that was downhill with a following wind. Compared with the Hurricane the Typhoon was a horrendous beast, much bigger and much heavier. There were no dual cockpit versions of the Typhoon so the first time you flew one was the time of your solo. There was no such thing as gaining experience with someone else at the controls. Even first running the engine was a pretty terrifying experience, the noise was so tremendous. That was the first introduction. The noise was so terrific, tremendous."

At the time, according to Armstrong, squadrons were moved around between different airfields to prevent the enemy from knowing their locations. "We flew from Manston, Thorney Island, Tangmere, and Martlesham Heath all in the course of eight months. Whilst we received our rocket training in Llanbeddr, a station in Cardigan Bay, Wales."

Richard Armstrong's first flight in a Typhoon was from Manston.

"After cruising around, getting the feel of the aircraft, I was coming in to land and the Airport Controller told me to go away because there was an air raid in progress," he recalled. "This was my first landing in a Typhoon and I couldn't see any enemy activity, the whole place was quite peaceful. My first thought was 'What the hell am I going to do now?' So I did the only thing I could. I flew around for a while at 7,000 feet. I wasn't used to that part of the world and I took care to keep in view of Manston, just flying around in circles thinking 'What am I going to do if it gets dark before I get to land?' In that case my first landing was going to be a night landing. Luckily it was just going dark when they told me I could pancake. I think that was about the best landing I ever did in my life."

Because of the Typhoon's enormous propeller pilots had to carry out three-point landings. "It was essential to keep the nose up to avoid taking chunks off the end of your prop and maybe do yourself some more serious damage at the same time," Richard Armstrong explained. "Luckily I was trained by the Royal Canadian Air force where it was a point of honor that every landing was a three-pointer, whether flying Hurricanes, Harvards or Tiger Moths. The Typhoon was not difficult to land. You had to level off at twenty feet, gradually pull the nose up to lose speed and the aircraft would then gently sink to the ground, landing with no shock at all. In theory you reached the point of stall just as your wheels were a foot off the ground. In general you could land them quite gently but you weren't always successful."

On March 2nd 1944, three months before the invasion, 198 Squadron attacked an enemy RDF tower in Ostend. "This looked like a big chimney," Armstrong explained. "It was heavily defended and it was a really hairy job. As we never attacked it again I presume we destroyed it. The enemy always concentrated their flak on the coastline and if you were at nought feet you could get into considerable trouble with their light armaments. This particular tower was built right on the very edge of the cliff and was well defended. The Germans always used tracer and, of course, you could see it. Luckily tracer isn't very good at finding out where your bullets are going. The tracer bullet is lighter than the ordinary bullet, because it is hollow and packed with powder. This causes the shell to follow a different trajectory. So if you see tracer coming up you can be certain that the real bullets, which will do more damage, are not on that trajectory."

In April 1943 the Squadron was based at Llanbedrr on the West Coast of Wales, on a rocket training course, using rockets fitted with cement practice heads, Armstrong explained, "Although it was difficult at first, as time went on, you got better and better. We practised at different angles of attack, sixty degrees, forty degrees and twenty degrees. The lowest was the easiest and most accurate. The range was a really amusing setup. The targets were out on the water, about 200 yards offshore, square rafts which you were supposed to sink. The firing area had to be approached at low level and this entailed crossing a single railway line. The line ran along an embankment at this point and the railway company installed two special signals to stop the train if we were practising on the range. So you had to wait for the signals to be favorable before you went in and did your attack. We had to make certain there were no trains in the way.

The Typhoon was a reliable aircraft by spring 1944, most of its problems had been ironed out but still engine failure was one of the biggest fears, along with flak and enemy fighters that Typhoon pilots faced. Armstrong described an unpleasant experience he suffered while returning from a sortie in late May 1944.

"The hairiest moment that I ever had was coming back across the Channel from an operation when the engine just stopped. I must have been hit by flak. I was just near enough to the cliffs to try to make it gliding in. If I had been fifteen feet lower I wouldn't have made it, I would have been into the cliffs. However I managed to put the Typhoon down right on the top of the cliffs, within twenty feet of the edge. That was by far the most frightening experience because I didn't know, until the very last moment, if I was going to make it. The Typhoon wouldn't glide for any distance, it usually came down like a flying brick but it would glide for a short distance. Luckily I was up at 7,000 feet when my engine stopped and you could cover, I don't know, four miles or so from that height.

"You just did your best and hoped like hell," Armstrong continued. "Luckily there was a small anti-aircraft unit just at the spot where I landed. The crew all dashed out to help me, one with a cup of tea.

"I probably had an oil leak after being hit by flak. The first thing you had to do on occasions like this was to open the ammunition bays to empty or unload the breech, 'cause there's one up the spout. When I opened the panels this time it was disconcerting to find there was nothing up the spout, the gun wasn't cocked and would never have fired. All four cannon were the same. I got hold of the chief and gave him a right bollocking when I got back.

The month of June 1944 began quite quietly for the pilots and ground staff of 198 Squadron. But one morning, when Richard Armstrong was on standby they had an unusual scramble. A new radar with great range had just been introduced that could detect when German aircraft were being scrambled in France. Armstrong was on standby in charge of a flight of two.

"The instructions of the Controller were to circuit base until the rest of the squadron could get into the air when we were then instructed to vector over the Channel and climb to 10,000 feet, or 'Angels Ten' as an unusually excited controller termed it. He told me that there were 'One hundred-plus enemy aircraft at twelve o'clock above'. It was a beautiful day, without a cloud in a bright blue sky. You could see for miles and not an aircraft in sight. We couldn't see a darn thing. Then "They're behind you turn 180 degrees" came the next instruction. We dutifully turned around and looked at an equally empty sky – nothing. Eventually, after being re-directed several times and flying up and down the English Channel for quite a while we were told to return to base and pancake. So we returned to base and landed. It was a few days later that we discovered that the whole fiasco was due to the new radar they had introduced and which they were not used to. We had been all over the Channel, trying to catch a bunch of seagulls with rings on their legs that had been flying off the coast of Kent."

Like the description of May 1944 the one for June is taken from the Squadron histories, usually written shortly after each sortie by the intelligence officer, during or after debriefing. The intelligence officer was a pilot assigned to diary duties.[72] The figures, such as altitude, cloud cover, airspeed etc., are taken from that document and must be considered to be as accurate as possible; though in some cases it seems hard to understand how the pilots can calculate the height of a smoke column, for example.

Throughout the month of May and into June the tempo of operations increased and the pilots often found themselves on standby.

"In the days before the squadron was transferred to the Second Tactical Airforce, in readiness for the invasion, our principal duty was South Coast Defense," Armstrong explained. "This required each flight, and we had two, to take alternate shifts in a state of readiness, alternating between morning and afternoon shifts. Whilst on readiness each flight would have to provide two pilots on 'Instant Readiness', sat in the cockpit of their Typhoons, two on 'Three Minutes Readiness', sat in the Dispersal, but fully dressed and ready, whilst the remainder of the flight remained within the immediate vicinity, on 'Standby'. The Instant Readiness pilots had to remain in their cockpits, strapped in and on oxygen, occasionally running the engine to keep it warm, for two hours. After their allotted time they would change over with the Three Minutes Readiness pilots for the next two hours. Instant Readiness could be extremely boring. The majority of the time you just sat there all morning doing nothing except maybe reading a book but, on the other hand, if you were scrambled it could be the entire opposite. The signal to scramble came by red flare, fired from the control tower. We prided ourselves in being airborne within 13 seconds of the signal."

Pilots from 198 Squadron attacked a wide variety of targets. "On the whole Rhubarbs were great fun because they allowed you to do anything you wanted. Attacking railways more than anything and attacking enemy aerodromes, which, if you could catch aircraft on the ground, were a piece of cake apart from enemy flak. The flak wasn't all that dangerous because they had no experience of an aircraft flying as fast as the Typhoon. They were used to aircraft flying at 280 or 310 mph but suddenly to appear over the airfield periphery doing 440mph you were gone before they knew you were coming. I think that was our salvation really. You went in as low as you could, 30 or 40 feet maybe. Below the level of the hangars. The lower you were the safer you were because their guns couldn't traverse fast enough.

"Trains were the most fun because they were utterly defenceless. A speeding engine, with steam up trying to avoid you, created a spectacular explosion if you hit it with cannon fire. Trains were best attacked from three quarters, flying along the length of the train, raking it with cannon fire, and hitting the engine last of all. An average train was only doing about 40 or 50 miles an hour and was a sitting duck. The real aim was to block the line as well as destroying the enemy's means of transport. We could only strafe with cannon as we hadn't yet been equipped with rockets in those days."

The Typhoon was equipped with four 20mm cannon, two in each wing. "The cannon were usually concentrated on a firing zone 200 yards ahead. A special sight, reflecting off the windscreen, was fixed on this same distance. The theory was that the wingspan of the opposing aircraft could be set into this sight and when his wings filled the measurement indicated on the sight she was in range and you could fire. However there was little time for such niceties and you just fired and hoped. That's where armchair theory goes out of the window."

The first day of the month opened with no operational flying, only Flying Officer Hardy and Flight Sergeant Petherbridge carrying out practice tail chasing. A few days before the invasion the Wing had a visit from General Eisenhower who stood on a box to talk to everyone as Armstrong described: "It was one of these efforts where the speaker says, 'Come on, gather round lads' and then proceeds to stand on a box. It was,

I suppose, intended to increase morale before the invasion. It really did the reverse because we all thought we didn't need any Yanks to improve our morale. After he'd finished his speech 'to the boys' the Squadron was suddenly scrambled. We had to dash to Intelligence for a quick briefing on the operation. We were to attack a 'Noball' target in France, The launching ramp, or ski site, of a V1 rocket. We all knew that this particular site was already utterly destroyed, as indicated by the red pin on a nearby wall map. A yellow pin indicated that it was in course of construction whilst a green pin that it was ripe for destruction

"The entire briefing, observed by the General, was crazy. There were no safety courses home, no emergency channels, nor any other relevant information that was usually supplied as routine. The whole squadron took off whilst the General stood and watched. We had been asked to take off with our canopies open so that he could see us better. Half way across the channel we were ordered to return to base. The General had gone. The whole show was just for his benefit. God knows what could have happened whilst we wasted our time crossing the Channel, just for his amusement. That didn't help to improve morale at all, it just made us angry."

The following day was different when the first operation took place at 1515hrs with 9 Typhoons taking part in a 123 Wing attack on a radar installation at Dieppe. The Typhoons took off from Thorney Island, 198's home, and sped across the Channel to the target. Wing Commander Brooker DFC led the whole formation. The 198 Section split into two groups with Squadron Leader J Niblett taking three other Typhoons in for a low-level attack and Flight Lieutenant R. A Lallemand attacking in a dive from out of the sun. "Our rocket attacks we were very low at around 150 feet," Armstrong recalled during the interview. "You would cross the English Channel at nought feet and when you were two miles off the French coast you'd climb up to 7,000 feet or higher and then dive over the coast. The idea being that it was too high for German light Ack Ack and too low for the heavy Ack Ack.

"Rocket attacks were carried out, more or less, in a gentle dive, nothing spectacular," Armstrong explained. "It had to be a rock steady approach. Steep dives were entirely ineffective as far as rocketry was concerned. Steep dives were only used in dive-bombing or in attacking enemy aircraft depending on the situation. There could be no violent movements during a rocket attack."

"We'd been targeted to destroy a French château on D-Day, which was reputed to be a German Army Headquarters and we flew back over the beaches. We saw hundreds and hundreds of ships offshore with major battleships firing rockets inland. It was a fantastic sight. We flew down the beach and then turned across the Channel to get home to Thorney Island. When we landed back home we ran into the dispersal to switch on the radio to hear the news, but there was no mention of the invasion. The news didn't break for ages. The invasion was no surprise really because we had been confined to base for ages, unable to go on leave or visit the local pub because we knew it was about to happen. The night before the invasion there were hundreds of aircraft flying overhead, crossing the Channel. Literally hundreds of them. Gliders and all sorts. The place had been oozing with troops for days. You could hardly see any wharves from the air because there were so many ships anchored there."

Light flak from enemy anti-aircraft fire peppered the sky. As Niblett bored in on the target his aircraft was rocked by flak. Suddenly he was hit and his aircraft exploded into a mass of flames and crashed into the cliffs. The rest of the Squadron formed up after the attack and headed back home, minus their Commanding Officer. "This sudden loss of our Commanding Officer was quite a blow to the squadron," wrote the Squadron diarist. "Squadron Leader Niblett has been with us ever since our Manston days when he was a Flight Lieutenant and had command of 'A' Flight where he earned for himself the D.F.C. His sudden loss will be felt deeply by the whole of the Squadron."

Despite the loss of Niblett, operations continued and later in the afternoon at 1715hrs another section of Typhoons was up heading for France. This time, Flight Lieutenant Harding led Flight Sergeants Linter, Morley and Petherbridge, Flying Officer Hardy, Pilot Officer Allen, Flight Lieutenant Pye and Pilot Officer Pye on a raid on the radar installation at Cap Gris Nez. Attacking the target with real ferocity, rocket hits were seen in and around the target area.

They were back at base at 1915hrs and no more flying took place that day. As a snapshot of daily life in the squadron it is interesting to note that, although they had just lost their Commanding Officer, the 123Wing Officer's Mess Dance went ahead as scheduled. Even thought Niblett's loss would be deeply felt, they could not afford to stop and mourn for him. It was carry on and let off steam as the diarist relates. "The whole evening proved a riotous success and a very good time was had by all and sundry. There was an unusually high attendance by the ladies and dancing continued into the earliest hours. The only thing that our pilots are dreading now is a call early in the morning, round about dawn!"

Thankfully, the early morning call didn't come and pilots were able to sleep it off. The first operational flight of the 3rd of June took place in the afternoon when eight Typhoons took off from Thorney Island at 1520hrs. Wing Commander Brooker led the formation back to attack the radar station at Dieppe. With Brooker leading Sergeant G. S. Madgett, Flight Lieutenant J M Plamondon and Warrant Officer A R Hallett Flight Lieutenant Lallemand led Flight Sergeant Stratford, Flight Lieutenant D Sweeting and Pilot Officer D W Manson. Rolling into a shallow dive the pilots released their rockets and strafed the target area as they levelled off, pumping cannon shells into the buildings. Several strikes smashed into the installation and hit the surrounding area. Climbing rapidly away the pilots watched the explosions. Forming up, they roared back across the Channel with all aircraft returning safely.

The next flight of the day saw Flight Lieutenant Harding leading another section of 198 Squadron Typhoons back to the radar installation at Cap Gris Nez where they fired their rockets at the target achieving several hits. No flak came up to greet them and all aircraft returned to base. That evening the Squadron discovered their new Commanding Officer was to be Squadron Leader I J Davies who had been a Flight Lieutenant with 609 Squadron.

The following day, though sunny, saw no operational activity for the Typhoons of 198 Squadron. But the following day, Monday, 5th June, operations began early.

Pilots were out of bed at dawn, the engines run up on their Typhoons and their wheels lifted off the runway at 0755hrs. Squadron Leader Davies flying as Blue leader led Flying Officer Armstrong, Flight Lieutenant Plamondon, Free French Squadron Leader Ezanno, Flight Lieutenant Lallemand (Green Leader), Pilot Officer Mason, Flight Lieutenant Sweeting, Sergeant Madgett, Flight Lieutenant Harding (Black Leader) Flight Sergeant Petherbridge, Flight Lieutenant Pye and Flight Sergeant Linter on a Ramrod to attack the radar site at Fecamp.

Levelling off, the pilots could see orange flames rise into the air as the rockets exploded. Light flak arched up at them as they climbed away. The flak became heavier as it chased the Typhoons out to sea. All aircraft returned to base unharmed.

Later that same day on another 123 Wing show, Davies was again in the air leading Allen, Stratford, Flight Sergeant Morley, Harding, Petherbridge, Flying Officer Rainsforth and Flight Sergeant Linter on a Ramrod to attack a German HQ in a château near Bricquebec. Climbing into the evening sky at 2110hrs they headed out to sea at low level to avoid radar. Crossing the French coast, Davies climbed the formation and spotting the target, attacking from north to south.

The Typhoons dove on the HQ at high speed pouring cannon fire and rockets into the target. The pilots saw their rockets hammering the main building, starting fires as they exploded. Cannon shells ripped into the main building and the outbuildings. The main building was left charred and almost entirely destroyed from the attack while fires burned in the outbuildings as the Typhoons roared away.

At the same time, two aircraft from 198 Squadron accompanied aircraft from 609 Squadron to attack another château in Northern France but they were unable to find the target due to considerable flooding in the Lire River Valley. Turning to their secondary target, they attacked the railway line between St Lô and Carenten where two rockets smashed into the line and two more were seen to strike the embankment. They all returned to base unharmed.

"Late that evening, all the pilots of 123 Wing were given a briefing on activities that we can expect early in the morning," wrote the Squadron diarist.

D-Day for 198 was, unsurprisingly, not a stand down. "The long awaited attack on Europe started today, with landings on the beaches between Le Havre and the Cherbourg Peninsula," the diarist recorded. The entire squadron was up very early to carry out a rocket attack on enemy coastal gun positions but to the disappointment of everyone, the attack was called off and the Squadron was placed on 30 minutes readiness.

They didn't have long to wait. At 0825hrs 12 Typhoons from 198 Squadron climbed into the morning air and headed for France. Wing Commander Brooker took Armstrong, Plamondon, Madgett, Davies, Stratford, Sweeting, Flight Sergeant Sellman, Lallemand, Mason, Ezanno and Flight Sergeant Milne on a Ramrod to attack a château in the St Lô area.

Though the cloud cover was low, they crossed the beaches flying at 2,000 feet, pinpointed the target and rolled into their dives, releasing their rockets. Smoke and flames were seen billowing from the ground floor windows by the last Typhoon to leave the scene. Crossing the coast as they headed for home the pilots reported seeing intense activity on the beaches below.

"We'd been to destroy a French château which was reputed to be a German armoury headquarters on D-Day and were flying back over the beaches," Richard Armstrong recalled. "We saw hundreds and hundreds of ships offshore with major battleships firing rockets inland. It was a fantastic sight. We flew down the beach and then turned across the Channel to get home to Thorney Island.

"Then when we landed we ran to the mess to switch on the radio but there was no announcement and it didn't come for ages but we knew it was coming because we had been confined to our bases and we couldn't go on leave or anything.

"The night before we saw hundreds of aircraft flying over ead going across the Channel, literally hundreds of them. Gliders and all sorts. The place had been oozing with troops. But coming back across the channel you could hardly see the wharf because there were so many ships there."

Itching to get back across the Channel to help out with the invasion the pilots of 198 Squadron had to hang around until late in the afternoon when they were detailed to attack enemy transports. Lifting off at 1715hrs they roared across the Channel with Wing Commander Brooker leading a 123 Wing formation to hit enemy vehicles on the road from Falaise to Caen. The 198 Squadron section included Linter, Crouch, Stokes, Harding, Petherbridge, Hardy and Pye.

Catching the enemy on the road, the Typhoons roared down on them, firing their rockets and raking the area with cannon fire. Explosions from the rockets destroyed armoured fighting vehicles and transport vehicles. Pilots from 198 Squadron claimed seven Armoured Fighting Vehicles destroyed and one transport vehicle smashed by their rockets. They claimed another five damaged.

The fighting wasn't finished for the day. At 2040hrs Squadron Leader Davies took Flight Sergeant Stratford, Flight Lieutenant Sweeting, Warrant Officer Hallett, Flight Lieutenant Lallemand, Flying Officer Milch, Pilot Officer Mason and Flight Sergeant Milne on an armed recce of the Caen Sector where they attacked two tanks and several other enemy vehicles. Releasing their rockets as they levelled off, the projectiles pounded the target area, ripping into trucks, tanks and armoured cars. Shells from the four cannon on each of the Typhoons smashed into the vehicles. They claimed one truck completely destroyed, two tanks and several armoured cars severely damaged. They were back at base by 2300hrs.

Flying on the 7th began early. Squadron Leader Davies took Pye, Petherbridge, Allen, Harding, Flying Officer Lane, Rainsforth, Stokes, Hardy, Linter, Crouch and Morley on an armed recce to the Lisieux area. They took off at 0820hrs climbed into the morning sky and formed up over the Channel, heading for France. Crossing the French coast, they roared towards their patrol area and spotted enemy armoured fighting vehicles north west of Cormeilles which they immediately attacked with rockets and cannon fire, leaving them burning.

South of Bourg Archard, the Typhoons sighted more enemy vehicles. These were armoured fighting vehicles, transports and some cars. Rolling into their dives, they plastered the area with rockets and cannon fire, leaving two AFVs destroyed, a transport in flames and the others damaged. Two tanks were also hit. Light flak peppered the air around them and W.O. Stokes' port wing was on fire. Pulling up to 1500 feet he jettisoned his hood but the Typhoon dived into the earth bursting into flames. "It is possible that W/O Stokes managed to bale out but no one reported having seen any sign of a parachute in the air and it is feared that W/O Stokes lost his life."

The next sortie took place at 1730hrs when Wing Commander Brooker led Sellman, Plamondon, Milne, Lallemand, Hallett, Ezanno and Armstrong on an armed recce to the Lisieux–Bernay–Evreux area. A stationary goods train was attacked with rockets and cannon fire causing severe damage as their projectiles smashed into the wagons, carriages and locomotives. Their cannon shells ripped into the train and as they left, dust and debris was seen to be rising in the smoke.

Breaking from this attack, 198 pilots spotted a convoy of six lorries on the Verneul Breteuil road and promptly peeled off, diving on the enemy vehicles. Releasing the last of their rockets, they levelled off and raked the area with cannon fire before rapidly climbing away, leaving two destroyed and the rest damaged. On the way back to base, before crossing the coast, another lorry was sited northeast of Lisieux that was raked with cannon fire and left badly damaged.

The last sortie of the day took place at 2115 hours when eight Typhoons from 198 Squadron took off to attack a large convoy in the Bretteville area. The convoy was stationary in the Vire to Bernay–Villiers Bocage road. This time Squadron Leader Davies led Pilot Officer Allen, Flying Officer Hardy, Flying Officer Rainsforth, Flight Lieutenant Harding, Flight Sergeant Petherbridge, Pilot Officer Crouch and Flight Lieutenant Pye to attack the vehicles. Spotting the convoy they roared down on the targets, releasing their rockets, strafing them with cannon shells. Two tanks received direct hits from the rockets and exploded, utterly destroyed, while three AFVs burst into flames. Three transports also exploded and burnt fiercely. Some of the vehicles managed to move off into the woods. When the aircraft left, the convoy was still stationary with so many vehicles damaged and unable to move.

On the following day, the first flight took place at 1425hrs when Squadron Leader Davies led Flight Sergeant Milne, Squadron Leader Ezanno and Flight Sergeant Madgett on an armed recce in the Caen–Lisieux–Falaise area where they attacked and destroyed two AFVs and a transport truck. Continuing their patrol they ran across several tanks, trucks and transports moving north on all roads in the Bernay–Villiers Bocage area.

Peeling off, they dove on the tanks attacking them with rockets and cannon fire. Two tanks exploded, the rockets blowing their turrets off, bursting into flames. A staff car suffered a direct hit and was left engulfed by fire, while another transport was also blown apart. Several vehicles were damaged but the Typhoons did not see the rest of the results from their rocket attacks.

Wheeling away, they headed for home when Flight Sergeant Milne suffered engine trouble and made for the British lines north of Caen. The squadron diarist (usually the intelligence officer) recorded that there was some controversy surrounding what happened to Milne. Squadron Leader Davies reported that he saw Milne gliding towards the British lines when about a mile away he dove into the ground. Squadron Leader Ezanno and Flight Sergeant Madgett thought that this was another aircraft that appeared out of the clouds and that Milne was still gliding; but his landing was not seen.

Last flight of the day was another armed recce into the Caen sector, this time with Wing Commander Brooker leading Flying Officer Milch, Flight Lieutenant Plamondon, Flying Officer Armstrong, Flight Lieutenant Lallemand, Warrant Officer Hallett, Flight Lieutenant Sweeting and Flight Sergeant Stratford. Flight Lieutenant Lallemand took his section of three into attack several tanks and armoured cars in Grunoult while Brooker's section attacked several scout cars moving north. Rockets and cannon shells poured into the enemy vehicles destroying one tank, two armoured cars and several scout cars. Two enemy vehicles were left damaged from this attack.

No flying took place on the 9th but on the 10th the Squadron was back in action again. At 1235hrs 12 aircraft from 198 Squadron and another 12 from 609 Squadron, all led by Wing Commander Brooker, headed across the Channel to attack the radar station at Fecamp, but the operation was aborted due to low cloud cover over the target. All the aircraft returned fully loaded.

Later in the evening, at 1800hrs the Squadron was again in action with aircraft from 609 Squadron. Wing Commander Brooker, (Black Leader) led Milch, Ezanno and Sweeting, while Squadron Leader Davies (Blue Leader) led Sellman, Plamondon and Hallett with Flight Lieutenant (Green Leader) leading Stratford, Mason and Madgett. Their targets were woods at Tourville near Caen that were reported to be full of troops but they were unable to find the woods because of low cloud cover. But they did find enemy transport on the Caen–Villiers Bocage road and roared into the attack, destroying one AFV and two transports.

No operational flying took place on 11th June. "The Squadron was released in the afternoon and some of the pilots made a sortie into Brighton with the usual results," the Squadron diarist recorded. "Flight Lieutenant Sweeting and Flight Sergeant Stratford reached home at 3 a.m. owing to having fallen asleep on the train."

Monday, the 12th was a busy day for the Squadron. Flying began at 0510hrs when Squadron Leader Davies taking 'A' Flight consisting of Flight Sergeant Linter, Flying Officer Hardy, Flight Sergeant Petherbridge, Flight Lieutenant Harding (Green Leader) Flight Sergeant Morley, Flying Officer Rainsforth and Flight Sergeant Battley on a Ramrod to attack the radar station at Cap D'Antifer.

They roared across the Channel and climbed rapidly to height as they approached the target. Peeling off, Davies led the dive on the enemy installation firing all his rockets into the target area. The projectiles exploded as they smashed into the buildings, sending smoke and debris into the air covering the target. The remaining five Typhoons fired their rockets at the smoke that obscured the target. As the last aircraft went in the gunners woke up and began pumping anti-aircraft shells into the sky. None of the Typhoons were hit and they all returned to base safely.

"'B' Flight was then dragged out of bed and 5 A/C led by Wing Commander Brooker D.F.C. took off at 0610hrs to attack the radar station at Cap de la Heve," the diarist recorded. With Brooker leading Ezanno, Lallemand, Hallett and Mason they headed for the target attacking it from north to south. The pilots saw no direct hits from their rockets but they did see several strikes on the target from their cannon.

The next sortie of the day took place in the afternoon. Squadron Leader Davies led eight aircraft from 198 Squadron to a wooded area east of Caen. Together with eight aircraft from 609 Squadron they attacked the woods, that were reported to have been an enemy vehicle concentration but they saw nothing on the attack except some smoke coming from the north corner of the woods.

At 1850hrs on the following day, the 13th, the first operation of the day took place. Having been on standby all day the pilots were finally airborne led by Flight Lieutenant Lallemand. Leading Flight Sergeant Stratford, Warrant Officer Hallett, Flight Sergeant Sellman, Flight Lieutenant Plamondon, Flying Officer Armstrong, Flight Lieutenant Sweeting, Flight Sergeant Madgett, Flight Lieutenant Harding, Flight Sergeant Thursby, Pilot Officer Allan and Flight Sergeant Petherbridge they headed for the target area a 1½ square mile patch at Villers-sur-Mer surrounded on three sides by Allied troops. Careful to avoid hitting their own sides, the Typhoons along with aircraft from 609 Squadron pumped rockets and cannon fire into the area sending smoke and debris into the air.

Next day was a busy one for 198 Squadron. At 0520hrs Squadron Leader Davies lifted off from Thorney Island on an armed recce leading Rainsforth, Crouch, Morley, Harding, Flight Sergeant Bartley, Hardy and Linter to the Valognes area in the Cherbourg Peninsula. One large enemy transport truck was attacked and destroyed by rocket fire north of Yvetot. Near Valognes the Typhoons attacked enemy armoured vehicles leaving one in flames and the others damaged. Near Bricquebec they attacked a staff car leaving it in flames. Falk burst around them as the Typhoons tore through the sky then they dove on the gun positions firing the last of their rockets and strafing them with cannon shells. One gun position was destroyed under the onslaught of rocket fire.

Suffering engine trouble, Pilot Officer Crouch headed for Allied lines escorted by Flight Sergeant Morley. One mile south of Monte Bourg, Morley saw him try to crash land but instead, Crouch hit a tree and burst into flames. "This is a very sad loss to the Squadron as he was one of the original members of the Squadron and had just come back to us after a rest," wrote the diarist.

At 1125hrs Wing Commander Brooker took off from Thorney Island leading Flight Lieutenant Lallemand, Flight Sergeant Stratford, Flying Officer Armstrong, Warrant Officer Hallett, Flight Lieutenant Sweeting, Squadron Leader Ezanno and Flight Sergeant Sellman on an armed recce into the same area as the earlier mission. Owing to an over-revving propeller Brooker was forced to turn back shortly after take off, leaving Lallemand to take over the mission.

Five miles north of Valognes they peeled off, diving on four stationary lorries and four army huts pounding them with rockets and cannon shells. Leaving them damaged and smoking they encountered light accurate flak from enemy gunners. Shells smashed into Sweeting's port mainplane and the pilots heard Stratford say over the R/T that he had been hit and that his oil pressure was dropping and he was going to have to make a forced landing. Though he was over Allied lines at the time, none of the pilots saw him go in.

Though most of their work was low-level rocket attacks they also escorted bombers. That was a much different proposition as Armstrong suggested.

"Escort duty was difficult, with both Marauders and Mosquitoes. The Typhoon was only effective at 400 miles an hour and, as you are escorting someone that can't do more than 250mph or so, it gets a bit difficult keeping back with them. You are flying all over the sky trying to keep yourself in position all the time. I think the Mosquito was the most difficult," Armstrong said. "They were nowhere near as fast as 400 miles an hour. They might have been with no bombs aboard and with all their armament removed but with a full load of bombs and a load of ammo they might have done 250mph, no more.

"Bombs make a big difference to flying speed and Mosquitoes were no different. We escorted them to Eindhoven to attack the Philips Battery Works. On the return journey there were three of them who must have been hit and were hanging back. The CO called me and told me to take Blue 3 and look after those chaps who were lagging behind. We could see a whole squadron of ME 109s way up above us and it was quite something trying to keep up sufficient speed to be able to tackle them if they came down and yet keep back with these chaps. Luckily they never came down. Why I don't know. I presume he wasn't all that happy about tangling with Typhoons because they were both faster and had greater firepower."

On the 15th operational flying didn't take place for pilots of 198 Squadron until the late afternoon. At 1705hrs Wing Commander Brooker took Flight Sergeant Bartley, Flying Officer Hardy, Flight Sergeant Petherbridge, Squadron Leader Davies, Flying Officer Lane, Pilot Officer Allan, Flight Lieutenant Pye, Flight Lieutenant Harding, Flight sergeant Linter, Flying Officer Rainsforth and Flight Sergeant Thursby on a Ramrod to attack two ferries across the Seine along with aircraft from 609 Squadron. Pilots from 198 Squadron went in low, attacking both jetties and the ferry at Duclair. In a line astern the Typhoons roared in on the target, releasing their rockets, achieving several direct hits. The ferry itself received poundings from several projectiles and was left burning fiercely.

"When we went into attack we were flying in a spread out formation," recalled Richard Armstrong. "We usually went into attack flying in line abreast formation from which you would peel off to make individual attacks. I think the theory was that if the aircraft were all higgledy piggledy all over the place the Germans wouldn't know where to fire but if you were in a line they would know exactly where to fire. We attacked from the same direction but not in any organized manner. What might be described as a loose formation."

Flak burst all around them as the Typhoons turned away from the burning ferry and headed for the gun positions on the hills north of the target. Even as flak shells burst around them, they dove down on the gun positions raking them with cannon fire, silencing the guns. But not before they had claimed a Typhoon. Flight Sergeant Bartley, hit by flak, baled out of his aircraft but his parachute was not seen to open.

Later in the evening, six pilots of 'B' Flight took off from Thorney Island heading for the radar station at Cap D'Antifer. Flight Lieutenant Lallemand, leading Hallett, Mason, Plamondon, Ezanno and Armstrong attacked the Coastwatcher buildings, the rectangular lattice structure south southwest of the semaphore station. In a line astern they roared down on the target, flak coming up at them and released their rockets. Several strikes were seen on the targets, while the gun positions were raked with cannon fire. All the aircraft returned safely to base at 2025hrs with the exception of Armstrong who returned at 1925hrs shortly after takeoff, due to mechanical troubles.

Only one sortie took place for 198 Squadron on the 16th that saw Squadron Leader Davies taking Allan, Hardy, Petherbridge, Harding, Lane, Rainsford and Pye on an armed recce. Their secondary target was to be petrol storage tanks at Maillaraye and this they attacked being unable to hit the main target due to low cloud over the area. Indeed, to attack the storage tanks, they dove through gaps in the cloud and saw several rockets strike the tanks but no fires were started. There were no massive explosions from igniting petrol so the pilots assumed the tanks were empty.[73]

The Squadron began to get ready to move to their new base at Funtington six miles north of Thorney Island. The move was put off until the following day so the pilots could get some sleep. That same day, Flight Sergeant Stratford returned from France to the relief of everyone having crash-landed north of Carenten. "The aircraft caught fire and he last saw it still burning," wrote the diarist. "He was picked up by some American soldiers and taken to a landing barge to come back to England. They stayed off the beach all night and were bombed once and next morning set sail and arrived at Portland after a 14-hour journey. He says that on several occasions the Americans mistook him for a German prisoner, apparently not knowing what an RAF uniform looks like."

The following day the Squadron took off at 0900hrs for their new home at Funtington.

Operational flying began at 1120hrs when Flight Lieutenant Harding and Flight Sergeant Morley went off on a weather recce over the Isigny–St Lô–Falaise–Cabourg area. Covered by 10/10ths cloud at 2/3,000 feet it was not suitable for operations.

The next sortie of the day took place at 1805hrs when Flight Lieutenant Lallemand took Flight Sergeant Stratford, Pilot Officer Mason, Squadron Leader Ezanno, Flying Officer Milch and Flying Officer Armstrong on an armed recce in the Caen–Villiers Bocage area. Flak came up at them as they attacked several enemy transports on the road, leaving one in flames the others severely damaged. The Squadron diarist then goes on to say that the pilots saw Flying Officer Armstrong's aircraft get hit by flak and go down. Indeed, the diarist states that they saw his aircraft "crash in flames."

But this cannot be true. Armstrong's own account of his forced landing is quite different. He was taken prisoner until the end of the war. Now, was there another Armstrong in the Squadron? There is no record of it in the Squadron history that there were two Armstrongs in the Squadron at the same time. Armstrong himself said he joined the Squadron in 1943 and the diarist writing in the Squadron history states, "He has been with the Squadron for nearly a year and it is made worse by the fact that his wife had a baby only a few days previously."

So it is very likely that this was Richard Armstrong and what the pilots saw was either another Typhoon or they did not see him bale out but saw his aircraft crash, assuming he did not get out.

Thinking Armstrong had gone down, Lallemand continued the patrol, attacking more enemy transport on the Caen–Falaise road while still under heavy fire from enemy gunners. Pilot Officer Mason called up after leaving the target area but had not been heard or seen since. "It is hoped he has landed in our lines north of Caen," wrote the diarist. A black day indeed for the Squadron as Stratford was also hit by flak in his ammunition bay and landed back at base with a 20mm shell still smouldering. Both Ezanno and Milch were also hit by flak.

Though there was no operational flying the next day, the 19th, but Squadron Adjutant Flying Officer Smith had a memorable experience. After consuming large amounts of alcohol Smith was led out to the Jeep and left in it to get some fresh air. The combination of alcohol and fresh air was too much and Smith fell asleep. "Some time later," the Squadron diarist recorded, "a mysterious stranger came out of the Mess and leapt into the Jeep and drove off into the night with the adjutant beside him. There was a loud crash and the next thing our adjutant knows is that he is being led down endless roads to a sick bay where he had some stitches put in and bandages put on and was then led back and driven to the Mess in the now rather battered Jeep."

There was no sign of the mysterious stranger.

The first sortie on 20th June saw Squadron Leader Davies leading Flying Officer Milch, Flight Lieutenant Plamondon, Sergeant Madgett, Flight Lieutenant Lallemand, Flight Sergeant Stratford, Warrant Officer Hallett and Flight Sergeant Sellman on an armed recce on railway lines in the

Bernay area. Taking off at 2000hrs crossed the coast, found their railway line and followed it. At Quittebeuf they found 15 to 20 closed rail wagons and some flat cars that they immediately attacked. Peeling off, they dove on the targets, releasing their rockets. The projectiles hammered the area completely destroying two wagons, damaging others and striking the track itself. Turning, the Typhoons came back again, firing bursts from their cannon along the length of the stationary wagons before climbing away. Southeast of Bacquepuis they attacked one locomotive and several wagons hitting the track ahead with several near misses on the train.

As the light was waning, another four Typhoons from 198 Squadron took off from Funtington. Flight Lieutenant Harding led Flight Sergeant Hammond, Flight Sergeant Petherbridge and Flying Officer Rainsforth on a Ramrod to attack railways around Lisieux. Over the Channel they formed up with aircraft from 609 Squadron and headed for France. The first target was a tunnel and rail line west of Lisieux that they plastered with rockets and cannon fire. Several hits were scored in the mouth of the tunnel and on the line itself. At St Martin and St Julian they attacked the line again, destroying signal boxes with their remaining rockets. The pilots reported last seeing Petherbridge attacking a target south of the rail line at St Aubin Sur Algot when there was a big flash on the ground, starting a fire. Rainsforth, Petherbridge's No.2, called him, but was met with silence. Leaving the target, Rainsforth called Petherbridge again and received a reply; following the flash it must have been a great relief. However, despite Petherbridge saying he was OK, he did not return to base with the others and nothing further was heard of him.

Low cloud over France made operational flying on the 21st impossible and in the afternoon, the Squadron was told they were moving to Hurn so they spent the afternoon packing up. At 0830hrs the following day the Squadron took off and landed at their new base.

While unpacking took place, the first operational sortie of the day took place in the early afternoon when Squadron Leader Davies took Flight Lieutenant Pye, Pilot Officer Allan, Flying Officer Lane, Flying Officer Hardy, Flying Officer Rainsforth, Flight Sergeant Morley, Flight Sergeant Linter, Flight Lieutenant Lallemand, Flight Sergeant Stratford, Squadron Leader Ezanno and Warrant Officer Hallett along with aircraft from 609 Squadron to Cherbourg providing close support for the Americans who were beginning their attack on the town. They took off from Hurn at 1205hrs and tore across the Channel. On take off, Flight Lieutenant suffered a burst tyre peeling off; they rolled into their dives releasing their rockets on a variety of enemy targets. The projectiles ripped into flak positions, barrack blocks, railways and roads and on a wireless station as the Typhoons swarmed over the area. Intense, light and heavy flak filled the sky as they attacked and Davies' aircraft was hit. Turning his aircraft he tried to make for the American lines but was losing height too quickly as his engine died. The other pilots from 198 Squadron watched him bale out of the stricken fighter but his parachute did not open before he hit the ground.

Davies had been with the Squadron for a little more than a fortnight before he was killed. It was another sad day for the Squadron.

The last flight of the day took place at 1720hrs when Flight Lieutenant Harding led Lane, Rainsforth, Linter, Hardy, Morley, Allan and Pye on an armed recce in the Caen area where they attacked three lines of stationary rail wagons in sidings near Bencanville La Campagne. Peeling off, they roared up the line, firing rockets and cannon shells at the targets utterly destroying two wagons that burst into flame and damaging several others.

The following day, the Free French 23rd Squadron Leader Ezanno, holder of the Croix de Guerre, took over command. The Squadron had been at readiness all day but nothing happened until the evening when the light was beginning to fade. Taking off at 1230hrs, he took Barton, Allan, Linter, Harding, Pye, Hardy and Morley to attack targets in the Falaise–Argentan area. Five of the Typhoons peeled off, firing their rockets at several rail wagons and a signal box that was left burning fiercely from the attack. At Orville, two Typhoons came in low, firing their rockets and cannon at a stationary train. Shells and projectiles tore into the wagons and locomotive. Wheeling away, the pilots could see the wagons smoking.

Unfortunately, Flight Sergeant Barton, Ezanno's No. 2 were separated from the rest of the formation as they headed for home. Approaching the Isle of Wight Barton reported that his engine had cut and according to the Squadron diarist, Ezanno told Barton to switch to reserve tanks but it didn't work and he hit the water. Orbiting the positions where Barton's Typhoon had gone in, Ezanno searched for evidence that his No. 2 had survived but he could see nothing. Barton had only been with the Squadron a few days.

Flying began early on the 24th of June when Wing Commander Brooker led eight aircraft from 198 Squadron and 8 from 609 Squadron on an armed recce to attack railway lines in the Domfront–Lille area. At Evron, they pumped rockets and cannon fire into the area, striking several wagons as well as the lines.

At 1945hrs the same day, Squadron Leader Ezanno led Flight Lieutenant Sweeting, Flight Lieutenant Plamondon, Flying Officer Milch, Flight Lieutenant Lallemand, Flight Sergeant Stratford, Flying Officer Williams and Sergeant Madgett on an armed recce in the Domfront–Laval area. At Sille they attacked more than 50 rail wagons in sidings plastering the area with rockets and cannon fire sending dust and debris into air as the projectiles exploded, damaging several wagons and cutting the lines. On the way home they were shadowed by two Focke Wolfe 190s that were chased away by Thunderbolts.

Poor weather kept the Squadron on the ground over the next four days until June 29th when Squadron Leader Ezanno led Flight Sergeant Madgett, Flight Sergeant Stratford, Flight Sergeant Coulson, Flight Lieutenant Coulson, Flight Sergeant Hammond, Flight Lieutenant Sweeting and Flying Officer Milch to attack several tanks on flat cars at Mézidon. Forming up with 609 Squadron they headed for France but by the time they arrived over the target area, the tanks had gone. Instead they attacked parked rail wagons at Conches. Tearing in at high speed, they opened fire seeing several strikes on the wagons and rail lines. Turning for home, the Typhoons landed at airstrips in France to refuel, then took off again and landed at Hurn. All the pilots returned safely.

"Rocket attacks were always launched at very low level, around 150 feet," Armstrong explained. "It was general practice to cross the English Channel at nought feet until you were approximately two miles off the French coast and then climb rapidly to 7,000 feet or higher to dive over the coastline. The idea being that at 7,000 feet we were too high for German light Ack-ack and too low for the heavier guns. At least in theory."

The last day of this eventful month no flying took place and the Squadron prepared for their move to France.

CHAPTER TWELVE

198 Squadron, July 1944

We lost quite a lot of guys but it usually tended to be the new ones who were relatively inexperienced. The chaps who were experienced and knew what they were doing usually lasted for twelve months or more. Shall we say if you lasted a couple of months you would last at least six. There were some that were there when I joined the squadron and were still there when I left, but not many. There were also any number of chaps who had come and gone during the same period.

Flying Officer Richard Armstrong

This was the day of the move for 198 Squadron to Plumentot that would become their home in France. Everything had been packed and the Squadron waited for the Dakotas to arrive to take them across the Channel. At 1330hrs the Dakotas showed up, were loaded with tents, orderly room equipment, ground personnel, spare pilots and personal kit and at 1525hrs they took off for France and arrived one and a half hours later after an uneventful trip.

Things started happening when the Dakotas landed at Plumetot (B10) as the enemy started shelling the airfield. The adjutant's typewriter was smashed in the mud as the result of the shelling. The Dakotas were quickly unloaded and left as fast as they could, leaving the Squadron and the Wing personnel to fend for themselves under the enemy shelling. "It now appeared that a mistake had been made and 123 Wing personnel were told they had to go back to England immediately," wrote the diarist. "Within an hour of arriving the Wing personnel were on their way to B4 to be transported back to England. The remainder, the Squadron personnel proper, in pouring rain, erected the tents and after a good meal went to bed."

Back in England, those pilots remaining were briefed to take off in 20-minute intervals starting at 1830hrs but this was cancelled and the pilots remained in England, with only what they stood up in for one more night.

That night the landing strip was heavily shelled making it difficult for all personnel to get a good night's sleep.

Bad, wet weather hampered operations in France. Back in Hurn the pilots stranded there with no kit began to hear rumours coming back from B10 that the strip was waterlogged, was under constant bombardment and all their kit had been lost. However, in France itself the reality was different, as the diarist recorded. "Most of the day was spent digging in, by the evening most of the tents were surrounded by huge plots of earth. The air overhead is full of Spitfires on patrol and an occasional formation of Typhoons going over, usually met by intense enemy flak. Most of the boys have a smattering of French and are managing to get around in our local village of Plumetot but the inhabitants, with few exceptions, speak a patois."

The weather on 3rd July was still bad and none of the pilots had managed to get across to France or to get their kit; but relief came when Dakotas arrived from France complete with 123 Wing personnel, though the Squadron personnel, doctor, spare pilots, ground personnel and adjutant had all been left in France. There the strip was still waterlogged and much to everyone's chagrin, German tanks penetrated the area to within a mile and a half of the airfield. At the airfield there was nothing for the Squadron personnel to do without the pilots and aircraft and with the pour weather. "We play cards and drink whiskey and gin," the diarist recorded about life at the Plumetot airstrip. "The Messes are quite good but we miss bread, beer, papers and mail."

By July 4th the weather was clearing and the pilots, still at Hurn, were put on 60 minutes readiness and carried out practice flying, but no operations took place.

At Plumentot the highlight of the day was a Spitfire that did a belly landing on the airfield with the pilot walking away from the wreck.

Low cloud and rain made operational flying imossible until the 8th of July when it cleared enough for the Squadron to finally fly to France. At 0330hrs on the 8th the Squadron was called and took off for France in two parties of nine aircraft, landing at B5 Camilly, which was the base they would operate from while using Plumetot to sleep.

'Safely' in France, the first operational flight took place at 1030hrs with Squadron Leader Ezanno leading Flight Lieutenant Pye, Flying Officer Hardy, Flight Sergeant Morley, Flight Lieutenant Harding, Flying Officer Rainsforth, Pilot Officer Allan and Flight Sergeant Linter to attack camouflaged gun positions south of Caen. Now they were in France, the targets were much closer and the Typhoons would take off, form up over the sea, gain height and come roaring back in to attack their targets. Peeling off, they rolled into their dives, releasing their rockets that hammered into gun positions and the area around them along with shells from their cannon. Dust, smoke and debris covered the targets as the rockets exploded and the pilots could not see if the guns had been destroyed. All the time, the flak came up at them from different directions. Flight Lieutenant Pye was hit pulling out of his dive and his hydraulics packed up, forcing him to make a wheels up landing.

Later that afternoon, Wing Commander Brooker led 'B' Flight to attack enemy transport on the Bayeux to Caen road as the Germans were retreating into Caen itself. Leading Flight Sergeant Stratford, Flying Officer Williams, Flight Sergeant Sellman, Flight Lieutenant Plamondon, Flying Officer Milch, Flight Lieutenant Sweeting and Sergeant Madgett, he took off at 1610hrs and they headed for the target. Rain lashed their windscreens and nothing was seen on the roads but the Typhoons attacked them nonetheless to make them impassable for the enemy. Rockets pounded a crossroads northwest of Caen and one German transport was caught out and promptly destroyed by cannon shells and their remaining rockets. "The Squadron was released at 1930hrs and went by road to B10[74] and spent the rest of the evening sorting out kit and fixing tents to individual requirements," the diarist recorded. "All the rest of the Squadron have dug slit trenches in their tents and put their beds in them, so we are expecting the worst as we haven't the time or the energy to dig them ourselves."

They spent a quiet night except for a British artillery barrage that erupted at 0400hrs.

The following day, the pilots returned to Camilly and waited for flying to begin. By early afternoon the only operational sortie of the day took place when Flight Lieutenant Harding took Ford, Rainsforth, Pye, Hardy, Flight Lieutenant Shepherd, Allan and Thursby to attack tanks on the outskirts of Villiers Bocage in the Caen sector.

Light flak peppered the sky around them as their rockets exploded in the road. One tank received a direct hit and exploded burning fiercely. Another tank was badly damaged along with several transports. All the Typhoons returned to base safely.

On 10th July, 'B' Flight took off at 0905hrs to attack an enemy strong point around the village of Amaye-sur-Orne south of Caen. Flight Lieutenant Lallemand led Warrant Officer Hallett, Flying Officer Williams, Flight Sergeant Stratford, Flight Lieutenant Plamondon, Flight Sergeant Sellman, Flight Lieutenant Sweeting and Flying Officer Milch with Brooker leading the formation that included aircraft from 609 Squadron. Low cloud over the area made it difficult to spot so Brooker climbed the Wing up to 7,000 feet above the cloud, spotting a hole in the cloud above the target area. Peeling off, the Typhoons dove through the cloud opening encountering intense flak on the way down. Releasing their rockets, the projectiles pounded into the area, and as the Typhoons levelled off, one by one they strafed the enemy positions with short bursts of cannon fire. All aircraft returned safely to Camilly as the weather closed in stopping operational flying for the rest of the day.

The following day, the weather cleared in the afternoon for the Squadron to mount an attack on enemy troops and gun positions east of Caen on the River Orme. With Wing Commander Brooker leading Madgett, Plamondon, Flight Sergeant Coulson, Lallemand, Champion, Sweeting and Hammond they took off at 1435hrs soaring into the afternoon sky. Cloud cover lay at 3,000 feet but fortunately it was clear over the target area, and the Squadron orbited waiting for the red smoke to be put up by the Army to pinpoint the enemy's position. As they waited two ME109s bounced the formation but broke off without firing. One of the enemy fighters disappeared into the cloud while the other skimmed across the top. Releasing his rockets Flight Lieutenant Plamondon chased the enemy fighter, caught up with it and fired several short bursts of cannon fire. The pilot was seen to bale out as his stricken ME109 disappeared into cloud and was later claimed as destroyed. This was the first enemy aircraft to be destroyed by 198 Squadron since February. All the aircraft returned to B10 Plumetot where they were now to be permanently based.

Again, low cloud and poor weather kept the Squadron on the ground until the afternoon of 12th July. At 1500hrs Squadron Leader Ezanno leading Flight Sergeant Thursby, Pilot Officer Allan, Flight Lieutenant Lane, Flight Lieutenant Harding Flight Sergeant Ford, Flight Lieutenant Pye and Flight Sergeant Bryant took off on an armed recce in the Villiers Bocage –Everecy–Thury–Harcourt area. Climbing above the cloud base of 3,000 feet the formation sighted several enemy aircraft but did not attack. They did attack enemy vehicles caught on the road southeast of Villiers Bocage. Rolling into the dives, they peppered the area with rocket projectiles destroying one tank and a large transport vehicle. All the time intense light flak burst around them as they attacked. Three Typhoons were hit but they all returned safely to base.

Pour weather again played havoc with operational flying the next day and a show was finally laid on for the early evening. At 1810hrs Wing Commander Brooker took Milch, Plamondon, White, Lallemand, Champion, Hallett and Stratford to attack a ferry across the Seine River at Hautot. They climbed to 8,000 feet and peeled off through a break in the clouds, diving down to 2,000 feet. Four aircraft plastered the south jetty and the ferry moored alongside with rockets and cannon fire while the other four pulverised the north jetty sending smoke and debris flying into the air as the rockets exploded. Both jetties were covered with smoke and the ferryboat was severely damaged having been raked by cannon fire. On this raid there was virtually no flak. Was this simply luck or a sign of the weakening of the enemy's defences overall?

On the 14ᵗʰ low cloud kept the Squadron on the ground and there was no operational flying. However, the diarist wrote an interesting entry for that day about enemy aircraft activity near the airfield. Presumably the Typhoons were kept on the ground because low cloud made attacking ground targets very difficult. "The day was enlivened by enemy aircraft coming over from time to time to strafe the troops on the roads. About 1400hrs several came over near the airfield, two of which were seen to be shot down by Spitfires and two more by anti-aircraft fire," the diarist recorded.

"One ME109 came across at about 1,000 feet with flames pouring out of his long range tanks, eventually going straight in just beyond the airfield. A further three enemy aircraft were shot down by anti-aircraft fire elsewhere, making a total of seven aircraft for one mission."

The following day low cloud again kept the Squadron on the ground throughout the day. They heard this day that they were to join 123 Wing at B7 Martregny in a few days' time. During the night JU88s came over and strafed the airfield but did little damage.

The very low cloud continued into the 16ᵗʰ and the 17ᵗʰ and no operational flying took place for the Squadron.

By 18ᵗʰ July the weather had finally cleared to blue skies and the first sortie of the day was at 0745hrs when the Wing, led by Wing Commander Brooker took off to attack five enemy gun positions northeast of Caen. For 198, Squadron Leader Ezanno led Flight Lieutenant Champion, Flight Lieutenant Plamondon, Flying Officer Milch, Flight Lieutenant Lallemand, Flight Sergeant Stratford, Warrant Officer Hallett, Sergeant Madgett, Flight Lieutenant Sweeting and Flight Sergeant Sellman into attack. Several pilots saw their rockets smash into the gun positions along with their cannon shells. During the attack they experienced some light flak but no one was hit.

These gun positions had been holding up the Army's big advance on the morning of Operation Goodwood, so to ensure that they were knocked out, the Squadron returned to base, rearmed, refuelled and went back to the target area. At 0945 Brooker led the Wing back to the gun positions and the flak started earlier as he dove down on them. After this second attack, three of the gun positions were considered destroyed, so Brooker decided to refuel and rearm and go after the other two. One can only imagine the tension of the remaining German gunners, wondering if yet another attack was imminent.

It was, at 1220hrs, but this time the gunners were not unnaturally ready; heavy flak before they reached the target was fired up at them and light flak was fired from around the target area. Rolling into their dives they plastered the remaining two gun pits with rockets and cannon fire and by the time the Wing turned away all five gun pits were covered in smoke and considered knocked out.

Flight Sergeant Sellman was hit by flak as he pulled up from his dive and oil poured from his engine, covering his canopy. His engine stopped suddenly and he glided towards the British lines. At 1,500 feet he baled out, suffering a minor injury to his foot and was back at the Squadron by the afternoon.

The last flight of the day was led by Flight Lieutenant Harding who took off at 1740hrs leading Flight Sergeant Bryant, Pilot Officer Allan, Flight Sergeant Thursby, Flying Officer Hardy, Flight Sergeant Ford, Flying Officer Rainsforth and Flight Sergeant Morley on an armed recce in the Bretteville–Falaise area. One heavy transport, two tanks and a motorcycle were sighted on the Falaise–Thury–Harcourt road by the Typhoons who rolled into attack, firing their rockets at the enemy vehicles. Some hit the heavy transport causing it to burst into flames. Smoke poured from the destroyed vehicle. The tanks and motorcycle were damaged under the onslaught of the rocket attack, unable to move.

The following day the Squadron moved to Martregny (B7), their new home and no operational flying took place that day.

On 20th July, one sortie took place. Flying in the morning was virtually impossible with a visibility of 200 yards and a ceiling between 200 to 300 feet but by midday it had cleared and 'A' Flight took off at1335hrs on an armed recce to the Falaise–St Pierre-sur-Dives area. Flight Lieutenant Harding led Flight Sergeant Bryant, Flying Officer Hardy, Flight Sergeant Linter, Pilot Officer Allan, Flight Sergeant Thursby, Flying Officer Rainsforth, and Flight Lieutenant Lane on the patrol. At Moriers they spotted two enemy staff cars that were promptly pulverised by rockets and cannon fire, utterly destroyed. Wheeling away, the formation then attacked rail yards at Damblainville, pumping the last of their rockets into buildings, wagons and signal boxes. After their attentions the entire target was covered in smoke.

Throughout this raid the formation had experienced heavy, light and intense flak coming from the River Orme area. All the aircraft returned safely to base including Flight Sergeant Bryant who was hit by flak early in the mission and had to turn back.

On this day Flight Lieutenant Plamondon was posted to 197 Squadron as a Flight Commander.

Heavy rain the following day turned the airstrip into a quagmire and no flying took place. "The tents are leaking so life has become unpleasant all at once," wrote the diarist for this day.

No flying took place due to low cloud and rain for the next few days until 24th July when the low cloud cleared enough for an operational sortie to take place. At 1705hrs Flight Lieutenant Harding took Flight Lieutenant Shepherd, Flying Officer Rainsforth, Flight Sergeant Morley, Flying Officer Hardy, Flight Sergeant Bryant, Flight Lieutenant Pye and Flight Sergeant Thursby on an armed recce to the Mézidon–Pont L'Évêque area. At St Pierre, they spotted two enemy staff cars and peeled off, firing their rockets and cannon at the vehicles. One staff car exploded into flames from a direct hit while the other was seriously damaged. At Canon, two more enemy staff cars were attacked by the Typhoons with one being blasted apart by direct hits from rockets and the other heavily damaged. Continuing their patrol they attacked rail wagons at Le Breuil with rockets and cannon fire, leaving the target area covered in smoke. At Ouarville the last of their rockets were expended on a road and railway bridge but they did not see the results of their attacks as they came in at low level, firing short bursts of cannon. Throughout the patrol they encountered flak with heavy, intense and accurate anti-aircraft fire from the Aron area and light flak at St Pierre. Harding was hit by flak, a shell going through his radiator but the damage wasn't serious and he returned safely. Flight Sergeant Morley however, returned but ground looped, ripping off his undercarriage, owing to his tail wheel being damaged on takeoff and causing him to loop when he landed.

July 25th was a very busy day for the Squadron. 'A' Flight was briefed early in the morning on a mission to attack an enemy strongpoint east of Caen. Flight Lieutenant Harding was set to lead the mission but ended up taxiing into a water bowser, damaging his aircraft. Instead, Flying Officer Hardy led the formation taking Flight Sergeant Ford, Morley, Lane, Pye and Linter on the attack. Taking off in pairs the last section did not catch up to the main formation due to poor visibility and had to turn back so only five aircraft arrived at the target area where they orbited for 30 minutes looking for the red smoke that would mark the location of the enemy; but no smoke came so they returned to base without firing a shot. While they were orbiting, flak was quite intense and Ford was hit but not seriously.

At 0945 hours 'A' Flight took off again on an armed recce, this time led by Flight Lieutenant Harding[75]. But just as they crossed the bomb line they ran into heavy, accurate flak and Shepherd and Harding were hit. An anti-aircraft shell smashed into Shepherd's radiator and he turned for British lines streaming glycol. His engine seized and he crashed landed safely just inside the British sector and he was back with the Squadron by the afternoon. Flight Lieutenant Harding, streaming petrol from his nose tank managed to land safely back at base with the rest of the formation.

At 1300hrs Harding again took 'A' Flight into the sky on a Ramrod mission to attack enemy mortar positions south of Caen. Bryant and Linter both turned back due to technical trouble while the rest of the formation continued. Over the target, they spotted the red smoke and rolled into their dives, pouring rockets onto the enemy positions. As they attacked heavy, accurate flak came up at them. The pilots reported seeing their rockets smashing into the target area, saturating it, exploding on contact causing the whole area to be covered by smoke and debris. The mortar position was considered knocked out. But again flak took its toll and

Harding was hit in the nose tanks and fuselage while Flight Lieutenant Lane was hit in the fuselage. Both men managed to bring their aircraft back to base successfully.

This mission was typical of operations at that time, in that it lasted no more than 30 minutes because the airfield was not far behind the bomb line. This meant that pilots with damaged aircraft had a better chance of getting back to base than if they had to fly across the Channel to land in England.

The last flight of the day saw 'B' Flight having its turn with Flight Lieutenant Lallemand taking Flight Sergeant Stratford, Warrant Officer Hallett, Flight Lieutenant Champion, Flight Lieutenant Sweeting, Flight Sergeant Madgett, Flying Officer Milch and Flight Sergeant Coulson on a Ramrod to attack enemy gun positions at Laize-la-Ville south of Caen. Arriving over the target, the Typhoons orbited searching for the red marker smoke to identify the target but none was fired. They were then redirected by the Forward Controller to a secondary target south of Bourguebus. This was an enemy stronghold that they pulverised with rockets and cannon fire, causing a massive fire. Light flak burst around them as they dove on the target and Flight Lieutenant Lallemand was hit in the undercarriage. One wheel came down and he put the other wheel down when he landed back at base, but at the end of the runway the undercarriage collapsed.

The 26th was another hectic day for the Squadron. The first entry for this day states, "183 Squadron have now arrived and 183 Wing is at its full strength of four squadrons (609, 198, 164 and 183) with Wing Commander Dring D.F.C. as the Wing Commander Ops."

The first operational flight took place at 1535hrs when 'A' Flight took off on an anti-train sweep between Yvetot and Charleville with aircraft from 183 Squadron. Wing Commander Dring led the formation as they swept over the area. Spying a goods train at Merville the Typhoons peeled off and swarmed over the train, firing their rockets and strafing it with cannon fire, leaving it a smoking wreck.

'A' Flight was up again at 1935hrs on an armed recce to the Mézidon–Falaise–Argentan–Lisieux area. The Typhoons roared down the runway with Squadron Leader Ezanno leading Flight Lieutenant Lane, Flight Lieutenant Pye, Pilot Officer Allan, Flight Lieutenant Harding, Flight Sergeant Bryant, Flying Officer Rainsforth and Flight Sergeant Ford but nothing was seen and they encountered heavy, accurate and intense flak near Mézidon. Ezanno was hit in the tail plane but managed to land safely.

For the third time that day, 'A' Flight took off, this time at 2140hrs to attack several enemy AFVs near Fontenay le Marmion. Under heavy anti-aircraft fire they orbited for three minutes over the target area, waiting for the red marker smoke to be fired. Finally, they spotted the red smoke and peeled off. Diving down on the targets, the accurate flak continued as they pumped their rockets into the target. The light was rapidly waning and they couldn't see the results of their work. Pye, Morley and Ford were all hit by flak but managed to return to base.

The 27th was the first day that the Squadron began to cab rank. Cab ranking involved a section of four aircraft patrolling a given area over the Allied lines waiting to be given a target by a ground controller who was right up at the front lines in an armoured car.

At 1320hrs four aircraft began cab ranking with Flying Officer Hardy leading Ford, Allan and Lane where they were given a target of camouflaged tanks in a wood near Rocquancourt which they immediately attacked with rockets and cannon fire. The rockets were near misses but they saw their cannon shells strike home. No flak was encountered at that time.

Only 15 minutes later, Green Section of 'A' Flight was vectored onto the same target by the forward controller. Flight Lieutenant Sweeting led Milch, Hallett and Coulson on this attack where they encountered heavy and accurate flak. Pressing home their attack, the Typhoon pilots released their rockets and strafed the target area. Their rockets ripped into the area leaving one tank smoking. Flight Lieutenant Sweeting was hit several times by flak but returned to base safely.

At 2115hrs Green Section were up again and given a target to attack and the visibility was pour due to low cloud so they returned without firing anything.

The following day no operational flying took place until the evening when Squadron Leader Ezanno took off at 2055hrs leading Blue Section Flight Lieutenant Lane, Flight Lieutenant Pye and Flight Sergeant Ford on a cab rank operation. Unable to attack the primary target they attacked an orchard north of Rocquancourt. Smoke could be seen coming out of the orchard as an enemy tank burst into flame from a direct hit by Flight Sergeant Ford.

At 2140hrs the same evening, Green Section led by Flight Lieutenant Harding went off on a cab rank attacking enemy tanks in a wood at Secqueville. Leading Flight Lieutenant Shepherd, Pilot Officer Allan and Flight Sergeant Morley Harding peeled off over the target area followed by the others. Roaring down on the wood they released their rockets, each projectile sending dust and debris in all directions leaving a fire blazing and a column of smoke rising into the air. Trees burn, so following such attacks in wooded areas it was often difficult to identify positive strikes on the enemy tanks.

On the 29th very poor weather, low cloud at 2,500 feet, made operational flying impossible until the evening. At 2110hrs 'B' Flight led by Flight Lieutenant Lallemand with Flight Lieutenant Champion, Warrant Officer Hallett, Flight Sergeant Hammond, Flight Lieutenant Sweeting, Flight Sergeant Coulson, Flying Officer Milch and Flight Sergeant Madgett took off to attack enemy transports on the Moyen–Villiers Bocage road. Pressing home their attack as light flak came up at them, with one transport suffering a direct hit from the rockets, bursting into flames. As the rockets exploded all around the enemy vehicles several others began pouring out clouds of thick black smoke as the enemy reeled under the onslaught.

The following day Flight Lieutenants Sweeting and Plamondon (with 197 Squadron) received news that they had won the D.F.C.; news that was duly celebrated.

Though poor weather kept the aircraft on the ground throughout the morning by late afternoon it had cleared enough for a sortie to be mounted. At 1600hrs Flight Lieutenant Sweeting (Blue Leader) and Flying Officer Hardy (Green Leader) and their six companions set off to attack enemy tanks reported to be moving on the road near Aunay Sur Odon. Unfortunately, the tanks had been scared away into cover by other Typhoons that were milling around the target area. Sweeting then led his section down to attack a wood with rockets and cannon fire but saw no results while Hardy took his section at low level scouring the countryside for the missing tanks but finding nothing. They returned to base without having fired off their rockets.

The last day of the month, the 31st of July, bad weather made the morning operation a failure as no worthwhile targets were sighted and the pilots of 'A' Flight attacked a wood near Villiers Bocage but saw no results.

A more successful raid took place later in the afternoon. At 1540hrs, 'B' Flight took off with Flight Lieutenant Lallemand leading on an armed recce in the Tourorvre–Mortagne area where they sighted ten flatbed wagons on the line at Tourorvre and attacked them with rockets and cannon fire. Several strikes were seen and they went on to attack the line to the northeast and southwest.

A goods train was caught at Mortagne that was ripped apart by rockets and cannon shells from the attacking Typhoons. Rolling into their dives they poured cannon shells into the wagons and locomotives, firing short bursts as they levelled off, flying at low level the length of the train, one after the other, firing their cannons. Several shells smashed into the locomotive and it exploded, utterly destroyed.

The next flight of the day was a disaster. Again 'B' Flight was to take off at 2045hrs on an armed recce to the Vire–Aunay area. Flight Lieutenant Champion flying No 4 position in the first section crashed on takeoff, blocking the way for the rest of the section so only the first three aircraft were able to get away. Champion died of his injuries shortly after being pulled from the wreckage and the other three aircraft were immediately recalled.

So ended the month of July 1944 that had seen several enemy motor transports, tanks, railway wagons, locomotives damaged or destroyed with the most memorable event – if not necessarily the most significant – being the destruction of an ME109 by Flight Lieutenant Plamondon.

Perhaps, the last word for this section on 198 Squadron should come from Flying Officer Richard Armstrong, who described some of the less harrowing memories that still remained sharp down through the decades of those relentless sorties, day after day.

"I'll never forget one incident when we were stationed at Thorny Island. They must have left the aircraft with the tails plugged into the rockets, which was strictly against safety instructions. The ground crew started an aircraft up and all the rockets went off into Thorny Island Sound. We were all in dispersal when this happened and someone shouted "Rockets" as we all rushed out. We could see the grey and black smoke clouds coming off the water. That was terrific enough until some poor bugger came out of the middle of it in a rowing boat and you've never seen anybody row faster.

"There was one of our chaps called Flt Lt 'Bluey' Dahl, an Australian, mad as hell but a good friend. I was flying as his number two on one occasion half way across the Channel in terrible weather when we were ordered back to base. We were based in Manston at the time. We couldn't see anything in spite of being very low, you could just see the coast as we passed. Then suddenly Bluey yelled 'Break!' as he broke to starboard and I broke to part. You don't ask any questions at such moments, you just do it. Then I could see Canterbury Cathedral and all I knew was there were a lot of balloons around the Cathedral. Anyway, I successfully flew around Canterbury and got back to Manston safely. I didn't know where Bluey was by then as I put the aircraft down, then he came in and landed. When he got out of the aircraft he leaned against it and I wondered what was the matter with him. So I walked across to see him. His aircraft must have caught a balloon cable between its cannons and severed the cable. It must have done because there were marks on both the top edge of the wing and underneath it, so the cable must have been broken. He was very lucky. The CO told him he'd better report what had happened. He duly reported it to Balloon Command and they said thank you very much. They came back to him half an hour later and asked him if he was sure. 'Of course I'm sure, the aircraft is marked.' 'Are you sure this is where you were?' 'Yes of course I am.' 'Well, we'll come back to your sir.' We all thought this was worth listening to so we all stayed on in Dispersal. They eventually came back and said he had got to be mistaken because there was no balloon missing. He went through the roof and told them that when one of their people winds his wire down tonight he'll find there's no bloody balloon on the end of it."

In another story about the mad Australian, Armstrong talked about an operation that had been cancelled due to snow and low visibility. "I went out on a show, again with Bluey Dahl, and again it was bad weather, snowing like mad, and we had to return. I got back to dispersal before him, hung up my parachute and two blokes near the door warned me that there was a parson waiting to see me. I thought it was a bit quiet in dispersal so I looked on the other side of the lockers and here was this parson. 'Mr Armstrong?' he enquired. I said I was and he went on, 'I see you signed on your form that you are a Methodist and we would like to welcome you to our congregation.' We were still at the back door of the Dispersal and in the middle of this preamble when Bluey Dahl burst in, dumped his kit on the floor and said, in a loud voice, 'Jesus Christ, what an abortion,' then he looked up and found himself about a foot from a Methodist Parson. The Methodist church didn't bother me anymore. That is the sort of thing you remember."

Life as a fighter pilot during the war was about the human side of things as much as it was about the fighting. "Many books that you read today make the whole thing sound cold and it wasn't, not by a long way. The human factor came into it all along. In terms of friendships. Things were getting very hairy in general operations and I remember standing in Westgate waiting for the transport to come, we were billeted in Westgate, and I looked at the bushes which were just coming into bud because it was springtime and I remember thinking you'd better take a good look at it Richard because you aren't going to see that again. Things like that stand out in my mind."

Armstrong remembered the apparently seductive power of the uniform.

"If you had a pilot's uniform on you could literally have any woman you wanted. It sounds unreal but it is true. You'd then find out, when you got back into civilian clothes that women wouldn't take any notice of you. You'd think it's still me, I'm still here.

"We had a squadron dance one week-end and by then I was married. Someone had invited a whole mess of Wrens up from Dover to Manston for this dance. I was sat at the bar drinking when the CO came up to me and said, 'You're sat by yourself Dickie and there's a Wren over there also sat all by herself. Don't you think that's wrong? Go over there and ask her to dance.' So I dutifully went over there and asked her to dance. She was in civvies and quite a bit older than I was but we spent quite a good evening together. As the evening was coming to an end all the chaps started to mysteriously disappear with various women and I found I was the only one left with this girl. I thought I had better show the flag and asked if she would like to take a walk and, to my surprise, she said yes she would. When we eventually came back to the transport she asked me if we ever got any time off. I said 'Yes we do,' and she said that we would be very welcome to come down to a party in Dover.

"About a couple of weeks later the whole Squadron was stood down and by popular demand I phoned my new friend up. She asked me when could we come down to Dover and I replied, 'Right now. I've got a party of about 15 blokes here, all raring to go.' She told me to come right up to the main entrance at Dover Castle and tell the guard who we were. I was really shattered to find out she was the CO Wrens at Dover Castle. We had a good evening and we got back in due course. I never dreamt she was the scrambled egg version. Morals were a little different when you didn't know if you would be living tomorrow."

WAAFs were often found driving wagons on the airfields doing their part for the war.

"When you ran the engine of a Typhoon above idling speed, perhaps to warm the engine, a member of the ground crew had to lay over the tail to keep it down, otherwise you'd lift the tail and the prop would hit the ground, which didn't do the aircraft much good," Armstrong said. "Well the poor chap on the tail had to put up with what would amount to a 200 or 300 hundred mile-per-hour wind. We had a couple of WAAFs who drove our Station Wagons. I can't remember their names now but the one we had allocated to B Flight was far too familiar. At least, I thought so. This particular lassie was always on about the quality of women and was a regular pain. Well, we were passing an aircraft being warmed up and one of the chaps told her that she couldn't do that. She immediately replied 'What is there to it?' So one of our chaps signalled the groundcrew member in the cockpit to close the throttle and changed places with him. She happily laid over the tail plane and he opened the throttle wide. She got hit with one hell of a wind and her skirt just blew away. All the chaps just stood around admiring the view. We didn't have any more trouble at all from her."

CHAPTER THIRTEEN

257 Squadron, July 1944

At the beginning of July 1944, 257 Squadron was based at Needs Oar Point in the New Forest, along with other Typhoon Squadrons. Like 197 Squadron, 257 Squadron was a bomb carrying Typhoon squadron. At this point they were about to move out of Needs Oar Point to Hurn.

The information that follows here is from the same source as the other day to day operations we have seen with other Typhoon squadrons. Is it accurate? We must remember that the debriefings of these events happened some hours after each flight and what was seen by the pilots flying at 400mph may be exaggerated. But, it is the only real record we have of what went on every day in 257 Squadron, just as it is the closest we will get to the real events of the other squadrons in this book.

However, the first two days of the month were blighted by pour weather so no flying took place except for a 20-minute air test flown by Flight Sergeant Blair on the 1st. Rain came down even harder with very poor visibility while haze hung over the French coast.

Despite the rain, the pilots and ground crew moved to Hurn by road because there was no sleeping accommodation at Needs Oar Point.

The first operational flight of the month took place on the 3rd in the early evening. During the day low cloud made visibility difficult but by the evening it had cleared enough for the Typhoons to take off so at 1910hrs Squadron Leader W.C. Ahrens lifted off from the runway at Hurn with two other Typhoons and the rest following behind. Leading Flight Lieutenant R.G. Smith, Flying Office E.J. Whitfield, Flight Sergeant R. R. Blair, Flying Officer S.J. Eaton, Flight Sergeant W.H. Upperton and Flight Sergeant W.B. Whitmore, Ahrens took them across the Channel where they dive-bombed marshalling yards. Over the target area, they peeled off, diving down from 6,000 feet to 1,000 feet where they released their bombs and scored direct hits, cutting the railway line. Several wagons in a siding caught fire and as they headed for home, they caught an enemy transport on the road and peppered it with cannon fire, leaving it damaged. They were back at Hurn at 2035hrs.

The first two operations of the following day were abandoned because of bad weather over France but in the evening, Squadron Leader Ahrens took Flight Sergeant A.W. Horner, Pilot Officer P.D. Jenkins, Flying Officer J. A. Smith, Flight Lieutenant R. G. Smith, Pilot Officer P.W. d'Albemas, Flight Sergeant B.J. Spragg and Flight Sergeant W.H. Ewan on a Ramrod to attack buildings and troop concentrations on the south bank of the Seine near Elbeuf. Splitting into two sections the first section attacked the south bank east of Elbeuf while the second section attacked rail and road bridges in the north end of Louriers where they achieved two near misses. Wheeling away they remained low, strafing three staff cars and anti-aircraft guns with cannon fire.

Again low cloud during the day on the 5th stopped any operational flying until later in the day when it cleared enough for flying to take place. Wing Commander Baldwin took off at 1950hrs leading 146 Wing with Squadron Leader Ahrens leading Flight Sergeant A.W. Horner, Flying Officer J.M. Cullingham, Flying Officer J.A. Smith, Flight Lieutenant J. R. Wistow, Pilot Officer P.W. d'Albenas, Flying Officer A.T. Sennett and Flight Sergeant Spragg to attack two rail bridges and a tunnel north of Elbeuf. Thick cloud down to 500 feet made visibility over the target area very difficult. Wing Commander Baldwin and several others of the Squadron turned back, unable to drop their bombs while six aircraft, led by Flight Lieutenant Wistow stayed the course, boring in at low level and dropped their bombs, scoring a few hits on the rail lines near the tunnel. As they roared in flak arched up at them, bursting all around them. They were back at base by 2130hrs as the light was fading.

The following morning, the first operation of the day took place at 1055hrs when Wing Commander Baldwin took pilots of 146 Wing, including 197 Squadron and Flight Sergeant K.E. Button, Flying Officer J.M. Cullingham, Flying Officer A.T. Sennett, Flight Sergeant R.W. Snell and Flight Sergeant Bragg from 257 Squadron on a low level mission to attack a rail bridge over the River Risle south of Beaumont Le Roger. The Typhoons roared in on the target at high speed, firing short bursts from their cannon then releasing their bombs as they flew over the bridge. Two direct hits were observed at one end of the bridge cutting the line, while at the other end, a crater still not repaired from a previous attack now made the bridge useless. Bombs and cannon shells smashed into the supporting arches of the bridge as the Typhoons attacked. They all returned to base by 1230hrs.

The next sortie of the day saw Squadron Leader Ahrens, taking off at 1620hrs from Hurn leading Flight Lieutenant Smith, Flying Officer R.

Logan, Flight Sergeant A.B. Campbell, Flight Sergeant A. Shannon, Flight Sergeant Blair, Flying Officer W.B. Richardson and Flight Sergeant M.E. Marriott on an armed recce over the Caen sector. Though the mission brought the Squadron very little joy it brought mostly grief. Attacking an enemy transport Flight Sergeant Blair, flying as Ahrens' No. 2, must have dived too low as they both bombed the enemy vehicle. The Squadron diarist recorded, "it is believed the blast and rubble from his own or the CO's bomb damaged his aircraft and started a glycol leak."

No flak burst around them as they attacked and it was subsequently discovered that the enemy vehicle had already been hit in a previous attack. Blair tried desperately to make for the beachhead and Squadron Leader Ahrens ordered the No. 4 of the section, Flight Sergeant Marriott to escort Blair as far as he could. "But a few minutes later Bob called up in a calm, sure voice that his engine was on fire and that he was baling out," the diarist recorded. Blair's Typhoon crashed and blew up. A few minutes later, Marriott flew over the crash site and reported that he could see Blair lying very still, face down. "It is believed that the parachute did not have time to open due to lack of height," according to the diarist for 257 Squadron.

On the 7th operational flying took place later in the afternoon. At 1515hrs Squadron Leader Ahrens led an attack on a road junction near Caen. Lifting off from Hurn, they roared into the afternoon sky, forming up over the Channel they raced across to France. Over the target area, Ahrens peeled off, diving down on the road junction, releasing his bombs as the rest of the flight did the same. Bursting bombs plastered the area, with five dropping directly on three of the four roads and the junction. Two enemy transport trucks on one of the side roads leading away from the target area were attacked by the Typhoons. As they tried desperately to get away, the fighters came down on them, strafing them with cannon fire leaving both vehicles burning wrecks.

Later, at 1955hrs Wing Commander Baldwin led a wing operation with 193 Squadron and 257 Squadron to attack road and rail bridges in the Caen Sector. Squadron Leader Ahrens took Flying Officer P Onysko, Flight Sergeant A.W. Horner, Flying Officers Cullingham and Sennett, Flying Officer J.D. Lunn, and Flight Sergeants Spragg and Ewan as 257's contingent. Taking off from RAF Hurn the Typhoons climbed rapidly into the evening sky and headed for Normandy. Crossing the French coast they turned towards the target and Baldwin peeled off followed by the rest. Flak from enemy gunners below burst around them as they dove down on the bridges, letting their bombs go and strafing the area with cannon fire. One direct hit at the western end of the road bridge smashed into some houses destroying four and blocking the main road with debris. But the rest of the results were not seen by the pilots as the area was covered in dust, smoke and debris.

A few minutes later the Typhoons struck again, this time it was the railway yards at Serquigny where they strafed more than fifty wagons with cannon fire. Shells ripped into the wagons, setting some on fire, damaging and splintering others. All the time, moderate flak burst around the Typhoons as they attacked. None were hit and they all returned to base at 2140hrs.

The following day the Squadron had the news that they would be operating from France while still stationed at Hurn. "Early in the afternoon, 'B' Flight led by the Wing Commander and the C.O. made the first Squadron landing at B15 near Ryes, Normandy," the Squadron diarist recorded. "The strip consisted of a few cornfields rolled flat and was a bit tricky for landing due to a large and very formidable dip halfway along its length. We returned to RAF Station Hurn to find that 'A' Flight had been enjoying a very easy time."

The following day, bad weather and low visibility caused the first operation of the day to be aborted and the flight had to jettison their bombs near Trouville before returning to B15. The only item of note in the Squadron diary for this day is the entry about Flight Sergeant Button, who overshot his landing at B15 and ended up in the middle of an ammunition dump. Fortunately for him nothing exploded and apart from shock and a sore thumb he escaped serious injury. The pilots stayed the night at B15 and were kept away by the artillery barrage and air bombardment on enemy positions in Caen.

On the 10th, Squadron Leader Ahrens led Flying Officer Lunn, Flight Sergeant Snell, Flying Officer Sennett, Flight Sergeant Spragg and Flight Sergeant Horner to attack a village south west of Caen. The targets were enemy mortar positions that had been harassing British troops in the advance on Caen. The Typhoons roared away from B15 lifting into the morning sky at 0550hrs. Several minutes later they were over the target area, where they rolled into their dives and dropped on the target area. Six direct hits were seen on the road where the enemy positions were while four fell short. As they pulled out of their dives, they strafed the area with cannon fire. That was the only operation of the day and the pilots returned to RAF Station Hurn for the rest of the day.

That day Flight Lieutenant J.F. Williams D.F.C. joined 257 Squadron from 198 Squadron and flew his first 257 Squadron show the following day, the 11th, which turned out to be aborted due to poor weather and low cloud. However, the next flight was more effective. At 1445hrs Flight Lieutenant Williams took Flying Officer F.H. Broad, Flight Sergeant W.H. Upperton, Flight Sergeant Shannon, Flying Officer W. Richardson, Flight Sergeant Marriott, Flight Sergeant Snell and Flight Sergeant Jones to attack enemy tanks and troop positions at Feugarolles. Taking off from B15 they climbed rapidly away and were over the target minutes later where they peeled off and dove on the enemy positions releasing their bombs and strafing the enemy as they pulled out of their dives. Bomb after bomb burst in the target area exploding on impact damaging several tanks, covering the area with smoke and debris. Most of the flight returned to B15 but some pilots from 'B' Flight returned to RAF Hurn across the Channel in England. The Squadron diarist does not give a reason why the flights were split in this way.

With some pilots at B15 and others at Hurn operational flying took place on the 12th in the late afternoon. At 1750hrs Typhoons from 257 Squadron took off from B15 heading for the railway yards at Alencon. Only five aircraft, Flying Officer Broad, Flight Sergeant Jones, Flight Sergeant Whitmore, Flight Sergeant Campbell and Flying Officer Richardson reached the target, which they dive-bombed. Releasing their bombs the pilots reported seeing two hits on the tracks themselves the rest falling in the target area.[76]

An interesting incident during that flight was recorded in the Squadron history. "Mustangs of the U.S.A.A.F. made a dart at us on the way back and actually had the nerve to fire. Flight Sergeant Whitmore collected a .5 bullet in his mainplane. We returned very disgruntled to B15."

The entry for that day goes on to state that three pilots of 'B' Flight managed to return to RAF Hurn in very bad weather and while others attempted to do so, they eventually returned to B15 due to very low cloud.

The following day on the 13th the Squadron was on readiness for most of the day and didn't fly until late in the afternoon when Squadron Leader Ahrens led Flight Sergeant Shannon, Flight Lieutenant Williams, Flying Officer Richardson, Flying Officer Logan, Flight Sergeant Marriott, Flying Officer Cullingham and Flight Sergeant Snell to dive bomb the rail yards at Verneul. Dropping their bombs in the target area, the pilots were unable to see the results due to smoke and dust over the target area. However, on their way back, according to the Squadron diarist, they bounced thirty-plus ME109 fighters. In the dogfight that ensued one ME109 was shot down in flames, another was left diving away smoking and listed as a probable while four others were reported as damaged by cannon fire. Flight Sergeant Marriott flying No. 2 position to Flight Lieutenant Williams was hit and forced to bale out. As he floated down in his parachute he was harried by five ME109s while Williams, completely out of ammunition, could do nothing to stop it. Overhead six Spitfires were seen by the Typhoon pilots but they gave no assistance to the hapless Marriott. The diarist does not say if he landed safely, was taken prisoner or killed in the entry for this day.

With the exception of an aborted scramble from B15 on the following day, no dive-bombing missions took place and the Squadron returned to Hurn. The following day bad weather stopped any operational flying from taking place, though Flight Lieutenant Wistow with Squadron Leader

Ahrens led an armed recce but had to abort and landed at their new base near Croix Sur Mer. "This airfield is a great improvement," wrote the diarist. "It is one of the first constructed in the beachhead."

On the 16th Squadron Leader Ahrens led Flight Sergeant Snell, Flying Officer Sennett, Flight Sergeant Horner, Flight Lieutenant Wistow, Flying Officer Lunn, Flight Sergeant Spragg and Flight Sergeant Ewan on an armed recce in the Thury-Harcourt–Lisieux–Falaise area. Taking off at 1935hrs they climbed into the evening sky to begin their patrol. On the road at Bois they dive-bombed enemy motor transports caught in the open. Ahrens released his bombs as he pulled out of his dive at low level, flying through his own bomb burst. His aircraft damaged from the debris of the bomb burst, he climbed away, trying to gain height but eventually was forced to bale out east of Caen. His parachute was seen to open but did not fill and he was lost.

On the same sortie, Flight Sergeant Ewan baled out as his aircraft suffered engine trouble. "He landed safely south of St Lô and was seen to be walking about two miles south of the town," the diarist recorded. "Squadron Leader Ahrens had not been our C.O. very long but he was respected by all and a good leader."

At 1640hrs the following afternoon, Flight Lieutenant Wistow led Flight Sergeant Snell, Flying Officer Sennett, Flight Sergeant Horner, Flying Officer Onysko, Flying Officer Lunn, Flying Officers Cullingham and Smith to dive bomb enemy troop positions at Amaye-sur-Orne. Climbing to 8,000 feet over the target, Wistow peeled off, rolling into a dive as the rest of the formation followed. Roaring down on the target area in a shallow dive due to low cloud, they rapidly lost height, firing short bursts of cannon fire as they levelled out at 2,000 feet and released their bombs. Explosions ripped into the orchard where the troop concentration was. As the Typhoons shot over the target area, they strafed it with canon fire before climbing rapidly away. All the time, the sky around them was mottled with bursting flak from enemy gunners but no aircraft were hit and they all returned to base.

The 18th of July was full of action for the Squadron with the first sortie taking place at 0855hrs. Wing Commander Baldwin as Red One led the Wing to dive bomb enemy troop concentrations at Secqueville la Campagne. For 257 Squadron, Flight Lieutenant Williams led Flying Officer Eaton, Flight Sergeant Whitmore, flight Lieutenant Wistow, Flight Sergeant Spragg, Flying Officer Sennett and Flight Lieutenant Lunn in on the target. Rolling into their dives, they roared in on the village releasing their bombs. Twelve bombs landed in the village while the rest were near misses. Pilots from 257 Squadron had two bombs under-shoot and two bombs were hung up, remaining under the wings. As the explosions tore through the village they kicked up debris and smoke. All the aircraft returned to B3 at 0935hrs safely.

At 1130hrs the Wing Commander again led the attack, this time it was a low-level bombing mission on a château used as a German HQ at St Pierre, south of Falaise. Flight Lieutenant Williams was again leading for 257 Squadron, taking Flight Sergeant Upperton, Flying Officer Tennant, Flight Sergeant Jones, Flight Lieutenant Wistow, Flight Sergeant Snell, Flight Sergeant Horner and Flying Officer Onysko on the mission. Pulling out of their dives, the pilots saw to their disappointment many of the bombs bouncing on hard earth and overshooting the target area before exploding. No direct hits were achieved on the château, though the aircraft strafed the building with cannon fire as they pulled out of their dives. On the way back, they carried out an armed recce over the Argentan–Falaise area and attacked some enemy trucks and a tank with cannon fire. They reported several shell strikes on the vehicles, which were stopped under the onslaught of fire from the Typhoons. Both the truck and the tank were claimed as damaged by pilots of 257 Squadron. They hadn't moved when the Typhoons wheeled away back to base.

Another armed recce was carried out by pilots of 257 Squadron in the Bretteville–Mézidon–Falaise area that afternoon. Taking off at 1450hrs, Flight Lieutenant Williams led Flight Sergeants Shannon and Jones, Flying Officer Broad, Flight Lieutenant Wistow, Flight Sergeant Spragg and Flying Officers Sennett and Lunn on the recce where they spotted 12 to 15 motorised and horse-drawn transports south of Glatigny. Seven Typhoons peeled off, rolling into their dives and roared down on the vehicles that had stopped as the troops had taken cover in the village. Bombs whistled down on the road, hammering the area, leaving at least three vehicles burning and others severely damaged. The Typhoons levelled out at high speed and followed the road, firing their cannon as well. The rest of the bombs cratered the road filling it with debris, making it difficult for the Germans to move through the village. One aircraft bombed the crossroads in the Bretteville–Falaise area but did observe the results.

The last flight of the day took place in the early evening, when Flight Lieutenant Wistow led Flight Sergeant Upperton, Flight Sergeant Jones, Flying Officer Eaton, Flight Sergeants Snell and Horner and Flying Officer Onysko to dive bomb an enemy tank concentration in a wood near Secqueville. Forming up with 193 and 197 Squadrons they dropped into their dives, tearing down on the targets marked by red smoke and released their bombs, all of which fell in the target area. Light flak burst around them as they dove down on the target and levelled off. Below, several explosions were seen with some vivid red flashes. The last Typhoon came roaring back over the target to look at the bombing results and reported seeing thick black smoke rising from the wood. They were all back at base by 1920hrs.

The following day, the new Commanding Officer, Squadron Leader W.J. Johnson D.F.C. arrived, having been posted from 197 Squadron.

The airlift party for the Squadron was preparing to move over to France, to B3, their new home on the Continent. "The atmosphere is tense for it is rumoured that the squadron airlift party will move to France tomorrow. Many last minute arrangements are to be made including the attachment of two aircraft armourers to RAF Hurn owing to their unfitness for overseas duty."

On the 20th the Dakotas touched down at B3, the new home of 146 Wing, with the rest of the Squadron airlift party that included the ground personnel and any pilots who had not been flying from France. "All the boys seemed to thoroughly enjoy the trip, which was very smooth and uneventful," the diarist recorded.

At 1330hrs that same day, the new C.O. Squadron Leader Johnson led an armed recce east of Caen via Pont L'Évêque–Lisieux–Vimoutiers and bombed a crossroads. Four bombs burst on the crossroads while the remainder hammered the immediate area, with one direct hit that badly cratered the junction. A few bursts of enemy anti-aircraft fire was the only opposition the Typhoons met. They returned to base at 1450hrs. The ground personnel were busy putting up the tentage for the squadron in torrential rain.

The rain continued into the following day providing a respite to operational flying. An entry in the Squadron history provides a glimpse of day-to-day ground personnel work at the new airfield. "The Squadron administrative staff, Pilot Officer L.H. Warren, Squadron Adjutant and Corporal E.A.D. Woodcock were busy picking the site for the orderly room lorry at dispersal point – a difficult job considering that freedom from dust was an important consideration,' wrote the diarist. "An excellent spot was found and the offices of the Squadron Commander and Flight Commanders, with the Orderly room, were organised during the morning."

Because of rain, low cloud and mud no operational flying took place until 24th July when the weather cleared. The only flight to take place that day was at 1655hrs when Squadron Leader Johnson led an armed recce in the Mézidon–Falaise–Bretteville area. Weather in the western part of their patrol area was bad so they swept east to Mézidon where six aircraft dive-bombed a road and rail bridge. Though they scored no direct hits there were many near misses and the target was eventually obscured by smoke and debris from their explosions. Two Typhoons also dropped their bombs on the track 300 yards south of the bridge achieving one direct hit. They spotted several enemy transports throughout their patrol and one that was parked behind a hedge was strafed by two aircraft but no results were seen. They all returned to base at 1805hrs.

The next day saw three missions taking place. The first was a wing Ramrod led by Wing Commander Baldwin directed against an enemy ammunition dump in a wood south of Falaise. Mechanical failure kept

Flight Lieutenant Wistow and Flying Officer Smith on the ground, but the rest of the pilots, Flying Officers Logan, Richardson and Whitfield, Flight Sergeant Campbell, Flying Officer Sennett and Flight Sergeant Snell formed up with Typhoons from 197 Squadron and headed for the target. All their bombs exploded in the target area, causing several explosions to rip through the wood; but the pilots made no claims when they returned from the sortie.

The next operation of the day took place at 1545hrs when Squadron Leader Johnson led Flying Officers Tennant, Broad and Eaton, Flight Sergeant Jones, Flight Lieutenant Wistow, Flight Sergeant Snell and Flying Officer Onysko attacked an enemy strong point at Secqueville. Over the target, moderate and heavy flak from mobile guns west of the village began to burst around them as they dropped into their dives. Releasing their bombs the pilots saw them burst in the target area with two failing to explode. As the explosions smashed into the village, the pilots were unable to see the results due to the smoke and debris.

The last flight of the day was a washout with pilots seeing nothing. They took off at 1805hrs sweeping the area from the Beachhead to west of Paris in the Evreux–Mantes–Chartres area but they returned with all their bombs.

Beneath the Typhoons, the 25th saw the launch of *Operation Spring* around Caen, which would be the costliest effort for Canadian forces of the entire war, with 1,500 men killed. Overall Allied casualties during the three-day push were 18,444, 5,021 dead: which explains why the Typhoon sorties continued without pause, day in, day out, any haitus the result of poor weather alone.

The 26th saw another three operations taking place for the Squadron. The first was at 1230hrs, an armed recce in the Yvetot–Malaunay–Buchy area. The mission was carried out successfully but no enemy were sighted.

At 1520hrs the next operational flight took place with Wing Commander Baldwin leading a formation of Typhoons from 197, 193 and 257 Squadrons to attack the rail marshalling yards at Bernay. Flight Lieutenant Williams with Flying Officers Whitfield, Eaton, Smith and Onysko and Warrant Officer N.E. Burlow were the contingent for 257 Squadron. Approximately fifteen to twenty wagons were parked in the yards when the Typhoons arrived overhead. Rolling into their dives, they released their bombs but only four burst near the wagons while another six landed on the tracks and the rest landed on a road south of the target area. "Bombing was bad and the Wing Commander suggest immediate improvements – or else!" the diarist recorded.

In the evening, at 2000hrs aircraft from 197, 193 and 257 Squadrons led by Wing Commander Baldwin flew an armed recce in the Mézidon–Bernay–Argentan area. Squadron Leader Johnson led Flying Officer Cullingham, Flight Lieutenants Wistow and Williams, Flight Sergeant Campbell and

Flying Officers Tennant and Broad on the operation. With bad weather in the Mézidon–Argentan area they returned to the marshalling yards at Bernay achieving excellent results. Eight direct hits exploded among the wagons parked on the siding and smashed into the track while the rest of the bombs hammered the target area causing havoc. Several wagons were damaged and left smoking.

Climbing away from the target Blue section, led by Flight Lieutenant Williams, encountered 8/10ths cloud 10 miles east of Caen. Reaching the cloud base, intense flak opened up on them and almost immediately, Williams was hit.

"He reported over the R/T that he had been wounded and was paralysed," the Squadron diarist recorded. "He was exhorted to try and make base but a few seconds later, he half-rolled and went straight into the ground from 3,000 feet and blew up."

Flying Officer Tennant, Blue 3, was also hit by flak, his engine leaking glycol. Losing height, he fought with the stricken fighter and managed to make a forced landing by a canal north east of Caen. "He returned to the unit, complete with R/T crystals within a few hours," the diarist wrote.

The following day was one of intense activity with the Squadron mounting no less than six operations throughout the day. The first began at 0640hrs with Squadron Leader Johnson taking Shannon, Eaton, Whitfield, Wistow, Snell, Sennett and Onysko to divebomb an enemy troop concentration in a wood near Rocquancourt. They bombed and strafed the target area, with eight bombs smashing into the wood and exploding while the other eight fell just short. Meagre flak burst around them but all aircraft returned safely to base at B3.

Johnson was up again at 1010hrs leading Smith, Cullingham, Lunn, Richardson and Jones to dive bomb enemy troops and vehicles south of Caen. However, bad weather made it impossible for them to identify the target so they dropped their bombs in an unidentified wood near Auray sur Odon. No results were seen.

At 1320hrs the next set of aircraft took off from B3 with Squadron Leader Johnson leading Upperton, Campbell, Logan, Wistow, Snell, Sennett and Burlow to dive bomb tanks and troops in and around Rocquancourt. Rolling into a shallow dive, Johnson led the formation down onto the target. Firing short bursts of cannon fire they strafed the target as they dove. Six bombs smashed into the target causing a fire that poured heavy white smoke into the sky. North of the village the pilots reported seeing several German Tiger tanks engaged with British Shermans. They returned to base at 1400hrs.

One and a half hours later, Squadron Leader Johnson was up yet again leading Onysko, Cullingham, Logan, Richardson, Broad, Whitmore and Jones to bomb an enemy strongpoint, again at Rocquancourt. Diving through cloud, they dropped their bombs in the target area with two smashing into the town but the rest were unobserved due to poor visibility over the area.

At 1740hrs Squadron Leader Johnson took another section of Typhoons on an armed recce to the Thury–Harcourt–Bocage area but it was aborted due to bad weather and they jettisoned their bombs in a wood before returning to base.

The last operation of the day saw Flying Officer Richardson taking off at 2015hrs leading Broad, Upperton, Jones, Sennett, Snell, Cullingham and Smith to bomb enemy gun positions south of Caen. (One can only wonder what Squadron Leader Johnson thought he was playing at, shirking again. He had after all only been up five times that day.) Though the target was obscured by clouds they dropped their bombs in the general area achieving one direct hit on a road west of the target, and two in the woods but other results were not seen. Throughout this attack moderate flak burst around them as they dove on the target, strafing it with cannon fire before releasing their bombs in a mission that lasted only 20 minutes.

Low cloud made operational flying impossible until the evening of the following day when Squadron Leader Johnson led Flying Officers Logan, Eaton and Whitfield, Flight Lieutenant Wistow, Flying Officer Onysko, Pilot Officer Spragg and Warrant Officer Burlow to dive bombs guns and mortar positions at Belengreville. Taking off at 2030hrs they formed up with aircraft from 193 Squadron and a few minutes later were over the target area. Peeling off, they dove on the enemy positions releasing their bombs and strafing the target area as they levelled out. Bombs burst throughout the target area, covering it completely with dust and smoke as the Typhoons roared away. The cloud then closed in making any other such operation of the day impossible.

Three missions took place on 29th July. The first one was at dawn with Squadron Leader Johnson taking off at 0640hrs leading Flying Officer Lunn, Pilot Officer Horner, Flight Sergeant Snell, Flying Officer Richardson, Flying Officer Broad, Flight Sergeant Campbell and Flight Sergeant Whitmore to attack enemy gun positions north of Bretteville. According to the Squadron History, Wing Commander Baldwin led the formation on the attack. Climbing to 6,500 feet the Typhoons were above the cloud base and the target was identified through gaps in the cloud.

Rolling over on one wing, Baldwin dove through a cloud gap, followed by the first section. As the height wound rapidly down light flak burst around them as they fired short bursts of cannon fire, strafing the target. Releasing their bombs, the Typhoons levelled off at 1,500 feet following Baldwin and climbed rapidly away while the second section dropped into their dives. Bombs hammered the target area and a vivid orange flame erupted as the bombs exploded. When the last Typhoon had finished attacking the pilots saw thick black smoke from the target area reaching up as high as 1,500 feet.[77]

The next mission took place at 0905hrs when Flight Lieutenant Wistow led Warrant Officer Brown, Flying Officer Cullingham and Onysko, Flight Sergeant Upperton and Flying Officers Logan, Eaton and Whitfield on an armed recce to the Vire–Flers–Domfront area. Heavy cloud cover forced Wistow to drop below the cloud for a few moments spotting an enemy transport which was immediately bombed and strafed and left smoking. At Briouze, Wistow led the section through the clouds to bomb a road / rail bridge. Some near misses were seen but the full results of the bombing were obscured by low cloud as well as the smoke and debris. "Warrant Officer Barlow had engine failure after takeoff and dropped his bombs live on the beachhead near Caen," wrote the Squadron diarist. "He made a successful landing and returned quite unperturbed, there is no word if the bombs caused any casualties." The rest of the Squadron landed back at base at 1020hrs.

At this time, 257 Squadron was short of aircraft armourers. "Yet another armourer deficient," the diarist recorded. "The total deficiency in this trade is five aircraft armourers, the reason being that an aircraft armourer had to return to England for a major operation on a Specialist Medical Officer's instructions. We are now doing our utmost to get this one and only trade of armourers brought up in strength to the approved establishment of nine Aircraft Armourers."

The final flight of the day took place with Squadron Leader Johnson leading an attack an enemy infantry concentration in a wood near Caumont. Low cloud and rain made visibility difficult, but the formation pressed on, augmented by aircraft from 197 Squadron. Over the target, the Typhoons rolled into shallow dives to release their bombs but the bad weather made visibility very difficult. Aborting the dive, Johnson wheeled the formation away so he could attack the target from a different direction. Dropping into a shallow dive he approached the target but soon realised the rain and low cloud would make bombing too hazardous to undertake, so he aborted the mission and the aircraft returned to base with all their bombs.

At 1130hrs on 30th July a section of Typhoons roared into the morning sky. At the head of the formation was Flight Lieutenant Wistow leading Warrant Officer Burlow, Pilot Officers Spragg and Horner, Flying Officer Richardson, Flight Sergeant Shannon, Flying Officer Eaton and Flying Officer Whitfield on an armed recce via Thury-Harcourt–Flers –Caumont. Southeast of Vire, the formation spotted six large enemy transport trucks on the road towards the village. Climbing to 8,000 feet the first section dove through the clouds, bombing and strafing the enemy vehicles. Pulling out at 2,000 feet they tore overhead at high speed, then turned and climbed as the other section dove on the hapless enemy. Two direct hits smashed into the road, while others ripped apart houses on either side. Cannon strikes were seen on all the transports, four of which were utterly destroyed and left smoking. A Typhoon examined the target area, investigating the damage and the pilot reported that only two trucks could be seen, the rest were covered in debris from the bombing. Continuing their patrol, another large transport truck was strafed near Pontfarey and damaged. At St Cecile the Typhoons with bombs remaining attacked a road rail bridge but no results were seen, apart from one Volkswagen hit.

At 1620hrs, Squadron Leader Johnson took off, leading Flying Officer Lunn and Cullingham, Flight Sergeant Upperton, Flying Officer Tennant, Flight Sergeant Whitmore and Flight Sergeant Campbell on the second show of the day. The primary target was not identified but the pilots attacked several enemy tanks on the road near Annoy. Dropping into their dives, they bombed and strafed the enemy vehicles that appeared to be heading south away from Annay. One bomb exploded directly in front of a tank and the blast flipped it over leaving it upside down in a crater. It was claimed destroyed by the pilots. At Annoy a road bridge was bombed by one section of Typhoons with three or four very near misses claimed. Flak from Annoy peppered the sky around them but the Typhoons climbed rapidly away from the target area, up to 9,000 feet while the flak burst at 7,000 feet. They were back at base by 1725hrs.

The last flight of the day saw Squadron Leader Johnson taking off at 2040hrs leading Flying Officers Logan, Horner and Smith, Flight Lieutenant Wistow, Flying Officer Onysko, Pilot Officer Spragg, Flight Sergeant Snell, Warrant Officer Brown, Flying Officers Eaton and Broad and Flight Sergeant Campbell as part of a larger formation with aircraft from 193 and 197 Squadrons led by Group Captain Gilliam D.S.O., D.F.C. and A.F.C. to attack a formation of enemy tanks in a wood near Trouville. Intense light flak burst from 3,000 to 6,000 feet 1 mile northeast of the target area following the formation as they attacked. In a loose line abreast the first section of Typhoons dove on the target, dropping their bombs at different heights, firing their cannon. Levelling off at different times, each Typhoon climbed away above the flak while other sections carried out their attack. Seven to eight direct hits were seen on the target area and a vivid orange flash was seen followed by a massive explosion. Smoke poured into the sky as the Typhoons headed back to base. On this raid, Warrant Officer Brown was on his second operational trip when he burst a tyre on takeoff. "He managed to get airborne but unfortunately his 'D' doors were down to so he had to jettison his bombs and wait for the Wing to return to base," the diarist recorded. "He then made a successful forced landing on the emergency strip beside the runway. Good Show!"

The following day two missions took place. The first was at 1030hrs when Squadron Leader Johnson took Flying Officers Smith, Lunn and Onysko, Flight Lieutenant Wistow, Warrant Officer Burlow, Flying Officer Cullingham, Flight Sergeant Snell and Pilot Officer Spragg on a wing mission led by Group Captain Gilliam. Together with Typhoons from

197 Squadron they attacked an enemy headquarters near Bernay. It was a very hot day with clear visibility and over the target area the Typhoons dropped into their dives section by section. Strafing the building with cannon fire, they released their bombs and every one, bar one hang-up, smashed into the building exploding on impact, completely obliterating the structure. Following behind 257 Squadron's Typhoons, 197 aircraft finished the job, erasing anything that was left of the HQ leaving it a smoking pile of rubble. It was one of the most successful bombing raids 257 Squadron had carried out so far.

The last flight of the day took place against a tank park in a wood near Trouville. Taking off at 1540hrs Squadron Leader Johnson led Flying Officer Richardson, Warrant Officer Brown, Flying Officers Whitfield, Broad and Logan, Flight Sergeant Shannon, Flight Lieutenant Watts, Flying Officer Tennant, Flight Sergeant Whitmore and Flying Officer Cullingham towards the target area. Together with aircraft from 193 and 197 Squadron the whole formation was led by Group Captain Gilliam.

Seventy-five per cent of the bombs landed in the target area from the attacking Typhoons and brown smoke was seen rising to 200 feet. In the western part of the wood four to six bombs exploded, resulting in more thick smoke rising into the sky. North of the target area, two bombs blew apart some huts. Several Typhoons flying at high-speed at tree-top level strafed a large building north of the huts with cannon fire leaving it smoking and ruined.

Throughout the whole attack that lasted 35 minutes, the pilots experienced only moderate flak between 3,000 and 6,000 feet and all the aircraft returned safely to base at 1615hrs.

For the month of July 257 (Burma) Squadron had flown a total of 362 operational flying hours. "There is, however, still much to be done and it is our wish that the squadron is as successful in its future operations as it has been in the past," the diarist recorded. A sentiment echoed, no doubt, by the poor bloody infantry on the ground.

CHAPTER FOURTEEN

257 Squadron, August 1944

On the first day of August 1944 haze over the airfield kept the aircraft of 257 Squadron on the ground until the late afternoon. At 1710hrs a formation of Typhoons roared away from B3 into the French afternoon sky to attack enemy troops and mortars in a wood near Garcelles. Flight Lieutenant Watts led Flying Officer Whitfield, Flight Sergeant Upperton, Flying Officer Eaton, Flying Officer Richardson, Flying Officer Broad, Flight Sergeant Campbell and Flight Sergeant Whitmore for 197 Squadron with aircraft from 193 Squadron to attack the target. As the Typhoons attacked 80% of their bombs were direct hits in the southern part of the woods and thick brown smoke was seen to rise into the air from the target area.

The next day was frantic for the Squadron with four missions carried out. The first took place at 1515hrs with Flight Sergeant Snell, Pilot Officers Snell, Spragg, Horner and Jenkins, Flying Officers Onysko, Cullingham and Smith flying as part of a formation with other Typhoons from 193 and 197 Squadrons to attack troops and guns in a wood southeast of Caen. Unfortunately the target was obscured by cloud making it difficult to see if their bombs landed in the target area.

At 1715hrs Flying Officer Smith, Pilot Officer Jenkins, Flying Officers Onysko and Sennett and Pilot Officer Horner took off on a mission with aircraft from 197 led by the Wing Commander to attack troops and gun positions at Rocquancourt. Diving on the targets, they bombed the enemy concentration, seeing ten direct hits while the rest of the bombs landed in the target area. The bombing run was difficult due to 7/10 cloud at 2,500 feet and they encountered some light flak during the dive. The pilots reported seeing ten suspected gun positions in an orchard near the target area. While this raid was taking place Flight Lieutenant Wistow and Flight Sergeant Snell took off at 1745hrs to act as fighter escort for rocket-firing Typhoons from 266 Squadron on an armed recce in the Caen to Vire area. One armoured car was attacked and destroyed by rockets on this operation.

In the evening, Flight Lieutenant Watts led Flying Officers Whitfield and Richardson, Flight Sergeant Campbell, Flight Sergeant Shannon, Flying Officer Tennant and Flight Sergeant Jones on an armed recce around Conde Sur Noivear where they spotted 15 enemy tanks and 50+ transport trucks on the main road. Immediately, they rolled into their dives, dropping on the enemy in a line astern formation dropping their bombs in succession. Three tanks suffered direct hits and exploded into flames, completely destroyed while a staff car was ripped apart by bombs and cannon fire and left smoking. "Almost every man in the squadron damaged at least two tanks with cannon fire," recorded the Squadron diarist. The trucks, mostly soft-skinned vehicles, were riddled with cannon shells as the Typhoons strafed the road, before climbing rapidly away and landing back at base.

For the last show of the day, Flight Lieutenant Watts led Flying Officer Eaton, Flight Sergeant Upperton, Flying Officer Logan, Flying Officer Richardson, Flying Officer Whitfield, Flight Sergeant Campbell and Flight Sergeant Whitmore on an operation with aircraft from 193 and 197 Squadron led by Group Captain Gilliam.

The air was filled with the sound of Typhoons roaring into the evening sky as they took off at 2100hrs in hazy weather to attack the retreating Germans in the Conde area.[78] "Unfortunately, it was too dark for really good bombing but several direct hits were observed in the target area," the diarist entered. "Flak was heavy and very accurate."

Haze hung over the airfield on the morning of 3rd August and flying didn't take place until it cleared in the early afternoon. At 1340hrs Flight Lieutenant Watts took Flying Officer Logan, Flying Officer Tenant, Warrant Officer Brown, Flight Sergeant Whitmore, Flying Officer Whitfield and Flight Sergeant Jones on a Wing operation along with aircraft from 193 and 197 Squadrons to bomb a factory being used by the enemy as an ammo dump southeast of Caen near Troarn. Using bombs with 11-second delay fuses, 257 Squadron aircraft went in first. Rolling into their dives, they strafed it with cannon fire, attacking across the length of the building. Bomb after bomb smashed into the building sending dust and smoke pouring from the windows. Climbing rapidly away the 257 pilots later found out from pilots of 193 and 197 Squadrons that the factory had exploded just after they left. They all returned to base safely.

Next show of the day saw Flying Officers Richardson, Eaton and Logan, Flight Lieutenant Watts, Warrant Officer Brown and Flight Sergeants Campbell and Shannon on another Wing mission led by the Wing Commander to attack a wood reported to be containing enemy tanks and troops southeast of Annoy. Taking off at 1700hrs they roared into the afternoon sky, formed up over the sea and then came tearing inland at high speed heading for the target area, where they encountered intense light flak as high as 8,000 feet. The pilots reported seeing their bombs explode within the target area but no results were seen because of the smoke. They all returned safely to base 40 minutes later.

The following day morning haze kept the aircraft on the ground until 1220hrs when eight Typhoons lifted off the runway in pairs on an armed recce to the Falaise–Argentan–Flers area. Flight Lieutenant Watts led the attack on the village of Placy where 15+ enemy transports were headed. Light flak burst nearby as they rolled into their dives, bombing and strafing the vehicles. One transport truck suffered a direct hit and exploded, bursting into flames while others were badly damaged under the firestorm of shells and bombs. Two Typhoons sustained light damage from the flak but they all managed to get back to base by 1310hrs.

The next flight of the day was in the evening when Flight Lieutenant Watts led the same pilots on another armed recce in the same area. Taking off at 2005hrs they shot into the sky accelerating rapidly away as the light was beginning to wane. A few minutes later, they attacked a road leading to a bridge northeast of Flers. Intense flak burst around them as they came down one after the other, dropping their bombs and strafing the area. One direct hit burst on the road leading to the bridge, cratering it. Others were near misses on the bridge itself. Fifty minutes after the last pair had taken off, the Typhoons were back at base. That night they threw a party for the nursing sisters in the officer's mess "and the beer and whiskey flowed like water."

Fortunately, for all concerned there were no operations the following morning, the 5th of August, so those with sore heads were able to nurse their hangovers. The first and only show of the day was a Wing mission with 193 and 197 Squadrons. At 1930hrs, Squadron Leader Johnson led Flight Sergeant Campbell, Flying Officer Tennant, Flying Officer Logan, Flight Lieutenant Watts, Warrant Officer Brown, Flying Officer Richardson and Flying Officer Broad for 257 Squadron. The Wing was to attack barges moving up the Seine River carrying supplies for the Germans. Unfortunately, the Wing couldn't find the barges so they bombed and strafed an ammunition dump in a wood at Pont L'Évêque that had been hit before, achieving one direct hit on a nearby house. "Probably shook something up," the diarist recorded. They encountered no flak and returned safely to base.

Low cloud the following day scrubbed any operations for the morning. At 1620hrs Group Captain Gilliam led an attack on some covered railway wagons in a siding near Mézidon. They could not find the target due to the low cloud but were directed by the Controller to bomb flak positions in an orchard near Bretteville. Though they bombed the target area they did not see their results as the target was obscured by smoke and low cloud.

On the 7th of August the morning haze gave way to clearer weather and the first sortie took place at 1215hrs when Flying Officer Tennant and Lunn, Flight Sergeant Button, Flying Officers Sennett and Onysko, Pilot Officer Horner, Flying Officer Smith and Warrant Officer Barlow carried out an armed recce in the Bretteville–Falaise–Argentan–Mézidon area. They saw no movement but dropped their bombs on a road and railway bridge near Argentan. "The Medium bombers were seen to be taking a pounding from flak close by at Bretteville," the diarist recorded. "Six flamers went down. Bad luck for the bomber boys.

"Pilot Officer Spragg did not get off and Flight Sergeant Smith had engine failure on take off and tried to lob his aircraft down the runway. Unfortunately, only one wheel came up and he went over on his back. By a stroke of luck he got away with a shaking but the aircraft was a complete write off."

The next mission took place at 1515hrs when Squadron Leader Johnson led Flight Lieutenant Watts, Warrant Officer Brown, Flight Sergeant Upperton and Flying Officers Broad, Whitfield and Eaton with Group Captain Gilliam on an armed recce to attack enemy tanks near Falaise. None were found but instead they found four very large tank transporters. But just before they attacked Warrant Officer Brown had engine failure and began to go down, rapidly losing height. Dropping 4,500 feet his engine finally kicked in again and he headed for the base. In the meantime, the rest of the formation had rolled into their dives and attacked the transporters plastering them with bombs and cannon fire. The enemy transporters suffered several direct hits as the bombs smashed into them destroying them. Clouds of dust and smoke obscured the target area as the last of the Typhoons roared away leaving the wrecked transporters smoking and burning.

The final operation took place at 1800hrs when Squadron Leader Johnson led an armed recce to the Vire–Conde–Falaise area. "No red smoke was seen coming from any of our targets," wrote the diarist. "The Army could not seem to make up their minds."

Eventually, the formation peeled off and dive-bombed a bridge near Falaise. Attacking the length of the structure, several direct hits smashed into the approaches blasting the area, creating craters while several bombs were near misses on the bridge itself. There was virtually no flak on this operation and all the aircraft returned to base.

The first mission of the 8th was against a German HQ château 20 miles East of Bretteville. At 0945hrs Squadron Leader Johnson led Flying Officer Lunn, Pilot Officer Spragg, Flying Officer Onysko, Flying Officer Sennett, Pilot Officer Horner and Warrant Officer Burlow as part of a Wing show with aircraft from 193 and 197 Squadrons. Johnson took 257 Squadron aircraft in first, diving on the target, and firing short bursts of cannon fire. They released their bombs and levelled out, then climbed rapidly into sky. The first four bombs smashed into the château, direct hits, exploding on impact. The smoke from these explosions acted as a marker for the rest of the aircraft and 90% of the bombs hammered the area, completely destroying the château. Columns of thick black smoke poured from the wreckage and reached as high as 6,000 to 7,000 feet[79]. The pilots reported seeing strikes from their cannon shells over the whole target area.

The next mission was at 1120hrs with Johnson up again leading the same pilots on another Wing operation to attack a heavily defended orchard. Moderate and intense flak burst all around them as they bombed and strafed the area. Warrant Officer Burlow had his canopy shattered by light flak which knocked him unconscious. The aircraft immediately rolled over and dropped into a dive but he regained consciousness around 1,000 feet and managed to pull out. But his eyes were filled with blood and muck from various cuts and scratches. Sorting himself out, he levelled off and headed back to base.

The third mission of the day was uneventful. 257 Squadron bombed and strafed a wood but they saw no results.

The last operation of the day took place at 1950hrs when Squadron Leader Johnson led Flight Sergeant Snell, Pilot Officer Jenkins, Flight Lieutenant Wistow, Pilot Officer Spragg, Flying Officer Sennett, Pilot Officer Horner and Flying Officer Lunn on what the Squadron diarist referred to as a "Red Smoke Job" in the Squadron history. "We lobbed all our bombs in the target area that was enveloped in smoke and dust," the diarist recorded. The pilots reported seeing a large explosion in the north east corner of the target area.[80]

This had been a record-breaking day for 146 Wing. They had flown a total of 158 sorties, the largest ever since the Wing had arrived in France.

The following day, the 9th was just as busy and the first section took off at 1130hrs with Squadron Leader Johnson leading Tennant, Broad, Watts, Upperton, Whitmore, Logan and Richardson to a village near Thury Harcourt. Encountering some light flak, the Typhoons dove on the enemy positions defending La Groulais and all the bombs landed in the target area, pulverising the Germans leaving the village covered in dust and debris.

Johnson was up again at 1600hrs leading Flying Office Lunn, Pilot Officer Jenkins, Flying Officer Onysko, Flight Lieutenant Wistow, Flight Sergeant Snell, Flying Officer Sennett and Flight Sergeant Button to dive bomb enemy positions dug in at Rouvres northeast of Falaise. This was a Wing mission and they were joined with aircraft from 263, 193 and 197 Squadrons. Again, 257 Squadron Typhoons dove on the enemy first, strafing their positions with cannon fire and releasing their bombs before levelling off. Explosion after explosion ripped through the village as the Typhoons attacked. A large fire started and shortly afterwards thick brown smoke poured into the sky as the bombs burst in the target area.

The third operation for the day was another Wing mission led by the

Wing Commander with Flying Officer Broad, Flying Officer Tennant, Flight Lieutenant Watts, Flight Sergeant Upperton, Warrant Officer Brown and Flight Sergeants Jones and Shannon to attack enemy gun and mortar positions at Pons. With aircraft from 193 Squadron they peeled off, rolling into their dives, attacking in a loose line abreast formation all the while braving the light moderate flak that burst around them. Strafing and bombing the target they left a large fire pouring thick black smoke into the sky from the edge of the target area. This effort earned them hearty congratulations from the Army.

The following day, the 10th, Squadron Leader Johnson Lunn, Horner, Button, Wistow, Spragg, Sennett, Onysko and Jenkins on an armed recce in the Cambrouer–Lisieux area. Lifting off at 1045hrs their main goal was to attack transport but none was seen except for a few ambulances so they were redirected by ground control to attack a small bridge over a railway near Mézidon. They scored several near misses on the bridge and some direct hits on the line. They all returned safely back to base having encountered no flak.

The next mission took place at 1540hrs with Flight Lieutenant Wistow leading Flight Sergeant Whitmore, Flying Officers Whitfield, Logan and Richardson, Flight Sergeants Shannon, Campbell and Jones and Flying Officer Tennant enemy mortar and forming up points at Ouilly-Le-Tesson. Forming up with aircraft from 193 and 197 Squadrons over the sea, they roared inland, heading for the target area. Red Section led by Flight Lieutenant Watts went in first, diving on the enemy positions below. Releasing their bombs, they strafed the area with cannon fire, levelled off and climbed away. Behind came Blue Section led by Flying Officer Richardson who used the smoke from Red Section's bombing as a guide for him to drop his bombs. The bombing was very accurate and the target was riddled with cannon fire as the Typhoons roared in at low level.

The last flight of the day was at 1850hrs when Squadron Leader Johnson led Pilot Officer Jenkins, Flight Lieutenant Wistow, Flight Sergeant Snell, Flying Officer Sennett, Flying Officer Onysko, Pilot Officer Spragg, Flying Officer Lunn, Pilot Officer Horner and Flight Sergeant Button to attack the same château they'd attacked a few days before. Forming up with aircraft from 263 Squadron, the formation was led by Wing Commander Baldwin. Though the château was still burning and smoking from the recent hammering enemy resistance around the area was still strong. Huts north of the ruined château were enemy strongholds. There was moderate to light flak as the Typhoons peeled off and dove. As the height wound rapidly down Johnson began firing short bursts from his cannon, then released his bombs and levelled off, the rest of the formation doing the same. Bombs exploded in the target area, destroying several huts. As explosion after explosion ripped through the area several fires were started. Despite the moderate flak none of the Typhoons were hit so they turned around and headed for home. Once there, they discovered they were to go to Wales for a two-week course at Fairwood Common. They were to convert their 'Bombphoons' to rocket-firing Typhoons and over the next two weeks they would learn how to fight with rockets.

The Squadron arrived back in France on the 31st of August as a rocket-firing Typhoon squadron. They would continue to harass the Germans up to the end of the war.

CHAPTER FIFTEEN

The Fall of Caen and the Falaise 'Gap'

As we have seen in earlier chapters, Montgomery's plan was to engage the enemy armoured divisions in the Caen sector so that the Americans could break out of the Cherbourg Peninsula. That at least was the theory.

The Typhoons played a major part in keeping the enemy road and rail transport pinned down, attacking troops and armoured divisions during the day.

Caen was the hinge around which the Normandy campaign would either be a success or a failure. By July 7th British and Canadian forces facing Caen had been unable to dislodge the defenders who were well entrenched in naturally good defensive positions. Artillery barrages had failed to dislodge them, naval gunfire from ships offshore had also failed to force the enemy to retreat while the British and Canadian infantry kept plugging away at them, sustaining heavy casualties. The only response that might move the opposition from Caen was air attack. In this case it was to be the heavy bombers of RAF Bomber Command attacking in a tactical role for the first time.

So on the morning of July 8th at 0430hrs 467 heavy bombers arrived over Caen and began dropping 2,562 tons of bombs on enemy positions in the north of Caen. After the devastation of the air attack, artillery and naval gunfire followed. When that barrage was over the troops on the ground attacked. Where they had met stiff and bitter opposition only a day before now they moved with ease; by nightfall they were on the outskirts of the city. The next day they advanced into Caen itself and by the 10th they took the whole of the city north of the river Orme.

The population of Caen was 54,000. Now it was a tragic place with whole areas reduced to rubble under the onslaught of the Allied bombs and guns. Rubble, wreckage, debris lay everywhere and as the troops entered the city they were stunned by the carnage. Yet they found no malice or bitterness for such colossal damage amongst the population.[81]

Operation Goodwood which resulted in the capture of Caen by the British took place over the 18-20th of July 1944. It is true that the British had entered Caen by the 10th of July but they had not taken the entire city or the area surrounding Caen, the high ground and plain that was so desperately needed by the air force because it was such good ground for airfields. Nor had they taken the road to Falaise. Operation Goodwood was supposed to rectify this situation.

In his excellent book, *Caen: Anvil to Victory*, Alexander McKee goes into great detail about the battle. According to McKee, Montgomery had planned on taking Caen and the dominating heights behind the city by the evening of D-Day. Montgomery actually states in his memoirs that his original intention had been to secure the high ground between Caen and Falaise as early as possible but once he realised that to do this would mean very heavy losses he abandoned the idea, not seeing it as vital.

Montgomery planned a double-encirclement through Villier Bocage and the airborne bridgehead but 51st Highland had failed on the left and 7th Armoured on the right had been driven back in their first defeat since Alamein. With greatly increased forces he had then planned a tremendous right hook starting at Fontenay, which was to sweep round behind the city, via the Odon and the Orme to the heights of Bourguebus Ridge, directly in rear of Caen and dominating the rising plain and the dead straight road to Falaise. But 30 Corps, 8 Corps and 1 Corps combined had faltered and then come to a standstill under the impact of the German armoured strategic reserve. Dispensing with subtlety, Monty had then attacked Caen head on from the north with an overwhelming tonnage of bobmbs which had torn the city apart. Three divisions had ground to a halt in the rubble along the line of the water barriers which divided the city in half. He was in Caen but he had not taken Caen. The real prize, the dominating heights in the rear, the plain behind them and the road to Paris, which tactically were one, remained in German hands.

By the second week in July yet another failure imperilled everything they had done so far. The British and Canadian blood-letting went for nothing if the Americans failed in their part of the plan to break out of the bridgehead while the bulk of the German Army was elsewhere engaged and to swing the whole Allied line through an angle of ninety degrees with Caen as the pivot and so push the German Army up against the Seine. The Americans had failed again and again to break out. Their last attempt had been timed to coincide with the British and Canadian head-on assault on Caen of 7th July but by 10th July the Americans too had failed and General Bradley reported that he would be unable to try again until the 20th of July at the earliest and in fact it did not come until the 25th.

The Allies were therefore pinned in a narrow bridgehead ten to twenty miles deep which was barely one-fifth of the area they had planned to occupy and in fact needed to get by mid-July. If the situation remained as it was, the onset of autumn and then winter weather could have turned the stalemate into a disaster.

German infantry divisions so far held in reserve were being moved up to the front. In the period around the attack on Caen on the 7th of July four German infantry divisions reached the front and three of those went into positions facing the British and Canadians.

The German Panzer Group West had been pulled out of the line to rest and refit in preparation for a massive counter-offensive to split the narrow offensive and destroy the British and Americans separately. There was a strong danger of a break-in as the Germans began to move their armour away from Caen towards the American front, which they reckoned would be an easier proposition. Since the American drive on St Lô had failed it would take them 15 days before they undertook another offensive and if the German armour was allowed to re-group in front of the delayed American offensive there was a very real possibility of the Allies being slowly pushed back into the sea. Visions of Dunkirk all over again.

Something had to be done and holding the Germans at Caen was imperative, so they could be cracked there. From this emergency situation came Operation Goodwood that would finally give the British a little more breathing space and allow them to push on to Falaise.

As far as the infantry was concerned the heavy fighting in Normandy had taken its toll and the time was fast approaching when there would be no infantry reinforcements. Around early July the situation was that for every two infantry casualties there was only one man to take the place of both.

So the answer to that was using tanks. The armoured divisions had lost many tanks but not many tank crews, as most were able to bale out like some pilots could. This consideration and the fact that the infantry were exhausted and depleted was the main emphasis behind Goodwood, supported by air.

There were three armoured divisions available to the British and Canadians that were equipped with light fast tanks with 500 reserve tanks in Normandy and plenty of tank crew reinforcements coming online. On top of this, in England there were two more armoured divisions, one Canadian and one Polish getting ready to come over to France.

But the problem lay in the difficult countryside that was not conducive to fast, mobile tank battles as in North Africa. This countryside meant that they required a higher ratio of infantry to tanks and the type of tanks that could deal with the German Panther and Tiger tanks. The route that the British and Canadians would take to attack the Germans was where the British already had a bridgehead over the water barriers running into Caen from the southwest which continued to the north at Ouistreham.

The constricted corridor east of the Orme and the Caen Canal overlooked by the high ground of the Bois de Bavent to the Caen suburb of Colombelles was the main area decided upon. Yet so narrow was the front that advancing in a line abreast they could only advance one behind the other. However, once they had gained ground south of Caen they could fan out and start advancing properly. In effect, this attack on Caen came from the northeast, travelling in an arc starting due south and ending up facing southwest and west. Along the left flank were several fortified villages and for six miles the flank would be exposed to short-range German fire. On the right flank were heavily fortified villages on the outskirts of Caen, Colombelles, Mondevilles and Comelles. The fortified villages on the left, Cuverville, Giberville, Sannerville, Toufreville, Démouville, Bannerville, Manneville, Emieville, Grentheville, Frenouville, Bellengreville and Cagny they would have to pass through to get to the main objective.

Before the attack could begin, the area would have to be softened up from the air. On 18th July, 942 aircraft, 667 Lancasters, 260 Halifaxes and 15 Mosquitos set out to bomb five of those fortified villages in the hope of making the Army's task easier. At dawn, under clear conditions, the aircraft took off and climbed to 9,000 feet. Then, flying between 9,000 feet and 5,000 feet, they identified the targets. Bomb bay doors on the Lancasters, Halifaxes and Mosquitos opened and the bombs fell onto the villages below. During the raid they dropped 6,800 tons of bombs on the villages. Bomber Command dropped 5,000 tons and the American bombers dropped the rest. As the raid continued, no flak arched up at the bombers largely due to army artillery and naval gunfire smashing the enemy flak positions. Only five Halifaxes and one Lancaster were shot down and the Luftwaffe was nowhere in sight.

Under this onslaught of explosives the 16th Luftwaffe Field Division and the 21st Panzer Division suffered tremendous losses, particularly the former. On the ground, the army moved some four miles southeast of Caen, finally gaining some room to move.

One incident that shows how much air superiority the Allies had was the attack on Rommel. Rommel had been in conference on 17th July at II SS Panzer Corps HQ and left early at 1600hrs because he was in a hurry to return to his own HQ at La Roche-Guyon, As was usual, he went through Livarot, passing many German vehicles burning by the side of the road that had been pulverized by bombs and rockets mostly from Typhoons. Taking evasive action, his driver turned down several side roads until he managed to get back onto the main road. Believing they had not been spotted Rommel's entourage carried on, but RCAF Spitfire pilot Charley Fox strafed the car from about 300 yards. Rommel's driver swerved the car around into a side turning a few hundred yards ahead, but it was too late. A few yards behind the wrecked and burning car lay Field Marshal Rommel, unconscious in the road. His driver was dying and his aide,

Major Neuhaus was wounded. Sergeant Holke and Hauptmann Lang had both jumped out of the car before it turned over. Land managed to find a car to get Rommel to a hospital. His head injuries were severe, with multiple skull fractures. Charley Fox had found what must the ultimate 'target of opportunity'.

It will come as no surprise that there were other claimants to the strike, among them 193 Squadron led by Wing Commander Baldwin. According to the Operational Record Book Pilot Officer Ben Lenson and Flying Officer J. W. Darling attacked a staff car and an armoured car that day on a bombing and strafing sortie east of Caen. A Reuters correspondent in Brussels reported in August that it was Typhoons that hit Rommel. There are other claimants, notably Squadron Leader J. J. 'Chris' Le Roux of 602 Squadron. The balance of probabilities points to Charley Fox: but that didn't stop 193 Squadron, following the Reuters report, dubbing themselves the 'Rommel Killers'!

Back to the softening up process. Each wave of the bombers dropped smoke signals after dropping their bombs to show the area where the next wave should drop theirs. Target indicators were being dropped by the Pathfinder Force to ensure accuracy. On the ground were the markers who marked the target area for the Pathfinder Force to drop their indicators. On the left flank, bombs rained down on the farming villages of Toufreville, Sannerville, Banneville, Manneville, Guillerville and Emieville where the British thought 16th Luftwaffe Field Division were but where in fact a German Battle group was, strengthened by the Heavy Tank Battalion and the 200 Assault Gun Battalion. British Intelligence thought all of the 21 Panzer Divisions were near Colombelles but there was only part of Panzer Regiment 22 and the Tiger Battalion.

Throughout the bombing raid Bomber Command concentrated on armour and anti-tank guns rather than the infantry who were far more vulnerable.

When the bombing raid began, the Germans on the ground dove under the tanks or armoured cars for protection as the bombs came down all around them. So many came down it was like a "carpet of bombs" one German soldier wrote,[82] coining a phrase.

Bomb after bomb fell down on them, each explosion thundering in their ears. The screams from the wounded and those driven mad by the explosions could be heard amid the firestorm of bursting bombs that ploughed up the fields. Every high pitched whistle of approaching bombs and the sudden thunder-crack as they exploded brought death closer. Over and over it went on for hours.

In McKee's book Werner Krotenhaus describes the holocaust that fell from the sky all around the Germans. For some their nerves cracked, afflicted with a kind of temporary insanity while the earth erupted all around them. "The stunning effect temporarily incapacitated everyone.

Nerves and emotions were drained, it was impossible to think."

Entire fields with their barns and farmhouses were expunged, replaced by a barren moonscape of brown craters. Tanks were blasted into the earth, one 60-ton tiger tank was blown upside down, others were buried in the muck and mud and others caught fire as they suffered direct hits from the bombs. The bombers continued to roar overhead, flying low, their bomb aimers lining up the targets and then letting their lethal cargo go.

In contrast to the confusion and chaos on the ground up in the bombers it was all quite peaceful. The crew waited in anticipation for the flak to find them and drop them from the sky but on this early morning there was no flak at all. They had taken off at 0400hrs from England and as they lumbered over the target, light was just spilling above the horizon turning into a beautiful day. The sky was filled with aircraft, those going to the target area and those coming back. From 5,000 feet it all seemed so straightforward.[83]

On the ground, all the Germans could do was wait for the bombing to stop. While it went on there was nothing they could do. The flak batteries, instead of pointing up to the sky, were now being used as anti-tank guns and placed along the Goodwood line of advance. On the Bourguebus Ridge were 78 of these flak guns, pointing down at the roads. This was the same tried and tested technique that Rommel had used in Africa against the British that had stopped them time and again before Montgomery came out to turn the tide. Yet Bourguebus was not programmed for the RAF bombing campaign and was out of range of British artillery. It was to be the American Flying Fortresses and Liberators that would have Bourguebus as one of their targets.

As Bomber Command's campaign came to an end the US 8th Air Force bombing campaign began. The Lancasters and Halifaxes had gone in at low level, around 5,000 feet, to ensure they hit the targets. Their formations were loose and their bombing was very accurate. Now, the Americans came in much higher in tighter formations. The B17 Flying Fortress had been designed for deadly accuracy from a very high altitude and had a bomb-sight which the Americans boasted could put a bomb in a barrel from 20,000 feet.

Aside from Bourguebus the Americans were to bomb Bras, Soliers, Hubert, Folie, all clustered beyond the Caen to Vimont railway on the approaches to the higher flat ground that the Allied air forces wanted so badly for new airfields. Yet, in the most vital area of all, that of Bourguebus, where the 78 anti-aircraft guns were pointing towards the British advance, the American attack was ineffective.

So the guns remained intact, the German positions there still consolidated; though where the bombs had fallen, their condition was appalling. Some German units had been completely wiped out. The bombing on Démouville by American medium bombers had eliminated 1 Battery, 200

Assault Battalion, while 1 Battalion the Panzer Grenadier Regiment had been destroyed. Men of the 16 Luftwaffe Field Division were either dead, wounded or so stunned they were incapable of fighting. In other places, men were trying to dig their tanks out of the earth with their bare hands, the vehicles so covered in debris and rubble that their engines had fouled or their air coolers had clogged with dust and earth. The shaking nervous wrecks that had before the bombing begun been experienced soldiers didn't know what to do. Should they tend to the wounded or tend to their useless tanks?

It was into this atmosphere that the British advanced.

Unfortunately, the bombing had not destroyed the enemy resistance despite its ferocity and it would not be until nearly a month after Goodwood ended, on August 15th, that the British and Canadians would reach Falaise, enemy resistance was that hard.

This massive bombing raid in support of Operation Goodwood was the second such raid in support of ground troops made during the battle for Normandy. The first had been the bombing raid on the 7th to dislodge the enemy from positions north of Caen. The third massive raid by heavy bombers supporting the armies was on July 25th when 1,495 heavy and 388 fighter-bombers of the US Air Forces attacked enemy positions on the Périers–St Lô highway that would lead to the American breakout from the Cherbourg Peninsula. Another air attack took place on 30th July, when the RAF sent 693 Lancasters and Halifaxes with more than 500 medium and light bombers to drop 2,227 tons of bombs on enemy positions that were blocking the British 2nd Army from moving forward.

The fifth attack was the first tactical heavy-bomber attack that took place at night. On 7th August targets were pinpointed by green and red-coloured shells fired from 25-pound guns on the ground and overhead the bombs began to rain down on the enemy positions as the RAF 'heavies' arrived and began pounding the area. After thirty minutes the ground forces moved forward and another fifteen minutes later an artillery barrage supported their advance. The following day, Fortresses and Liberators of the US 8th Air Force continued the attack bombing enemy positions wherever they could but some of their bombs fell amongst Allied troops who were separated from the enemy by a few miles only. That same day, fighter-bombers from the 2nd Tactical Air Force, Mustangs, Mosquitos, Spitfires and Typhoons roared in, dropping their bombs and pulverising the enemy with rockets and cannon fire. In all, more than 5,000 tons of bombs were dropped; but by 9th August the ground troops were held up again, having moved only eight miles down the Falaise road from Caen since the end of Operation Goodwood. Another eight miles separated them from the actual town of Falaise.

A fresh Allied air attack took place during the day on 14th August when Typhoons and other fighter-bombers roared in on enemy positions on the Falaise front, pounding them with bombs, rockets and cannon fire. After the fighter-bombers the British and Canadian armoured divisions advanced at noon under a smoke screen laid right, left and in front of their artillery. That afternoon at 1400hrs 811 RAF heavy bombers came lumbering over the battle area, bombarding the enemy dug in at Quesnay Wood and Potigny, pulverizing the area with their incendiaries, high explosive and fragmentation bombs. At Quesnay some 20% of the 3,720 tons of bombs went astray into Allied lines. But the bombing worked and the Canadians managed to punch through the strong enemy positions and by nightfall had reached the northern heights above Falaise. By 16th August the Canadians were in Falaise and by the following day it was cleared of the enemy. But the town itself was a mess. The rubble was cleared by bulldozers so the tanks, armoured vehicles, trucks and other vehicles could pass through it. Despite all the destruction above the town the castle where William the Conqueror was born stood serenely, as if oblivious to the destruction below, its walls pockmarked by the ineffective gunfire used against it.

The American First Army had pushed the Germans back at Mortain while the American Third Army had gone behind the enemy who were facing the Canadians and by the 13th August were about 15 miles south-east of Falaise. By the 18th the British, Canadians and Poles from the northwest and the Americans from the south had encircled the Germans, leaving a gap only a few miles wide at Chamois for them to retreat through. By this time they had already begun retreating but it was too late for so many of them.

Rocket-firing Typhoons from 609 Squadron, 198 Squadron and others along with Bombphoons attacked the exposed enemy divisions in the Trun to Vinoutiers line of retreat. Fighter-bombers from the 2nd Tactical Air Force pulverised the enemy and the carnage below, as we have seen from Ken Adam's interview, was terrible. By the 19th the gap was closed and those troops left inside were either dead, wounded or eventually taken prisoner.

Fierce fighting continued outside of the gap and the Luftwaffe tried to intervene as the German Seventh Army tried to cross the Seine but the enemy's air force was no match for the Allies. Fighters from the US 9th Air Force claimed 77 aircraft destroyed in combat and 49 on the ground. More than 3,000 enemy vehicles were destroyed between the 25th and 29th August, with several thousand enemy soldiers killed during the river crossings.[84] On one occasion 2,000 enemy vehicles were caught out by medium bombers of No 2 Group as they waited to cross the Seine and were immediately pounded from the air by the Mitchells and Bostons. More than 1,800 vehicles were destroyed and many German troops killed. The Luftwaffe had been driven from its Normandy airfields as the Allies advanced and by the 29th they were pushed back to more distant airfields, closer to home, to Germany, where they could make a stand.

Caen had fallen, and the Caen sector had been taken. Sixteen miles down the road from Caen, Falaise too had fallen and the Typhoons had harried the retreating enemy divisions in the Falaise Gap to terrible effect.

Typhoons played a key role in bringing about the enemy's defeat at Caen by attacking any vehicles, troop concentrations, gun positions and installations with rockets, bombs and cannon fire. They were not the main reason for victory but they were a key part of it. Without their onslaught from the air the Allies would have had an even more difficult time breaking out of the beachhead.

As the Typhoons blasted away any enemy strong point or concentration that was holding up the Army's advance there was very little the Germans could do to stop the attacks. Richard Armstrong said the Germans hated the Typhoon because they had nothing that could stop it. Only accurate, heavy and highly concentrated flak made any difference; and there wasn't enough of it.

APPENDIX 1

The Prisoner

Flying Officer Richard Armstrong who flew Typhoons with 198 Squadron was one of the pilots hit by flak who didn't come back from the sortie. He was luckier than most as he managed to walk away from his wrecked Typhoon and ended up as a prisoner of war. Many British pilots lost their lives.

Some people might ask why put this section of Armstrong's war into the book? Because it shows just how dangerous and precarious life was attacking ground targets over Caen in the summer of 1944 and shows what could happen to pilots who survived being shot down.

As we have seen from the official Squadron history of 198 Squadron, they believed he had been shot down in flames. But during the low-level rocket attacks that took place around the Caen sector there was a lot of air activity and what his colleagues saw could have been another aircraft. So this is the true account.

His engine seized after being hit by flak on 18th June while on an armed recce attacking enemy tanks near Caen. "I reported four or five days before that I was having trouble with the engine. I gave the aircraft an air test and reported it as being OK but the engine just stopped," Armstrong said during our interview. "It was flying a bit rough and I had been fighting with the engine for a few minutes trying to get things right, oil pressure all over the place, temperature all wrong. The other blokes all went down but I didn't go down, I was nursing the engine.

"Suddenly the engine stopped and it's a bit disconcerting to see the prop in front of you because that means the engine has seized up. I decided I had to go down and made as much distance as I could to the coast but all the ground was wooded. It is pretty disastrous to land amongst trees but there is sod all you can do about it. I was lucky because suddenly a field opened up in front of me so I thought I'll put it in there. I was carrying eight rockets and thought I better get rid of them so I fired them all off and glided through the smoke into this field, which was quite small. I must have landed at about 250 miles an hour and walked away from it."

As he was having engine trouble rather than being shot down, how is it that the other pilots of his Squadron thought he went down in flames? Armstrong continues: "I think the blokes who saw the incident saw me fire the rockets and thought it was me that was exploding, that's why I was posted as killed," he said. "I landed with my wheels up and you would simply nose over if you landed with your wheels down.

One of the first things a pilot was supposed to do after crash landing behind enemy lines was to set his aircraft on fire so that it could not fall into enemy hands. "They gave us little pointed fireworks. The idea was to hit the aircraft wing as hard as you could with the point of this firework to set it on fire. I couldn't get the damn thing to light. I thought I'd pull the parachute out and light it and I was half way through this when I heard people running across the field nearby, so I thought bugger this I'm going. So I disappeared."

On the run for ten days, the French resistance eventually picked him up. "A Frenchman saw me in a barn and I reckon he must have split on me. Because Jerry knew I was there when he finally came for me and that was it.

"I was taken by motorbike on a side car with two Jerries on the motorbike with his rifle at the ready. All very dramatic. They took me, I don't know where, somewhere in France and I was interrogated only mildly and then pushed into this small camp they had built for army prisoners they had captured since the invasion."

From there, he was put onto a train of cattle trucks and was transported up to Sagen in Silesia. "That was a long trip," he recalled. "Forty cattle or a hundred people they used to say, crammed into the cattle trucks that were full of straw and not all that comfortable."

This first camp he came to in Sagen was Stalag Luft Three which was in southern Poland.

The prisoners were not treated badly by the Germans. "I couldn't complain," Armstrong said. "The food was awful to non-existent towards the end."

British Red Cross parcels kept the prisoners going. "But you couldn't say much about the food because the German army didn't get much better. With our Red Cross parcels we got better grub than the blokes guarding us," Armstrong recalled. "I think they had respect for the British."

But they weren't always that well treated. "We used to stand six deep to be counted twice a day. One of the guards took a rifle and hit one of our chaps into line with the butt of a rifle. One of the German officers in charge of the parade saw him and he was ordered to the front and slapped across the face with his gloves and marched out of the camp. What happened to that German soldier I don't know but that was the German temperament, it was very peculiar. Of course we were all officers.

Life in the camps was fairly easy. "You played golf you could read, you could natter. I was on the hockey team and we played six-a-side hockey with home made balls, but you didn't have much energy because food wasn't plentiful. You got one meal a day that was a sort of soup and we lived off the Red Cross parcels. When you had been playing six-a-side hockey for half an hour you were buggered."

The prisoners did their best to confound the enemy in as many ways as possible.

"A German officer came to see our camp commandant and his office was in our compound. One of our blokes came round to the driver of the officer to say that the officer wanted to see him inside. So the driver goes in to the office and the officer said he didn't want him and when the driver came out there were no wheels on the car. The wheels had been whipped off.

"They searched that camp from end to end and couldn't find them. They had been dropped in the bog and fifty blokes had shat on them. Their reaction was that it was terrible that officers would do something like that, that they were letting the side down. That was their reaction."

Escape attempts were always taking place but Armstrong was not allowed to escape because he was one of the new ones. There were men who had been prisoners for much longer than he had and they would have first go. Armstrong was put on duties such as keeping a lookout for Germans while tunnels were being dug. "You would be asked to do two hours on duty by a hot window watching a window three huts down that had a towel out of it and if he pulled his towel in you pulled your towel in and that was the signal that the German goons were coming. They climbed into the huts to find radio sets and escape tunnels and so forth.

"I was involved in dispersing sand from time to time from tunnels that were being dug. I wasn't allowed to escape because there were a lot of blokes who had been there a lot longer than I had. I could help and I was on sand distribution and you would walk around with sand in your trousers with a piece of string round the bottom that was looped up inside your trouser pocket. When you were out on the walk around the perimeter you just walked round and there were hundreds of blokes always walking around and you pulled a string and the sand would come out and pour over your shoes and mingle amongst the other sand and the blokes behind you would trample it down.

"There was nobody in Stalag Luft three that I knew, at least not in my compound. You get hardened to it when your friends are not there at night. You wouldn't think you could but you do. And if you have never faced that situation you're wondering what the hell I'm talking about."

But as the Russian lines were advancing inexorably closer the Germans decided to march the prisoners out of Sagen.

"I was on the march out of Sagen when the Russian lines were advancing on us. We were forcibly marched for 40 kilometres because we were valuable and they didn't want us to fall into the hands of the Russian Army. They wanted to hang onto us for as long as they could. They marched us for about 40 kilometres and it was freezing cold, terrible. They put us up in barns and churches. There were about 2,000 blokes."

As far as escaping was concerned on the march there was no chance.

"We were ordered not to escape under any circumstances on the march because if we were together with two or three thousand blokes we were safe but if you are by yourself you're not. The war was over anyway so what's the use of wasting your life. Lots of women were inviting blokes to come into the house because a lot of women thought it was protection for them if they were looking after a British prisoner of war.

"On that march we weren't making the progress that the German armour thought we should have made. I think we were supposed to do 20 kilometres a day on the march and we were doing about eight. The guards we had were all old men because the young ones had gone off to the Eastern front I suppose, and they had nothing left except these old men. They weren't at all keen to guard these prisoners of war. The slower we went the happier they were. We used to have to wake them up and give them their rifles.

"One morning the SS turned up complete with two machine guns and set them up at the side of the field and threatened us saying unless we were off they were going to shoot the lot. Well I've never heard such a growl of anger from a couple of thousand blokes and the SS just packed up and went.

"There was such a suppressed roar of anger from these two thousand voices that they must have thought better of it. That was a hairy moment when you are looking down the spout of a machine gun.

"I think the Germans were shell-shocked to hell by then. The majority of them just wanted to get home and see if their lives were still there. They knew the war was over. There was hardly any Germany left."

After the march, they were, according to Armstrong, put back on trains again and shipped towards Lubeck.

"We were there for about a couple of months when they started moving us again because it wasn't the Russian Army that was coming, it was the British Army. They moved us up into Denmark and then one morning we woke up and all the guards had gone and the British Eighth Army rolled in. Well, you couldn't see any tanks for the mound of RAF prisoners of war all over the tanks; it was quite something. They rolled into camp and that was it."

Back home, Richard Armstrong was officially classed as dead. "I was going up to Hendon and I thought I would go to the RAF memorial chapel in the City and I went in there just out of, well, I wanted to see it. I saw these books of remembrance all over the place and my name was there and it gives you a bit of a turn to find out you were there. I never said anything to anybody because you can't really cross your name out."

As far as the authorities were concerned he was dead so to get his old life back and be officially alive took some doing. "It wasn't easy," Armstrong explained. "There are loads of systems to write you off the system but there aren't any to write you back on. I was back home by then."

When a pilot came back from the war he was debriefed and sent home. "On indefinite leave," Armstrong said. "They gave you rations and I used to have to go down to the food office and say 'look I'm living I'm here and they'd say no you're not, you're dead.' Not as silly as that but almost. I had one hell of a job to get written back on. It really was difficult."

APPENDIX 2

Sir Alec Atkinson

Although Sir Alec was flying Typhoons before the period we are looking at in this book, his experience with the mighty fighter is worth recording. He flew with 609 Squadron during 1942 and 1943 initially on Spitfires before 609 was re-equipped with the Typhoon. After his time at 609 Squadron, he went on to become a flying instructor. But his impressions of the Typhoon are a little different to the other veterans we have looked at.

"The Typhoons were rather big and lumpy after flying a Spitfire but they were very powerful and in their day they were the fastest aircraft low down in the war. We could catch any German aircraft," he recalled during the interview. "But it had a lot of vices initially that got fixed later on. The Typhoon developed into the Tempest and the Tempest didn't have any vices.

Talking about the dreadful fault of the tail coming off, the major fault in the Typhoon's early period, Atkinson said, "They put fish plates all around the tail and even that didn't cure it. It was subsequently discovered to be metal fatigue that they fixed in the end."[85]

When 609 was at Duxford they were flying Spitfires but by the time they arrived at Manston they were flying Typhoons. "That's where we were engaged in protecting the country against low level intruders," Atkinson said. "They used to send out ME109s and FW190s at low level to attack the coastal towns and we were able to protect the country pretty well against these raids.

However, it wasn't just protection, they also took the fight to the enemy.

"We did Rhubarbs and attacked German communications, which was invented by Roland Beaumont who was the CO of the squadron. He was a very good pilot, probably one of the best fighter pilots in the world."

This was before Typhoons were flying with rockets.

"They started off with twelve machine guns then they finished up with four cannon. The thing that was really exciting was that it could go so fast. Not only at low level but it could dive at very high speeds approaching the speed of sound."

Talking about his CO Roland Beaumont, who wrote several books about his time as a Typhoon and later a Tempest pilot, Atkinson remembered a story about Beaumont when he was a test pilot on Typhoons. The account provides an interesting insight into the robustness of the aircraft.

"He was a test pilot on the Typhoon; this was at the stage when they hadn't solved the problem of the tail and the engine. He was asked by the chief test pilot at Langley to go up to about 30,000 feet and to dive down vertically and see what happened. The object was to see if there were any signs of cracks in the tail and it might be for this reason the tail came off. He was an extremely brave man and the weather wasn't very good. Anybody else would have said the weather wasn't good but he went up anyway to about 30,000 feet. He was above Windsor and he could see a gap in the cloud and he could see Windsor Castle below him and he did a half roll and he went down vertically. Very soon the aircraft was going down at colossal speed and the controls seized up, you know, he couldn't move the stick. He kept on trying and when it got into the lower level with more concentrated air he managed to move the stick and he survived. I believe the Germans had faced this sort of problem and lost some of their best pilots."

Atkinson described how pilots had very little time once scrambled.

"We were sitting round in the dispersal hut and then we would be told by telephone to take off and they would direct us where we should go and quite probably see the enemy. I remember once being told the aircraft was a friendly aircraft. I'd flown Spitfires and I knew it wasn't a Spitfire and they said it was and so I asked Control if I could fire at it because I knew it wasn't a Spitfire. They said, 'If you are absolutely sure then yes you can,' and I said I was absolutely sure so I did fire at it. He started weaving and he turned back towards France and that was fatal for him because I could go much faster than him so I used him as a splash target and shot him down. I'm sure it was a 109."

As we have seen in a previous chapter the Typhoon had a tendency to swing to the right.

"We had a very nasty accident at Duxford because one of the Belgian flight commanders was taking off in formation early in the morning and his tyre burst and he ran into another aircraft and he was killed. It could have happened to any aircraft I suppose but it happened to him. People were a bit cautious about taking off in Typhoons because they were so big and lumbering if anything went wrong, it was rather dangerous to take off in formation but we had to because it was a grass airfield."

When the D-Day landings took place, Alec Atkinson was an instructor.

"I was at the occupational training unit. I was instructing on Hurricanes and then Typhoons. The Hurricane was rather like an earlier Typhoon and so it was sensible to put the pupils into that. When they arrived they hadn't got much flying experience and they'd mainly been flying with fixed undercarriage aircraft and so this was a good way of showing them roughly what was going to happen in the Typhoon and then they had to go solo in the Typhoon."

Landing the Typhoon was the same as landing the Hurricane only the Typhoon had a much longer nose. "You couldn't see where you were going so you landed on three wheels including the tail wheel. You put all the wheels down and you knew the position well enough to be able to go down gently. You could do that with the Typhoon."

When D-Day did take place he was happy to be instructing.

"I'd been in the Squadron a long time and had enough. I was posted because you weren't supposed to be in the squadron for more than eighteen months or so and I'd been in the squadron for three years. But I hadn't been in action the whole time because when we first went onto Typhoons we had some time training; I suppose it was about six months."

When he was in the Squadron flying low-level Rhubarbs over France they were often shooting up trains.

"I remember going off one night and the weather wasn't good. It was perfectly alright for taking off on this side of the Channel but there was a lot of cloud. I thought quite wrongly that the German defences wouldn't be very alert for that reason and I got over to northern France and I caught sight of a train. I could see its steam so I thought I'd better attack it so I did. I went down and attacked it and then I pulled up. I thought gosh there's probably an awful lot of wires around here. So I pulled up and just as I pulled up a searchlight came on me which must have been operated by radar and they started shoving cannon shells up the searchlight beam so I was scared stiff. I did what I could to weave away and fortunately I wasn't hit. That scared me a lot.

"It was a light enough night to see the smoke of the train. I can't remember what time of the year it was, I think it was probably in the autumn. You didn't have onboard radar to tell you where you were. You could see the coast and the waves. If it was a light night or a moonlit one you could feel the bump when you went over the coast. You knew roughly where you were. I don't know why but when you fly over the coast in a lightish aircraft you feel a sort of bump because I suppose the air has come up from the coast."

On early night fighter operations with Hurricanes, flames from the exhaust often dazzled pilots until they put metal plates above each exhaust to mask the flames. "We didn't get a problem with the flames from the exhaust dazzling us in the Typhoon," Atkinson recalled. "When you were flying at night they used to put a steel strip above the exhaust so you weren't dazzled.

"As a flying machine I preferred the Spitfire because it was lighter and you felt more a part of it but in the Typhoon you were controlling it but you didn't feel as if it was part of you."

A flying instructor up until the end of the war, Atkinson went into the civil service and ended up as a second permanent secretary in the department of health and social security. "It was about 25 years ago; I am 85 now."

APPENDIX THREE

Correspondence between Montgomery and Eisenhower

The letter that General Dwight Eisenhower, Supreme Commander of the Allied Forces, sent to Field Marshal Montgomery on the 7th of July began with the observation that at the beginning of the operation to take Caen "We demanded from the air that they obtain air superiority and that they delay the arrival of enemy reinforcements. Both of these things have been done."

Eisenhower then stated that the ground build-up had proceeded rapidly despite the storms of June and early July and some "hard luck". The British were approaching the limit of available resources and if the operation was not a success they would be reaching the limit of the capacity of the ports held by the Allies to receive any more American troops. Indeed, Eisenhower then pointed out to Montgomery that the Germans were increasing their strength.

"These things make it necessary to examine every single possibility with a view to expanding our beachhead and getting more room for manoeuvring before the enemy can obtain substantial equality in such things as infantry, tanks and artillery. On the left we need depth and elbow room and at least enough territory to protect Sword beach from enemy fire. We should be all means secure suitable airfields. On the right we need to obtain suitable small ports that are available on the north side of the Brittany coast and to break out into the open where our present superiority can be used."

Eisenhower then went on to say in the letter that he was familiar with Montgomery's plan of holding with his left to attract all the enemy armour, while his right pushes down the peninsula to get behind the forces facing the Second British Army.

But it wasn't enough and the purpose of this letter was to get Montgomery to start moving faster.

"The advance on the right has been laborious and slow, due not only to the nature of the country and the impossibility of employing air and artillery with maximum effectiveness but to the arrival on that front of enemy reinforcements. It appears to me that we must use all possible energy in a determined effort to prevent a stalemate or of facing the necessity of fighting a major defensive battle with the slight depth we now have in the bridgehead."

Eisenhower then went to say that no full-scale attack had yet been attempted on the left flank supported by everything the Allies could bring to bear. Good weather was needed in order to bring the maximum use of air power to Montgomery's aid. The Supreme Commander then told Montgomery that all the air power he needed was available to him even if they needed to resort to heavy bombing of enemy defences to soften them up before the ground attack.

As far as the right flank was concerned Eisenhower stated that the only thing he could envisage was an airborne operation at St Malo. He believed that it was possible because the enemy had thinned out considerably in that area.

"The First British Airborne Division is now available and if it could seize the port and a US Infantry Division could follow in quickly by sea, they could, from that position, assist in getting your right flank rapidly down the Cotentin Peninsula."

He then ended the letter to Montgomery by offering to back him up in any decision Montgomery made to break the deadlock, take Caen and move forward. He even offered Montgomery the use of an American armoured division.

As we have seen in the final chapter the British entered Caen on the 10th of July and by the 20th Caen had been completely cleared of the enemy.

The day after Operation Goodwood was officially ended by Montgomery, and Eisenhower had returned from Monty's headquarters, Eisenhower drafted a second long letter to Montgomery in an effort to impress upon Monty how important it was for offensive action to take place up and down the front.

Couched in conciliatory terms, Eisenhower stated he wanted to assure himself that he and Montgomery saw eye to eye on the big problems facing them at that juncture.

Eisenhower referred to Montgomery's letter, dated 8th July 1944, where the Field Marshal said that the Allies must control the Brittany Peninsula, which was essential from an administrative point of view. He went on to quote Montgomery's letter that stated, "We do not wish to get hemmed into a relatively small area. We must have space for manoeuvre, for administration and for airfields." Referring to Montgomery's third point that "we must engage the enemy in battle to write off his troops and generally to kill Germans," Eisenhower added, "You might well have added by means of breaking through his positions and cutting him off in sizeable elements."

Referring to Montgomery's report dated 10th July, Eisenhower quotes Montgomery again: "We are now so strong and are so well situated that we can attack the Germans hard and continuously in the relentless pursuit of our objectives. This will be done by both first and second armies."

Eisenhower now gets to the point of his letter, which is that they are both in full agreement. "I think that so far as we can foresee we are at this moment relatively stronger than we can probably hope to be at any time of the near future. Time is vital. We must not only have the Brittany Peninsula, we must have it quickly."

In short, Eisenhower wanted to hit the Germans with everything the Allies had and the point of his 21st July letter was to ensure that Montgomery had the same thing in mind and would act on that view.

"A few days ago, when Armoured Divisions of the Second Army, assisted by tremendous air attack broke through the enemy's forward lines, I was extremely hopeful and optimistic. I thought that at last we had him and were going to roll him up. That did not come about."

Continuing, Eisenhower told Montgomery that the Allies were pinning their hopes on the American attack in the west, which would take place on the first day of good weather. In fact, it was unleashed on the 25th of July four days after this letter to Montgomery was drafted.

However, the terrain in the area was difficult for infantry and armour to move through and the enemy directly facing the American main point of assault was stronger than ever, according to Eisenhower.

"I think it is important that we are aggressive throughout the front," Eisenhower continued. The recent advances near Caen have partially eliminated the necessity for a defensive attitude. So I feel you should insist that General Dempsey keep up the strength of his attack." The Allies had the strength on the ground and in the air to support an offensive along the entire front. Eisenhower wanted the British attack to be intensified at the same time as the American attack began until they could gain the space and the airfields they needed for the Allied air forces to start operations.

"We do not need to fear, at this moment, a great counter offensive," Eisenhower wrote in that 21st July letter. Essentially, Eisenhower was saying that he could see no reason why Montgomery was not pushing harder. He goes on to finish the letter by saying he is sure that "In this way we will secure the greatest results in the quickest possible time, which is our basic objective.

"Moreover, I am convinced in this way we will have in the long run the least number of casualties. This is another reason, in my mind, for getting the business straightened out quickly. Eventually, the American ground strength will necessarily be much greater than the British. But while we have equality in size we must go forward shoulder to shoulder, with honors and sacrifices equally shared."

By the end of August the Allies had taken Caen, the Brittany Peninsula and Falaise and were heading for Germany. Did Eisenhower's letters make any difference? That is questionable. Did they make Montgomery move any faster? Did Eisenhower have the same picture of the British situation as Montgomery did? What is known is the backbiting and criticising that went on at SHAEF about Montgomery's progress.

One thing, however, is sure, as we have seen throughout this book. The efforts of the 2nd Tactical Air Force made a big difference to the enemy's ability to mount a counter offensive as they were under almost continuous attack by day, not least from pilots flying the magnificent Typhoon.

APPENDIX FOUR

Analysis of Air Support for "Operation Goodwood"

In a secret 2nd Tactical Air Force document, 30317/63, the results of the air campaign that heralded the beginning of Operation Goodwood on the morning of 18th July 1944 are examined. Written by Air Commodore A.J.W. Geddes who visited the area shortly after Goodwood had ended it provides interesting insights into the Air Force's view of the operation.

Based on the discussions he had with Chief of Staff, Second Army, Brigadier Chilton, 11 Armoured Division Commander Major General Roberts and the Visual Control Point Tank Commander 2nd Lieutenant Roberts, among others, Geddes was able to come up with what he believed were constructive criticisms.

As far as the overall plan for Goodwood was concerned, he states that he believed it was a bad plan.

"It relied on an armoured thrust unsupported by infantry in its later phases against an area known from previous photographic evidence to be heavily defended by inter-supporting anti-tank positions."

His recommendations for further planning of similar operations was that the infantry should either be used alone or carried on tanks in order to quickly follow up any air bombardment, especially of enemy anti-tank guns, "... so that the neutralisation of such areas begun by air bombardment should be sustained to help the armour through."[86]

Visiting the area after the air bombardment Air Commodore Geddes was able to see first hand the effect of the bombing. In his report he stated that using fragmentation and blast bombs paralyses enemy communications and control for a short time without cratering the area, which would hold up a rapid armoured advance. This was certainly the case in regards to the Goodwood bombardment.

"The density of the fragmentation bombing appeared to be correct and there was no evidence of sympathetic air bursts, all bombs bursting on the surface as planned."

However, against well-established enemy gun positions, properly prepared with slit trenches or protected from the blasts by buildings, fragmentation bombing was not as effective according to Geddes. To get around this problem, the use of high explosive delayed action bombs was the answer. Detonating after they had fallen, these bombs were powerful enough to uproot buildings which would fall on the gun positions, close the slit trenches and bury the enemy, increasing the disruption of the command and control infrastructure and making it hard for the enemy to mount a resistance quickly after the bombing.

In Operation Goodwood, Geddes stated that the bombing in the outer areas of enemy defences was a terrific punch but "… did not put the same weight on his reserve positions around Bourguebus, which actually were more important from the anti-tank point of view, and later caused our attack, which was at this later stage entirely an armoured affair, to fade out."[87]

He recommended that future attacks of this nature should knit together the army's requirement for pounding the areas they can't reach due to their artillery being out of range, with the requirements of the air force for a quick turnaround and to keep up the momentum of the army attack as they move deeper into enemy territory.

In paragraph 12 of his report Geddes stated that the method of putting up requirements for each service worked well for Operation Overlord (D-Day) because everyone sat round the same table using the same information. "By the 'Overlord' method we all knew from hour to hour the latest intelligence of the enemy positions, because we all worked round the table and could all hear the appreciations of the Commanders concerned at the same time."

However, Geddes says that the timing of the attack in Goodwood was the key to the failure of the operation.[88]

"The air support programme was based on the estimated speed of movement of the armour," he wrote. "This estimated speed was never achieved due to delays in the corridor, by minefields, by the railway embankment and the surprise of sudden tank casualties of the area of Bourguebus reported by scout cars to be clear of opposition."

As we have seen in the Chapter, *The Fall of Caen*, the effects of the air bombardment on the enemy were dramatic indeed but those effects wore off before the British and Canadian armour moved into those areas. This resulted in the enemy defences in the bombed areas, especially those around Bourguebus, to regain much of their efficiency.

"It is true the fighter-bombers, attacking pre-arranged targets and available at call, were laid on to continue the air bombardment after the heavies had finished," Geddes continued. However, as effective as the 'Bombphoons', rocket-firing Typhoons and other fighter-bombers were, they could not neutralise a large area as the medium and heavy bombers should have been able to do.

"It was not sufficient to allow a large scale armoured attack to 'swan' about in an area heavily defended by anti-tank weapons, which had recovered itself from an earlier heavy air bombardment," Geddes stated in paragraph 14.

He recommended that in future attacks of the same nature, the timing of artillery and air support should be done carefully in order to ensure that each stage of the advance was completed before the artillery and air bombardment signalled the start of the next stage. According to Geddes, doing things this way would have had two advantages:

"The first would be to allow each stage to be an effective co-ordinated attack. The second would be to increase the possibilities of using more air support because we will be able to employ more bombers on the turn-round if they are wanted when, say, our guns are moving forward and the artillery potential is reduced."

Another criticism levelled against Operation Goodwood by Air Commodore Geddes was that the safety margins were unnecessarily cautious. He believed that the Germans were given too much "breathing space", allowing them to sort out their communications while the British and Canadians were still advancing across the safety area between the start-line and the bombed areas. He believed that the safety distances should have been cut down to 1,500 yards and that the Army should be willing to accept greater risks, something Montgomery was not prepared to do.[89]

In Serial 1 of his report Air Commodore Geddes stated that Air Vice Marshall Harry Broadhurst, Air Officer Commanding 83 Group, thought that the appreciation of the enemy's anti-tank gun deployment was wrong. The Germans had moved their guns south of the Caen-Mézidon railway line, which meant that the British advance had to engage them at each village; resulting in the armour being too weak to move forward by the time they reached Bourguebus.

Because of the traffic congestion from the opposition from the villages on either side of the corridor through which the British advanced, 7th Armoured Division got bogged down and did not arrive in the Bourguebus area until the evening, when the plan had been to take it by 1000hrs. By evening, the armoured divisions were supposed to be in Falaise, some 16 miles down the road from Caen. Broadhurst told Air Commodore Geddes that he understood that Montgomery was prepared to lose up to 400 tanks in the advance during Operation Goodwood but, in fact, stopped at 200 tanks lost. Geddes wrote that the plan for air support after the heavy bombardment was for the Visual Control Post (VCP) to be able to call on fighter-bomber squadrons such as 197 Squadron and 257 Squadron to knock out the enemy's anti-tank guns or armour that were stopping the British advance.

"For this purpose, 83 Group put up standing patrols of rocket-firing Typhoons over the enemy gun areas all day. Fighter bombers were also at call, with some following up the initial advance by attacking pre-arranged targets. They reported that the guns in the Bourguebus area had stopped firing after the initial high level attacks."

However, Geddes pointed out that the enemy was using flashless propellant in their anti-tanks guns, which gave off little smoke. The assumption is that the means of identifying their positions from the air and through aerial reconnaissance must have been more through movement than through muzzle flash.

Indeed, this is what Air Vice Marshall Harry Broadhurst told Geddes, who reflected it in his report.

"Any movement of anti-tank guns in the area was bound to be seen by the standing Fighter Bomber patrols, and A.O.C. 83 Group did not think that such movement had occurred. He [Broadhurst] considered that the anti-tank guns in the action were already in the positions accurately known from photographic reconnaissance."

What was the effect of the air bombardment on the enemy and on the operation itself as far as the Army was concerned? In Serial 2 of his report, Geddes wrote that after the initial bombardment from the air the enemy in Giberville, Toufreville and Démouville were still holding out. To neutralise these positions required an attack by the infantry of the Second Army, which cost the British and Canadians their momentum.

Geddes continued by stating that a large part of the value of heavy bombing, as far as the army were concerned, besides the damage to personnel and equipment, was the disruption of the enemy's command and control infrastructure. "A German officer captured at Le Mesuil north west of Cagny said that his troops were obliterated by bombs."[90]

As soon as the high level bombing from medium and heavy bombers finished the fighter-bombers moved in, attacking enemy positions throughout the Bourguebus area directed by the Visual Control Post who was with 29 Armoured Brigade and was actually responsible for knocking out six enemy tanks, leaving them in flames.

The V.C.P. for the attack began with Major Troan D.S.O. D.F.C. S.A.A.F. as the air force controller, according to Serial 3 of Geddes' report.

"The V.C.P. Sherman tank reached the embankment at Grentheville at about 1100hrs. 29 Armoured Brigade had then reached their concentration area north of Cagny and were held up after this (including the V.C.P.) between Cormeilles and Grentheville south of the Caen–Mézidon railway by guns and dug in tanks on the ridge near Hubert Folie and by long-range guns south of Bourguebus."[91]

During this operation Major Troan was wounded outside his Sherman tank as he was putting up the aerial. The job of controlling then fell to Second Lieutenant P.M. Roberts, 3 County of London Regiment, Royal Armoured Corps, Commander of the Sherman tank that took over as Visual Control Post for 83 Group. Though it was his first action, his crew were experienced and he managed to direct fighter-bombers onto several targets, which included pounding a concentration of Panther tanks in a wood near Bourguebus that left six of the enemy tanks on fire. Other targets he directed Typhoons and other fighter bombers to, were dug-in Panthers and Tiger tanks in houses in and around the Bourguebus area only six hours after the heavy bombing had finished. Using the Typhoon cab rank system, Roberts directed rocket-firing Typhoons and 'Bomphoons' to attack enemy tanks moving southeast of Bourguebus, where several were damaged and destroyed. He also directed Typhoons to attack the railway bridge near Soliers.

Roberts' actions were widely publicised in the press back in the UK on the 24 and 25th of July but he was not aware of this.

The Bomber Command effort was limited to the front edge or the areas to be cratered on the flanks of the advance while the medium bombers had been used to their maximum and the fighter-bombers had hammered the back areas as much as they could, as at Bourguebus, where most of the resistance had come from and had delayed the Second Army from reaching Falaise for several days[92].

As far as Air Vice Marshall Harry Broadhurst, Air Officer Commanding 83 Group was concerned, they should have bombed the whole of the enemy defences, completely destroying any chance he had of mounting an effective opposition, instead of bombing just the front part of his defences. "In the case of the day selected for 'Goodwood' this would not have been possible," wrote Air Commodore Geddes. "The high-level bombing effort would have been curtailed by 1400hrs, due to the weather, which finally closed down altogether in the evening."

According to the report it was Air Vice Marshal Broadhurst's opinion, not an official announcement, that if the Army had gone on accepting more casualties it could have arrived in Falaise on the evening of the 18th of July.

That, of course, was Broadhurst's opinion.

Endnotes

CHAPTER 1

1 These facts came from *Typhoon and Tempest At War.*
2 This information comes from *The Hawker Typhoon and Tempest* by
  Francis K. Mason published by Aston.

CHAPTER 2

3 Noball targets are the sites of the German V1 flying bombs. ('Noball'
  was spelled differently by different squadron histories and
  documents.)
4 He went on to be a Wing Commander commanding 146 Wing and
  was shot down in Korea flying an F86 Sabre while on an exchange
  programme with the USAF.
5 This would be 146 Wing, 84 Group according to the book *2nd Tactical
  Air Force* by Christopher Shores and Chris Thomas.
6 The standard rocket projectile in those days was the 60lb rocket that
  consisted of a 60lb warhead mounted at one end of a tube with a
  rocket motor inside and fins on the back.
7 This would be the flex that Richard Armstrong talks about in Chapter
  VII, The Typhoon Described.
8 This would have been four Typhoons but Warrant Officer Bavington
  had engine trouble just after take off and returned to base.

CHAPTER 3

9 Taken from the *Memoirs of Viscount Field Marshal Montgomery,* Collins.
10 Page 550 of *With Prejudice,* Marshal of the Royal Air Force Lord Tedder, Collins.
11 Air Marshal Moiri 'Mary' Conningham.
12 Page 557 of *With Prejudice.*
13 P560 of Tedder's book *With Prejudice.*
14 Taken from the same report by Montgomery to his subordinate officers
15 Extract from page 32 of Eisenhower's report dated 13th July 1945 to the Combined Chiefs of Staff from *The Memoirs of Viscount Field Marshal Montgomery,* page255, Collins.
16 According to Montgomery in his *Memoirs,* page 256.
17 Code name for the American break-out.
18 Page 569 of Tedder's book.
19 According to Tedder, *With Prejudice,* pp 570-571.

CHAPTER 4

20 Flying single engined Masters training aircraft.
21 This was usually the Squadron Intelligence Officer.
22 This is the spelling as written in the Squadron History form 540.
23 This is the spelling indicated in the squadron history form 540.
24 According to the entry for this day in the squadron history.
25 It must be noted at this point that there is no mention in form 540 for 197 Squadron for this day that the mission experienced any flak from enemy gunners. This could well have been the case but there is no mention here.
26 This is a section of seven because Flying Officer Mahaffey crashed on takeoff but was not injured.
27 A direct quote from the squadron history.
28 A direct quote from the squadron history so must be assumed to be as close as possible to what was said.
29 This statement is directly from the squadron history, which may or may not be accurate.

CHAPTER 5

30 This is the spelling that appears in the history though the typing is very poor so it could be somewhere else.

31 The figure quoted by the diarist in the squadron history, though normally the dive would be 60 degrees.

32 Again, it has to be noted that the typing on this section of the history is quite poor, making the accurate spelling of these names difficult.

33 These were bombs with delayed fuses. Instead of exploding immediately the fuses might be set for a few seconds after hitting the ground.

34 This is a claim made in the squadron history.

35 Presumably this is a ruse by the Germans but the author of form 540 does not elaborate on this.

36 A hang-up is when the bomb remains attached to is mooring under the wing on release rather than dropping as it should.

37 Though this is in the squadron history it must be remembered that it is the pilots who are reporting this and the diarist is recording what the pilots have told him.

38 The actual wording in the squadron history is; "it was the unanimous opinion of all the pilots that the target was completely destroyed."

CHAPTER 6

39 Taken from Smith's personal log book.

40 An estimate that appears in the squadron history.

41 This figure is an estimated figure and is taken from form 540, the squadron history.

42 A direct quote from the squadron history taken from the 7th of August 1944 entry.

43 This is the figure quoted in the history and must be assumed to be an estimate.

44 This would be the Falaise Gap or the German retreat from Falaise that ended in disaster for them.

CHAPTER 7

45 One must assume this is true as stated in *Typhoon and Tempest at War*, by Arthur Reed and Roland Beaumont published by Ian Allan Ltd., because of the date of the specification issued by the Air Ministry for two 400mp fighters.

46 This is taken from *Typhoon and Tempest at War*.

47 Taken from the *Hawker Typhoon and Tempest*, Francis K Mason, Aston Publications 1988.

48 From *Typhoon and Tempest at War*, Arthur Reed and Roland Beaumont, Ian Allan Publishing 1974.

49 This is due to little development being done on the engine by Napier according to *Typhoon and Tempest At War*.

50 ibid.

51 As outlined in Mason's *Hawker Typhoon and Tempest*.

52 Pilots nicknamed this version of the Typhoon "coffin door jobs" as per Derek Taylor's remarks at the end of this chapter.

53 625mph.

54 One of the major problems with the Typhoon was the carbon monoxide seepage from the engine into the cockpit. They never overcame the problem and pilots always wore oxygen from the moment they entered the aircraft.

55 Compared with the Spitfire and Hurricane, according to Reed and Beaumont's *Typhoon and Tempest at War*.

56 This refers to the clear bubble canopies on all the later versions of the Typhoon but it had no car doors.

57 Another term for the early car door versions of the Typhoon.

58 This would be with the engine running.

CHAPTER 8

59 From the interview with Sir Kenneth Adam, London 2004
60 According to Ken Adam it was decided by the Air Ministry and wasn't a local order.
61 This is a comment from the diarist writing the Squadron history and is not substantiated elsewhere as we do not know which villages they are referring to.
62 This is a claim from the pilots so must be considered to be fairly accurate. One has to wonder how they managed to count the hits while dodging flak.
63 Claimed destroyed by the pilots.
64 Davies had been a Flight Lieutenant with 609 Squadron before commanding 198.
65 Flying Officer C.A. Rowland

CHAPTER 9

66 This would have been at Martragny according to Annear during the interview in 2004
67 This is a claim made by the diarist who was the intelligence officer debriefing the pilots on their return from the sortie.
68 Referred to as cab ranking.

CHAPTER 10

69 This quote from the squadron history was in quotations in the history itself.
70 It is not clear if this statement, which is not word for word, was entered on the 9th or 10th in the Squadron history.
71 Flight Lieutenant Vandaele, Flying Officer Jaspis, Flight Sergeant Ken Adams, Pilot Officer Merrett, Flight Sergeant Annear, Flight Sergeant Pagnam and Flight Sergeant Billam.

CHAPTER 11

72 According to an entry in 198's squadron history.

73 This assumption is stated in the squadron diary as written by the intelligence officer.

CHAPTER 12

74 This is Plumetot.

75 Presumably this would be in a new aircraft, though the history does not make that clear.

CHAPTER 13

76 The entry in the Squadron history does not say why only five aircraft reached the target, nor does it indicate if more took off to attack the yards.

77 How the pilots worked out the height of the smoke is not recorded in the history but presumably it must be by judging the height of the smoke relative to the height the pilots were flying at the time.

CHAPTER 14

78 The phrase "to follow up the retreating Germans in the Conde area" is an actual quote from the squadron history 2nd August entry.

79 This could only be according to the pilots who were either at that height or above it. On many missions it was standard procedure for one last Typhoon to fly over the target to observe the results of their bombing so it could be from this that these figures come from.

80 There is no indication in the squadron history as to what the target was. It was a village but there is no mention of the name.

CHAPTER 15

81 The supposition is taken from *The Royal Air Force in the World War* Vol. 4, Harrap & Co Ltd, 1950.

82 This was taken from *Caen: Anvil of Victory* the soldier being Werner Krotenhaus.

83 Based on an account by Flight Lieutenant G.D. Linacre reproduced in McKee's *Caen; Anvil of Victory.*

84 All the figures here are taken from the *Royal Air Force in the World War* Vol. 4.

APPENDIX 2: SIR ALEC ATKINSON

85 See Chapter VII, The Typhoon Described, for a full description.

APPENDIX 4: ANALYSIS OF AIR SUPPORT FOR "OPERATION GOODWOOD"

86 Taken from the first page of 2nd Tactical Air Force document 30317/63/Air dated 26th July 1944, signed by Air Commodore Geddes; made available by the University of East Anglia.

87 This is from paragraph 10 of the same report by Geddes.

88 In Chapter IV, the arguments by the Air Command that Goodwood was a failure as opposed to Montgomery's viewpoint that it served its purpose is clearly stated; it is interesting to see the same attitude in this report as well.

89 See Chapter IV for Montgomery's position on Goodwood.

90 This quote is from paragraph 3 of Serial 2 of Air Commodore Geddes' report.

91 Paragraph 1 of Serial 3, the "Goodwood" visit report 2TAF/30317/63/Air.

92 According to paragraph 7, Serial 1 of Air Commodore's report.

Bibliography

The Official History of the Royal Air Force, Volume Two, Her Majesty's Stationary Office

The Hawker Typhoon and Tempest, Francis K Mason, 1988, Aston Publications Limited, ISBN 0 946627 19 3

Caen: Anvil of Victory, Alexander McKee OBE, 1964, Souvenir Press, ISBN 0 285 63559 X

Typhoon Tale, James Kyle DFM RAF (Retd), 1989, Biggar and Co Ltd., ISBN 0 7125 0058 8

The History of the Second World War, United Kingdom Military Series, The Strategic Air Offensive Against Germany 1939–1945, Volume II Part 4, by Sir Charles Webster K.C.M.G., F.B.A., D. LITT and Noble Franland D.F.C., M.A. D. PHIL, 1961, Her Majesty's Stationary Office

The History of the Second World War, United Kingdom Military Series, The Strategic Air Offensive Against Germany 1939–1945, Volume IV, by Sir Charles Webster K.C.M.G., F.B.A., D. LITT and Noble Franland D.F.C., M.A. D. PHIL, 1961, Her Majesty's Stationary Office

Typhoon and Tempest at War, by Arthur Reed and Roland Beaumont, 1974, Ian Allan Ltd., ISBN 0 7110 0542 7

2nd Tactical Air Force Volume One, by Christopher Shores & Chris Thomas, 2004, Ian Allan Publishing Ltd., ISBN 1 903223 40 7

2nd Tactical Air Force Volume Two, by Christopher Shores & Chris Thomas, 2004, Ian Allan Publishing Ltd., ISBN 1 903223 41 5

With Prejudice, The War Memoirs of Marshal of the Royal Air Force Lord Tedder G.C.B., 1966, Cassell and Company Ltd.

The Memoirs of Field Marshal The Viscount Montgomery of Alamein, K.G., 1958, Collins

The Second World War: Closing the Ring, Winston S. Churchill, 1951, Houghton Mifflin Company

Crusade in Europe, by Dwight D. Eisenhower, 1948, Doubleday & Company Inc.

War Diaries 1939-1945, Field Marshal Lord Alanbrooke, Edited by Alex Danchev and Daniel Todman, 2001, Weidenfeld & Nicholson, ISBN 1 84212 526 5

Official History of 198 Squadron, National Archives, Kew, London

Official History of 197 Squadron, National Archives, Kew, London

Official History of 257 Squadron, National Archives, Kew, London

Official History of 609 Squadron, National Archives, Kew, London

Index

123 Wing 3, 7, 10, 75, 113-16, 127-8, 130

146 Wing xv, 35, 141, 147, 158

Adam, Sir Kenneth xiv, 72-82, 84, 86,89, 91-4, 89, 91-4, 96-9, 101-2, 104, 106-7

Allied Expeditionary Air Force xv xvii

Amiens 1, 2

Annear T., Warrant Officer 67-8, 88-95, 97, 99-100

Argentan 24, 32, 48, 57, 83, 97, 103, 104, 105, 125, 134, 146, 149, 156, 157

Armed Recce xvi, 4, 2, 7,8,10,30,31, 32, 33, 34, 39, 42, 43, 44, 45, 47, 53, 55, 57, 60, 61, 78, 84, 85, 86, 90, 91, 92, 97, 98, 99, 101, 103, 104, 117, 118, 120, 122, 123, 124, 125, 130, 132, 133, 134, 136, 142, 145, 146, 147, 148, 149, 150, 151, 152, 155, 156, 157, 159, 170

Armentiers 12

Armstrong, R., Flying Officer 11, 68-70, 108-14, 116-18, 120-23, 126-7, 137-44

Atkinson, Sir Alec xiv, 67, 175-8

Avranches 25, 26

B2 82

B3 44-6, 48-9, 147, 149, 154

B10 (Plumetot) 86, 89-90, 126-30

B14 48

B15 43-4, 143-4

Baldwin, Jimmy, Wing Commander 4, 11, 36-8, 41, 43-4, 47-9, 51, 55, 58, 60-2, 141-2, 145, 147-8, 159, 165

Baker, J., Wing Commander xvi, 11, 28, 29, 32, 35

Battle of Britain xiv, 27, 64

Bayeux 10, 12, 30, 35, 129

Beaverbrook, Lord 64

Berek-Sur-Mer 12, 13

Bernay 30, 47, 49, 51, 54, 60, 61, 83, 96, 97, 117, 118, 124, 148, 149, 153

Bocages 23, 91, 118, 119, 123, 129, 130, 136, 150, 162

Bombphoons 3, 7, 11, 14, 27, 43, 70, 160, 168, 185,

Breteuil 36, 118

Bretteville, 51, 56, 92, 103, 115, 132, 146, 150, 157, 158, 159

Brittany 21, 24, 179, 180, 182

Brooker, R. E. P., Wing Commander 3, 5, 7, 9-10, 12-13, 78, 81-3, 85, 90, 113-14, 116-121, 125, 129-31

Bruge 12, 13

Cabourg 90, 122

'Cab ranking' 46, 96, 135, 187

Camm, Sir Sydney 63, 65

Canadians and Canadian forces xvii, 5, 9, 17, 20-23, 26, 31, 48, 84, 86, 101, 108-9, 161-3, 167-8, 184-6

Carentan 116, 122

Cherbourg Peninsula 11, 17, 25, 77, 117, 120, 161, 167

Churchill, Winston S. 19, 25, 47

Circus 2

Coastwatcher 12, 13, 14, 75, 76

D-Day xv, xvi, xvii, 1, 2, 3, 15, 17, 18, 23, 24, 28, 29, 30, 43, 62, 77, 87, 113, 116, 162, 177, 184

Dring, Wing Commander 98, 104, 134

Evreux 83, 84

Eisenhower, General Dwight D. 16, 17, 18, 19, 20, 21, 23, 24, 25, 26, 112, 179, 180, 181, 194

Falaise Gap 26, 106, 169, 191

Flers 32, 57, 99, 101, 103, 151, 152, 156

Fortress Europe xviii

Freya 10, 13, 75, 76

Friendly fire 92

Funtington, W Sussex 82, 122, 124

FW190 61, 71, 86, 175

Geerts, L. E. J. M., Squadron Leader 3-4, 6, 8-9, 12-13, 76-86,

89-91, 94-5, 98, 102-5

Harrogate 27, 78

Harvards 27, 74, 89, 109

Hurn 34, 41, 43-4, 83, 86, 88, 124, 126, 128, 140-44, 147

Hurricanes xv, 1, 28, 63-4, 68, 70, 89, 107-9, 177

Jobourge 11

Johnson, S. L., CO 9, 29-30, 32-3, 35-6, 39, 42-3, 45, 48, 147-53, 156-9

Lancasters 88, 102, 164, 166-7

Le Havre 3, 37, 113, 189

Leigh-Mallory, Air Chief Marshal 18, 21

Lightning, P-38 xviii

Lisieux 30, 38, 44, 45, 47, 55, 61, 77, 78, 79, 82, 84, 90, 97, 98, 103, 117, 118, 124, 134, 145, 147, 159

Losses, Typhoons xviii, 97

Lovell, Derek xiv, xvii, xviii, 27-8, 31-4, 36-9, 41-9, 54-61, 70-1

Luftwaffe xvii, xviii, 1-2, 17-18, 44, 47, 66, 106-7, 164-5, 167

Manston 6, 12, 37, 92, 108, 109, 114, 137, 138, 175

Mézidon 92, 126, 133, 134, 146, 147, 149, 157, 159, 185, 187

Montgomery, Field Marshal Viscount xiv, 16, 17, 18, 19, 20, 21, 22, 23, 24, 25, 26, 162, 179, 180, 181, 182, 185,190, 194

Mosquitoes 121, 164, 167

Mourieres 57, 132

Mustangs xvii, xviii, 92, 144, 167

Napier-Sabre 28, 50, 64, 65, 70, 74

Needs Oar Point xvi, 5, 6, 28, 29, 31, 32, 37, 38, 39, 40, 41, 42, 140

Niblett, J., Squadron Leader CO 4-5, 8, 11, 75, 113-14

Noball missions 3, 37, 113, 189

Operation Cobra 23
Operation Goodwood 22, 23, 131,
    162, 163, 167, 180, 183, 184, 185,
    195
Orme (River) 20, 21, 22, 24, 35, 39,
    129, 130, 132, 145, 161, 164,
Ouilly-Le-Tesson 57, 159

Plamondon, J. M. C., Flight
    Lieutenant 48-51, 53-8,61, 115-20,
    122-3, 125, 129-32, 136
Plumentot B10 86, 89-90, 126-30
Pont L'Évêque 47, 51, 52, 62, 97,
    133, 147, 152, 156,

Racquancourt 49, 50, 95
Ramrod 2, 3, 4, 5, 6, 7, 8, 9, 10, 12,
    13, 29, 34, 35, 36, 75, 77, 78, 81,
    83, 84, 115, 116, 119, 121, 124,
    133, 134, 141, 148
Ranger 1, 37, 75, 79, 123
RDF 9, 10, 11,12, 29, 109
Rhubarb 2, 60, 112, 177
Roberts, E. R. A., Flight Lieutenant
    75-9, 81-6, 91, 99, 101-2
Rodeos 1
Rouen 4, 5, 6, 7, 57, 59

St Germain 54
St Lô 116, 122, 145, 163, 167
SHAEF 20, 23, 24, 26, 182
Smith, A., Squadron Leader 47-8,
    50-61
Spitfires xi, xiv, xvi, xvii, xviii, 1, 6,
    63, 64, 68, 70, 74, 89, 92, 107, 108,
    128, 131, 144, 167, 175, 176, 178

Tancaville 4
Tangmere 4, 6, 43, 109
Tedder, Air Chief Marshal Lord
    16, 17, 18, 19, 20, 21, 22, 23, 24,
    25, 26, 190

Tempest xiv, xvi, xvii, xviii, 63, 64,
    65, 107, 175, 176, 189, 191, 192
Thiberville 41
Thorney Island 3, 8, 10, 28, 72, 82,
    83, 109, 113, 114, 116, 120, 122
Thunderbolts xviii, 92, 107, 127
Thury-Harcourt, 35-6, 91, 99, 101,
    130, 132, 145, 150-1, 158
Tiger Moths 27, 73, 89, 109
Typhoon
    armament 63, 65, 112
    maximum speed 68, 69
    problems with design 64, 65, 66,
    69, 70

Valery 9, 10
Vassey 55,
Vimoutiers 61, 168

Wurtzburg 12-13, 14, 75, 76